New Perspectives in Policy & Politics
Edited by Sarah Ayres and Matt Flinders

RETHINKING POLICY AND POLITICS

Reflections on contemporary debates in policy studies

Edited by Sarah Ayres

First published in Great Britain in 2014 by

Policy Press
University of Bristol
6th Floor
Howard House
Queen's Avenue
Clifton
Bristol BS8 1SD
UK
t: +44 (0)117 331 5020
tpp-info@bristol.ac.uk
www.policypress.co.uk

North America office:
Policy Press
c/o The University of Chicago Press
1427 East 60th Street
Chicago, IL 60637, USA
t: +1 773 702 7700
f: +1 773 702 9756
sales@press.uchicago.edu
www.press.uchicago.edu

Policy & Politics is a leading international journal in the field of public and social policy, published by Policy Press. Spanning the boundaries between theory and practice and linking macro-scale debates with micro-scale issues, it seeks to analyse new trends and advance knowledge by publishing research at the forefront of academic debates. It is published four times a year, and is ranked on the Thomson Reuters Social Science Citation Index. Please visit the website for more information: www.policypress.co.uk/journals_pap.asp

British Library Cataloguing in Publication Data
A catalogue record for this book is available from the British Library

Library of Congress Cataloging-in-Publication Data
A catalog record for this book has been requested

ISBN 978 1 44731 946 7 hardcover

The right of Sarah Ayres to be identified as editor of this work has been asserted by her in accordance with the Copyright, Designs and Patents Act 1988.

The statements and opinions contained within this publication are solely those of the authors and not of the University of Bristol or Policy Press. The University of Bristol and Policy Press disclaim responsibility for any injury to persons or property resulting from any material published in this publication.

Cover design by Policy Press
Front cover image: kindly supplied by Asif Akbar

Contents

List of tables and figures

Tables

Figures

Notes on contributors

Sarah Ayres is senior lecturer in policy studies at the University of Bristol, UK. She is a political scientist with expertise in public administration and theories of policy making. Her research is concerned with devolution and decentralisation in an international context, with a particular emphasis on analysing inter-governmental relations between central and local actors. This work has drawn upon theories of partnership working and network management to examine the formal and informal processes that shape the governance of territory.

Jonathan Stephen Davies is professor of critical policy studies at De Montfort University, UK. He researches critical issues in governance, public policy and urban studies and is currently working on international projects exploring the governance and contestation of crises and austerity. Jonathan published his monograph *Challenging governance theory: From networks to hegemony* with Policy Press in September 2011. He has published recently in *Environment and Planning A*, *Policy & Politics*, *Public Money and Management* and *Urban Studies*, with papers forthcoming this year in *Environment and Planning C* and *Journal of Urban Affairs*.

Menno Fenger studied public administration and organisational sciences at the Catholic University Nijmegen, the Netherlands. He finished his PhD on the implementation of social policies in 2001. From 2000 to 2006 he worked as assistant professor at the Department of Public Administration, Erasmus University Rotterdam. In 2006, he was a visiting scholar at the Centre for European Studies, Harvard University. From 2006 to 2008 he was a senior policy adviser at the Dutch Ministry of Social Affairs and Employment. In 2008, he returned to the Department of Public Administration, Erasmus University. He has published numerous articles and chapters on policy dynamics in the area of social policies. In 2010, he was leading a research project on the legitimacy of social policies for the Dutch Ministry of Social Affairs and Employment. He currently is member of the editorial board of the *Journal of International and Comparative Social Policy* and co-editor of *Social Policy Review*. He is the overall project manager of the INSPIRES research programme, an EU-FP7-funded research programme about labour market resilience in Europe.

Matthew Flinders is professor of politics at the University of Sheffield (UK) and director of the Sir Bernard Crick Centre for the Public Understanding of Politics. He is also Visiting Distinguished Professor of Governance at Murdoch University in Western Australia.

Valeria Guarneros-Meza is a lecturer in the Department of Politics and Public Policy at De Montfort University, UK. Her research has focused on local governance and on the impact that institutional changes and socio-political reforms have on the former. She is also interested in citizen participation, inclusion and accountability, in particular how these concepts and meanings affect the organisational structures of local government as well as the practices and behaviour of local government bureaucrats.

Peter John is professor of political science and public policy at University College London, UK. He is known for his work on the theory and practice of public policy, and is author of *Analyzing public policy* (Routledge 2012) and *Making policy work* (Routledge 2012). He is an expert in the use of randomised controlled trials to find out how to involve citizens in public decisions, many of which were presented in *Nudge, nudge, think, think: Experimenting with ways to change civic behaviour* (Bloomsbury 2011).

Sara le Cointre attained a research degree in public administration and organisational science in 2012 at the Utrecht School of Governance, the Netherlands. During her time there she worked on several studies, including public accountability and collaboration in youth care transitions. She worked briefly as a freelance researcher for the Netherlands School of Public Administration, resulting in publications on complex causality. She currently works as a civil servant in local government, mainly on improving organisational processes.

Vivien Lowndes is professor of public policy in the School of Politics and International Relations at the University of Nottingham, UK. Using an institutionalist perspective, she is currently researching the effects of austerity on local governance. She is the author (with Mark Roberts) of *Why institutions matter* (Palgrave Macmillan 2013).

Alex Marsh is professor of public policy at the University of Bristol, UK. Much of his research has examined aspects of English housing policy, with a particular focus on policy and regulation in the rented housing sectors. He has been managing editor of *Housing Studies* and a visiting academic consultant to the Public Law team at the Law Commission. His work has been published in a range of journals including *Housing Studies, Housing, Theory and Society, Local Government Studies, Urban Studies, Policy & Politics* and *Modern Law Review.*

Steve Martin is the director of the Public Policy Institute for Wales and professor of public policy and management at Cardiff Business School, UK. He was previously the director of the Centre for Local and Regional Government Research and has led a series of major research programmes on local government policy, inspection and public service improvement. Steve has served as an expert adviser to a range of UK government departments and the European Commission. He led the UK government's Expert Panel on Local Governance in 2009-2010 and is a member of the ESRC's Local Government Knowledge Navigator team.

Kerry McCaughie joined the staff at the University of Nottingham (UK) in September 2011 as a research assistant in the field of local government. Previously Kerry worked as a research assistant at De Montfort University after completing an MSc at Loughborough University. Kerry's areas of research have included community cohesion, institutional resilience and partnership governance. She is now employed in a research department for a national governing body for sport.

Janet Newman is emeritus professor in the Faculty of Social Science at the Open University, UK. Before becoming an academic she worked in local government and was involved in numerous social and political projects. Her research interests include questions of governance, politics and power. Her most recent book is *Working the spaces of power: Activism, neoliberalism and gendered labour* (Bloomsbury Academic 2012).

B. Guy Peters is Maurice Falk Professor of American Government at the University of Pittsburgh. He is also professor of comparative governance at Zeppelin University, Germany. He earned his PhD at Michigan State University in 1970 and has three honorary doctorates from European universities. He is currently co-editor of the *European Political Science Review* and on the editorial boards of a number of other journals. He is a frequent consultant for organisations such as the World Bank, UNDP and UNICEF. His recent publications include *Institutional theory in political science* (third edition; Continuum 2012) and *Rewards for high public office in Europe and North America* (with Marleen Brans; Routledge 2012) and *Strategies for comparative political research* (Palgrave Macmillan 2013).

Christopher Pollitt is emeritus professor at the Public Governance Institute, Katholieke Universiteit Leuven, Belgium. Christopher is author of more than 60 scientific articles and author or editor of more than a dozen scholarly books. The most recent were *New perspectives on public services* (Oxford University Press 2012) and *Context in public policy and* *management* (Edward Elgar Publishing 2013). He has undertaken extensive consultancy and advice work for a wide variety of organisations, including the European Commission, the OECD, the World Bank, HM Treasury, and a number of foreign governments.

Rod Rhodes is professor of government (research) at the University of Southampton (UK) and professor of government at Griffith University (Australia). He is the author or editor of more than 30 books including recently: (with Anne Tiernan) *Lessons of governing: A profile of prime ministers' chiefs of staff* (Melbourne University Academic Press 2014); and *Everyday life in British government*(Oxford University Press 2011). He is life vice-president of the Political Studies Association of the United Kingdom; a fellow of the Academy of the Social Sciences in Australia; and a fellow of the Academy of Social Sciences (UK).

Martijn van der Steen is vice-dean and deputy-director of the Netherlands School for Public Administration (NSOB) in 2002 and director of NSOB's Think Tank. He studied public administration and history at Erasmus University Rotterdam and was trained as a management consultant at a leading consultancy firm in the Netherlands. His research interests include network management, the use of forecasting and scenarios in policy making, public sector strategy, and the relationship between the media and government.

Mark van Twist is professor of public administration at Erasmus University Rotterdam and academic director (internal audit and advisory) at Erasmus School of Accounting & Assurance. He is also dean and member of the Board of the Netherlands School of Public Administration, an inter-university institute that provides public sector executive education and an independent centre of applied research, critical thought and strategic advice about politics and governance. He has published numerous contributions to books and journal articles, e.g. in *Policy Sciences, Public Administration, International Journal of Public Administration, International Review of Administrative Sciences, Public Integrity* and *Public Management Review.*

Acknowledgements

Policy & Politics published its first issue in 1972 and since then has been one of the leading international journals in the field of public and social policy. The origins of this book lie in the 40th anniversary *Policy & Politics* conference in Bristol in September 2012 (www.bristol.ac.uk/pp40). The 2012 conference was a huge success and attracted over two hundred world-leading scholars from 19 countries. The chapters in this book are derived from a selection of specially commissioned papers that were presented at the conference and subsequently published as a special issue of *Policy & Politics* (2013, volume 41, number 4). I would like to thank my academic co-organiser of the 2012 conference, David Sweeting, and conference administrator Emily Thomas, both of whom contributed enormously to making the event such a success. My gratitude also goes to all the plenary speakers and conference delegates who contributed to such a rich and compelling academic discussion over two days. Thanks, of course, to the contributors of this collection who have produced such timely, insightful and thought-provoking chapters and the two anonymous reviewers who helped to fine-tune the collection. Finally, I would like to acknowledge the support of the publishers, Policy Press, who have been a great help with the final production.

INTRODUCTION

Rethinking policy and politics

Sarah Ayres

In recent years the nature of policy and politics has undoubtedly witnessed significant transformations. This has included the so-called transition from government to governance, epitomised by the inclusion of non-state actors in the policy process and the increasing importance of global governance in shaping domestic policy. There has been a reframing of the state in delivering public services combined with rising public expectations about choice and quality. We have witnessed devastating civil unrest in vulnerable parts of the world that has placed the concepts of democracy, civil rights and a global duty to protect civilians in the spotlight. Concerns over the environment and climate change continue to grow, compounded by extreme weather events that have caused significant disruption in countries and major cities. Developments in science and technology have provided solutions to some of these problems, while also creating new inefficiencies and defects; for example, the rise of the 'mediatised' world, access to information and the global concerns over data security have all featured heavily in recent political and policy debates. Finally, the global economic downturn and associated austerity measures have had a fundamental impact on shaping macro political ideology and the design and delivery of public services in many parts of the world. Austerity politics has also raised important questions about equity and social justice in the provision of welfare and public services. All of these factors have forced scholars and practitioners to rethink policy and politics in the 21st century. In doing so they have challenged perceptions about the ways in which policy is studied, designed, delivered and appraised.

The aim of this book is to bring together world-leading scholars to reflect on the implications of some of these developments for the field of policy studies and the world of practice. In doing so, it provides a timely opportunity to think about recent changes in public and social policy and how this shapes academic endeavour in the field. The chapters provide critical reflections on the ways in which academia can engage with policy and practice to find solutions to ever more complex and multi-faceted social problems. All contributions emanate from a special anniversary issue of the journal (2013, 41, 4): 40 Years of *Policy & Politics:* Critical Reflections and Strategies for the Future, in which contemporary policy issues were examined while looking back at the policy lessons and experiences of the last 40 years. Authors were asked to reflect on how much is enduring, what has changed and how we might use past lessons to inform future policy. The chapters in this book represent subjects and specialisms that have shaped critical policy debates over the last 40 years and identify issues that are pertinent to the future direction of the field.

In Chapter One Christopher Pollitt argues that despite the UK's leading role in public management reform, and decades of continuous change, little has been learned of the final outcomes. Pollitt ascribes this to the methodological limitations in evaluating major management reforms – i.e. the difficulty in using orthodox, *ex ante* performance indicators in complex and constantly changing policy environments – and an apparent disinterest within government for finding out the results. Pollitt also notes the apparent ease with which large-scale reform takes place in the UK. This is the consequence, he argues, of a 'light touch' legal system and a style of politics that enable leaders to instigate public reform unchallenged. While the UK may have a leading role as a major exporter of public management ideas, Pollitt asserts that 'its prominence has been built upon shaky foundations' (p 7).

In Chapter Two Rod Rhodes joins Pollitt in raising questions about the production and quality of social science evidence to inform policy and practice. He considers the limitations of the dominant tradition of modernist-empiricism in political science with its roots in the natural science model and asks what lessons about public sector reform can be learnt from using political anthropology: more specifically, whether the various reform proposals introduced in the UK blend with the everyday beliefs and practices of Whitehall civil servants and their ministers. Rhodes uses the concept of 'storytelling' to examine the structures and procedures that guide working practices in Whitehall. He argues that would-be reformers would benefit from drawing on observational evidence so that they know 'what they are seeking to reform' (p 43). These insights, he argues, would be more effective than the rational, managerial approaches to reform that have predominated since the 1970s, with modest success.

Jonathan Davies (Chapter Three) also refers to the importance of everyday behaviours and working practices in his critique of the continued dominance of the neoliberal narrative and quest for possible alternatives. He refers to the concept of 'everyday making' to explore the possibilities for resistance and change within the capitalist system. Everyday makers reject system-oriented theories and campaigns, looking instead to invoke opposition by deciding in the first place just to act differently. However, Davies rejects the idea that we need to choose between everyday and systemic approaches and instead argues that they are complementary. He argues that a future challenge will be to grasp the dynamics of scale – the systemic implications of everyday struggles and vice-versa.

In Chapter Four Janet Newman echoes Davies' call for the exploration of creative and progressive responses to the politics of austerity. She considers 'how far actors with "progressive" social or political commitments are able to enact new worlds within the confines of the [neoliberal] present' (p 71). Newman argues that critical reflections alone are insufficient and goes on to explore the potential for new methods, actors and framing of the policy process to generate innovatory solutions in a period of cuts and austerity.

Both Newman and Davies recognise the importance of the individual (or agency) in exploring new pathways to post-austerity politics, as do Vivien Lowndes and Kerry McCaughie (Chapter Five) in their analysis of local government in the UK. They identify the emergence of creative responses to service redesign based on pragmatic politics and 'institutional bricolage' – the recombination and reshuffling of pre-existing components to serve new purposes. Lowndes and McCaughie agree with Davies and Newman in their observation of an apparent absence of radical new ideas in austerity politics. Instead, they observe new solutions emanating 'bottom up' as practitioners take the role of innovators and entrepreneurs in their daily practices.

Martijn van der Steen, Mark van Twist, Menno Fenger and Sara le Cointre also examine the role of contextual factors, local circumstances and practitioners in shaping policy outcomes (Chapter Six). More specifically, they examine the unintended effects of policy interventions in 'weak schools' in the Netherlands. Their chapter poses two central questions: what causes the differences in outcomes of similar policies in similar contexts and can patterns of causation be found in what seem to be unpredictable, instable and chaotic systems. They look at the roles of causality, feedback mechanisms and cyclical loops in the production of policy outcomes. Cumulative effects are viewed as inevitable and, hence, predictable. Along with other contributors to this book, they recognise the central role of local practitioners in predicting and identifying the local circumstances and causations that might affect policy outcomes in unique ways.

Other chapters in this book have explored the complex relationship between different modes of governance – markets, hierarchies, networks – in the policy process. In Chapter Seven Guy Peters examines the challenges of policy coordination in different contexts. Peters claims that hierarchical coordination is the 'default option for coordination'(p 142) but that it can be analysed in different ways. One is to understand coordination as a collective action problem based on an analysis of self-interest and resource dependency. Another is to view coordination as a form of cooperation and collaboration, whereby coordination is not based so much on rational calculation but on perceived needs to work together and shared beliefs. He goes on to explore the conditions and factors where these alternatives are most likely to be successful. Likewise, in Chapter Eight, Steve Martin and Valeria Guarneros-Meza consider the dynamics of hierarchy and coordination in their study of local partnership working. They explore the kinds of 'self-steering' required in order to address complex public policy problems and whether external (hierarchical) steering by government can help or hinder the process. They conclude that 'soft steering' – defined as the provision of government funding, information and expertise' – can have 'an important role in helping to establish and mobilise the local partnerships' (p 160) but that self-steering capacity is also vital. These examples illustrate the continued presence of hierarchy within in the so-called transition to networked governance and, interestingly, the potential complementarity of governance modes in the right context.

Peter John's chapter (Nine) on the 'tools of government' looks at the scientific developments that have taken place in the field over the past 40 years. John argues that the traditional tools of government, such as legislation, finance and regulation, are being redesigned or supplemented by low-cost behavioural interventions, such as 'nudge'. Nudge involves using information in a particular way that encourages citizens to behave in their own or society's interest. He notes that the tools of government have always had an informational component but that they 'are more informational now because of a growing awareness among policy makers about the power of signals and norms' (p 184). John's work provides a powerful demonstration of the impact of new methodological and scientific techniques on the policy process.

A number of chapters in this book have raised questions about the types of knowledge and evidence produced by social scientists and their variable impact on policy (e.g. Pollitt, Rhodes and Flinders). In Chapter Ten, Matthew Flinders reflects on how the academy should engage with policy and practice. He calls for 'engaged scholarship' and for academics to realise their 'political imagination' to ensure that academic knowledge has a clear role in 'promoting public debate, cultivating engaged citizenship and having some form of impact *beyond* academe' (p 210). He challenges the academy to reconnect with policy and politics and to embark on a different type of scholarship that is more accessible. Aside from meeting a public duty, he argues that this will be essential to the reputation and survival of political studies as a discipline.

There are obvious connections in the topics covered in this collection. In the final chapter (Eleven) Sarah Ayres and Alex Marsh draw out key themes and discuss them under four headings: (1) theorising policy, (2) evidence and the policy process, (3) transforming structures and processes, and (4) implementation and practice. The ways in which each chapter addresses the four themes is examined and points of commonality and departure across the collection are identified. They conclude by arguing for 'greater tolerance of diversity in theoretical and empirical enquiry' (p 232) and for continued reflection on the foundational assumptions of the field of policy studies.

Rethinking policy and politics brings together a breadth of scholarly knowledge and evidence to offer critical reflections on the recent history and future direction of policy studies. In doing so it seeks to advance the debate by rethinking the ways in which scholars and students of policy studies can (re)engage with pertinent issues and interested publics in pursuit of both scholarly excellence and practical solutions to global policy problems.

CHAPTER ONE

Forty years of public management reform in UK central government: promises, promises …

Christopher Pollitt

UK central government: a world leader in public management reform, 1970–2011

The core focus of this chapter is on the history of public management reforms by UK central government, 1970–2011. The argument will be that we have learned remarkably little from the almost ceaseless procession of reforms. In relation to the theme of this book this finding is somewhat paradoxical. On the surface there has been constant change. Below the surface, however, the reform process itself has changed far less, and the absence of firm knowledge concerning outcomes has remained stubbornly constant. The chapter falls into two main parts: the first one, in which lack of learning is identified and evidenced, and the second, in which a theoretical interpretation of these findings is proposed.

Since at least the late 1980s UK governments have seen themselves as international leaders of public management reform, and mainstream public administration academics have, by and large, agreed (Lynn, 2006; Pollitt and Bouckaert, 2011). Some, indeed, have seen the UK as 'hyperactive' (Moran, 2003; Pollitt, 2007). Dorrell was an example of ministerial boasting when he said that the whole world was following UK-style marketising reforms (Dorrell, 1993). The Anglophone academic literature is saturated with UK examples, and governments have themselves from time to time created special units in the Cabinet Office and elsewhere to sell British expertise internationally. British staff, ideas and cases have featured prominently in the management reform work of, *inter alia*, the OECD and the World Bank.

The first argument here is that while the UK may have been a leader, and a major exporter of public management ideas, its prominence has been built upon shaky foundations. The models and techniques UK governments have implemented at home and sold abroad have been products more of hubris and fashion than of science or carefully husbanded experience. Despite a massive amount of management reform, we have little reliable knowledge about the *outcomes* – especially of the 'flagship' programmes announced in white papers and trumpeted by ministers and Prime Ministers. As far as the results for citizens and society are concerned these huge and complex changes remain both contentious and obscure. If one looks hard for the final impacts one will usually find oneself hunting the snark. Furthermore, not only have reform governments not really known what they are achieving (or failing to achieve), they have not been terribly interested in finding out.

It is necessary to be clear about what is, and what is not, being claimed here. This chapter does *not* deny that we may have learned a good deal about the processes of management reform. Neither does it deny that organisational structures have been (repeatedly) remodelled or that processes have been radically changed. Nor is there any claim that the whole thing has been some kind of trick by either ministers or top civil servants. The argument does not rule out the possibility that many good things may have been achieved – there is ample evidence that in some specific cases they have. I am simply saying that, by the standards of orthodox, warranted social science knowledge we actually know very little about the end results of all these reforms – about what works in terms of outcomes, and why. Our knowledge of our own achievements (and failures) is generally fragile, fragmentary and deeply contested.

Methods

The chapter is essentially an interpretive historical essay. It draws on a close rereading of the major management reform white papers of the past 40 years, and an appraisal of a mass of scholarly commentary on those reforms, some of it very recent. In a minor way this material was supplemented by a few informal and unattributable interviews and conversations with senior officials. The interpretation advanced was also cross-checked against a recently-assembled database of studies of the impacts of New Public Management (NPM) reforms in Europe (including the UK), which helped to clarify what was unusual and what was not about management reform in UK central government (Pollitt and Dan, 2011).

The basic theoretic orientation is historical institutionalist (Pollitt and Bouckaert, 2009, ch 1) and most of its insights depend on taking a long view, and noting similarities and differences over an extended period of time. Unfortunately, such an approach has become quite scarce in contemporary public management scholarship (Pollitt, 2008). It has several virtues, including the potential for seeing patterns that are invisible, or less clearly visible, when scholars concentrate on one reform, or look across current developments horizontally. It stresses the importance of organisational structures and processes, and emphasises notions such as path dependence, punctuations/windows of opportunity, institutional layering and displacement (Pierson, 2004: Streeck and Thelen, 2005; Mahoney and

–

Thelen, 2010). This group of (mainly American) scholars are rigorously theoretical and spend a great deal of effort defining and distinguishing between an array of concepts for describing different patterns of temporal development. Another school of historical institutionalists are less strenuously theoretical, and instead stress tradition and culture, and describe how these durable features are strongly embedded in particular arrays of institutions (for example, Painter and Peters, 2010). Historical institutionalism has sometimes been criticized for understating the role of individual actors, although some of its leading proponents have explicitly incorporated agency into their theorising (Mahoney and Thelen, 2010). In this regard it is perfectly true that an alternative story of the UK reforms could be written on the basis of the personalities and interests of various Prime Ministers and senior ministers. What is striking, however, is, first, the way in which the main continuities identified later in this chapter are sustained through many changes of government and personality and, second, the extent to which the distinctive UK pattern of reform appears to be dependent on its particular institutional structure (Pollitt and Bouckaert, 2011; Pollitt, 2007). It is also the case that even the most forceful personalities are to some extent shaped by their institutional contexts – indeed, the most successful ones have often learned to take maximum advantage of the particular organisational situation in which they find themselves (Tuohy, 1999, 261).

The core reform documents: promises, promises...

For the first piece of evidence, we may consider a mini-history of central government reform based on five key white papers. Right at the beginning of our period came the white paper *The reorganisation of central government* (Prime Minister and Minister for the Civil Service, 1970). And at the end, 2011 brought us another, *Open public services* (Minister for Government Policy, 2011). In between we examine *Efficiency in government* (Lord President of the Council, 1981), *The citizen's charter* (1991) and *Modernising government* (1999). White papers are, of course, a particular kind of document. They are broad statements of policy and aspiration. They cannot be expected to report detailed evaluations, or pile up mountains of evidence. Yet at the same time they *are* the principal manifestations of the government's intentions, and they offer a condensation not only of *what* the government thinks but *how* they are thinking it. Furthermore, in the case of public management reform there is no systematic series of secondary publications underlying the white papers and giving more detail. Occasionally they will be backed up with supporting technical publications, but usually these are more 'how to do it' than evaluatory (for example, Cabinet Office, 1999).

There were (many) more reform white papers than these five, but these have been selected as flagship, broad-scope reforms at decade-ish intervals. Sectoral reforms, such as those which were applied to, *inter alia*, the NHS, schools, and the police, also had their white papers, but they are not considered in any detail here. In several notable cases, however, these sectoral documents shared all or most of the characteristics we are about to identify in our set of five pan-governmental examples (for example, Department of Health, Welsh Office, Scottish Home and Health Department and Northern Ireland Office, 1989; Department of Health, 1997; Home Office, 1993).

To begin, let us compare first and last: the 1970 and 2011 white papers. *The reorganisation of central government* set out a new set of procedures and structures for enhancing the strategic rationality of policy making. It was underpinned by the assumption that government knows its own business, and can improve if it strengthens the centre. *Open public services*, by contrast, regarded central government as the default position for the provision of public services – only to be resorted to when other potential suppliers are, for some special reason, not available. It sang a hymn of praise to decentralisation, public participation, diversity and competition. It also addressed itself not only to central government, but to the whole public sector, and beyond. If we look across all five white papers we can see certain trends over time. They became much longer, and their focus broadened from central government to the whole of the public sector, and beyond. A further trend has been that the figure of the citizen has become much mentioned since 1991, whereas the white papers of 1970 and 1981 hardly referred to citizens at all, presenting themselves as governments reporting on what they were doing to put their own houses in order (Pollitt, 2012).

It is perhaps tempting to see these changes over the sequence of documents in terms of a relatively neat succession of big models or epochs. It is often said that 1970 was towards the end of the era of central planning. Since then we have had the NPM under Thatcher and Major, networks and partnerships under early New Labour, increasingly punitive centralised targeting under later New Labour, and now a further round of decentralisation and diversification, bracketed by some as all part of the new model of 'governance' rather than 'government'.

Unfortunately, this view of the past 40 years as basically a 'parade of the paradigms', though not entirely fictitious, and certainly handy for textbooks and classrooms, is flawed. In fact each alleged era contains many examples of counter-trends, and at the same time some loudly trumpeted innovations are actually ideas which have been around before, though usually under different labels. Decentralising governments have also centralised. Pro-market governments have also increased hierarchical controls in some areas, and so on. It is also quite clear that some issues remain on the agenda for a long time, even if the label changes with each government. Thus, for example, both Heath in 1970 and Blair in 1999 wanted to improve horizontal coordination, and both wanted more of what is now usually called 'evidence-based policy making'. Both contained visions of modern, rational and partly de-politicised policy making (Cabinet Office, 1999; Johnson, 1971). And the 2011 white paper from the Coalition government shares far more with its Blair 1999 predecessor than its ministers would probably care to admit (Painter, 2012; Pollitt, 2012).

Despite many changes of theme and appearance (and length) there are also some strong common threads running through all five white papers. Four quite striking continuities directly concern our problematisation of management reform knowledge. Across all five white papers there are four *absences* of what might be considered key management information:

- First, an absence of any systematic evidence of the alleged problems identified, or, indeed, for the solutions proffered
- Second, an absence of targets
- Third, a total lack of costings
- Fourth, none of the white papers builds any formal process of evaluation into their reforms, except for a partial exception in the case of the *Citizen's charter*, which did at least envisage development over a decade, including a process of review

To begin with, none of the five documents offers any systematic evidence for its claims. *Efficiency in the civil service* does have an annex giving some cost figures for government overheads, and the white papers of 1991, 1999 and 2011 contain some mini case studies illustrating how the proposed reforms might work. But there is nothing even remotely comparable with the marshalling of evidence one would expect to see in reform documents in some other policy sectors. Second, none of them articulated a set of measurable targets against which success or failure could have been assessed. One might find this particularly curious for the 1999 document, because it came at a time when the Blair administration was in the process of unleashing an unprecedentedly comprehensive, detailed and publicised set of performance indicators upon almost every major public service (Barber, 2007) and was busy praising 'professional' and 'evidence-based' policy making (Cabinet Office, 1999). Third, none of the five white papers contains any costings. It has always been known that reforms carry costs – one cannot restructure organisations, move around and retrain staff, install new technology or put in place new procedures without spending both time and money. Yet the proposals in public management white papers seem to float in an alternate universe where lunches are free. Fourth, the *Citizen's charter* was the only one of the five to put in place an explicit, extended public review process (see Prime Minister, 1996; Prime Minister and Chancellor of the Duchy of Lancaster, 1995; Public Service Committee, 1997). For the other four white papers the absence of targets was complemented by an absence of any visible process of evaluation.

A recent National Audit Office report summed matters up for 2005–2009, but it appears that the NAO's remarks could be applied to almost any part of our 40-year period:

> We reported in March 2010 on central government reorganisations between May 2005 and June 2009. We found widespread failure by departments to specify the expected benefits of these reorganisations clearly and make sure they materialise, and similarly to identify and control costs. (National Audit Office, 2012, 5; see also White and Dunleavy, 2010)

Though short on evidence, our white papers have not been short on promises. In 1970 *The reorganisation of central government* promised a more coordinated and strategic approach to policy making, with special units and procedures to ensure more rational, evidence-based decision making. In 1981 *Efficiency in the civil service* assured us that by the adoption of modern business techniques waste would be cut back and the entire government would henceforth operate more efficiently. In 1991 *The citizen's charter* said that explicit standards would be set for public services, better information would be provided, streamlined complaints procedures would be installed and citizens would be offered more choice. In 1999 *Modernising government* held out a menu of joined-up government, evidence-based policy making, increased partnerships and enhanced responsiveness to citizen–consumers and to business. In 2011 *Open public services* promised decentralisation, transparency, equal opportunities and competition among a wider range of public service providers.

What can we say about the fulfillment of these promises? The 1970 promises are almost impossible to track, but in general terms one could say that a coordinated strategy was not the hallmark of the later stages of the Heath administration. Rather there was a U-turn in industrial policy and an unfolding mess in employment and energy policies, one that eventually helped to bring the government down. The Prime Minister appeared increasingly cut off and 'bunkered' as the tide of economic and industrial events overwhelmed his government. The large departments that were created to help reduce 'siloism' turned out to be very difficult to manage, and, contrary to the stated expectation in the white paper, neither the giant Department of Trade and Industry (DTI) nor the equally elephantine Department of the Environment (DoE) remained as stable groupings for very long. Among other departures from the model, in 1974 the Department of Energy was carved out of the DTI, and in 1976 the Department of Transport was extracted from the DoE (Pollitt, 1984).

Many people believe that the Thatcher administration delivered on its promises of greater efficiency in the civil service. Certainly there were notable instances of achieved savings – such as those flowing from the Rayner efficiency 'scrutinies' (Metcalfe and Richards, 1987; Pollitt, 1984, 120–1). And civil service numbers were substantially reduced. However, the big picture remains moot. Subsequent scholarship showed that the Thatcher cuts had not had much impact on public expenditure totals (for example, Dunsire and Hood, 1989). Recent – and very detailed – work by Hood and Dixon points to an absence of any noticable fall in departmental running costs between 1980 and 2000, and questions any assumption of major efficiency gains (Hood and Dixon, 2013). Rayner Scrutinies and other initiatives may have saved significant sums here and there, but there was probably no large, general gain in efficiency – or, at least, there is no solid evidence of such.

Interestingly, the 1991 *Citizen's charter*, much maligned at the time, comes rather better out of this kind of analysis than some of the other white papers. First, it was announced as a long-term programme with a five-year review – which duly took place. Second, there can be no doubt that it directly affected many aspects of public services over a number of years – and, significantly, it was picked up by the incoming New Labour administration in 1997 and re-branded. Nevertheless, the overall impacts were hard to distinguish from other parallel developments (Public Service Committee, 1997, para 25, xviii) and the views of the public themselves were not systematically recorded.

Of the 1999 white paper one permanent secretary wrote that 'the whole *Modernising government* agenda was simply dropped after the 2001 election because none of the players by then involved in public sector reform had any interest in it' (personal email to the author, 12 April 2012). Furthermore, observers of the later Blair administrations might find it hard to credit that an administration characterised by 'sofa government' and a deep divide between the Prime Minister and the Chancellor of the Exchequer could claim to be a model for 'joining up' (although this is not to deny many examples of more or less successful joining up at lower and local levels). As for the partnership theme, it has continued, but has been accompanied from the outset by a variety of concerns about accountability, risk-sharing and high transaction costs (Pollitt, 2003, 52–74). All in all, the varied menu of ideas in *Modernising government* can be said to have led to a varied assortment of outcomes – some positive, some negative and many obscure and unevaluated.

One particularly intriguing aspect to our story was the way in which New Labour's espousal of evidence-based policy making could apparently coexist with a dearth of evidence around many big management reforms. An examination focused on white papers cannot hope to get to the bottom of this, but the literature does afford some clues. First, there is an acknowledged extra difficulty in evaluating broad policies as compared with specific programmes and practices (Davies et al, 2000). Second, though, there was a difference between central and local government. Some of the management changes in local government were quite extensively evaluated (for example, Hartley, 2008). Not for the first time, central government would seem to have exempted itself from its own strictures. Additionally, third, there seems to have been a degree of difference between substantive policies (for education, health etc.) and public management reform – at least for central government. In her review of the role of evaluation in the New Labour administration, Sullivan (2011) mentions many evaluatory initiatives, but none concerned with the reforms we have in focus here. As she suggests, administrative doctrines 'are generally not evidence driven' (2011, 508). Finally, it is too soon to give any kind of final verdict on the 2011 white paper. We must wait to see whether in fact 'our reforms give power to those who have been overlooked and underserved' (Minister for Government Policy, 2011, 5). Currently the most media-prominent elements of the reform appear to be controversies over the actual or proposed contracting out of public services to large corporations – hardly the transfer of power to the underserved. Once again, future investigations of this issue will be handicapped by the lack of targets and – in all probability – evidence.

Why so little hard evidence? First reason: difficulties of designing and implementing monitoring and evaluation

If it is correct that there is a glaring lack of evidence, costings and outcome data for most major management reform programmes these lacunae cannot by any means be blamed entirely on the ministers and senior officials who created them. There are considerable technical and methodological problems in evaluating such reforms, perhaps especially the kinds of structural and process changes which have been so popular with successive UK governments (Boyne et al, 2003; Pollitt, 2009).

Two interconnected problems are that the design of reforms does not stand still, and neither does the context in which they are being implemented. To come to full fruition, a major structural reform is likely to need years rather than months, and during that time the original design is highly likely to be adapted (Wallace and Fertig, 2008). Many reforms are, in effect, redesigned during implementation because new aspects or difficulties are discovered 'on the ground'. And at the same time the context in which the reform is taking shape may alter drastically. A period of economic growth may be replaced by a period of austerity. Scandals and accidents may reduce the appeal of an efficiency drive and increase the attraction of measures to enhance safety and/or accountability. In the 1990s the businessman appointed as a reforming Director of Prisons hit nearly all of his performance targets, but was nonetheless dismissed by the then Home Secretary because of ministerial embarassment at high-profile prisoner escapes. He subsequently won substantial out of court damages for unfair dismissal (Lewis, 1997). The political colour of the government may change, and the newcomers may wish to 're-badge' if not actually scrap the reforms beloved of their predecessors. Blair, for example, re-badged the *Citizen's Charter*. The goals of reform – often only vaguely expressed in the first place – may shift during implementation.

All this means that the orthodox model of evaluation, in which a defined instrument is introduced in order to achieve a defined goal, often cannot be applied. The goals are vague and priorities are shifting, while the design – sometimes for good reasons – is continuously adjusted during implementation (Sullivan, 2011).

Nor is this all. Even if a reform is clear and reasonably stable, and even if outcomes are measured, it may well be exceedingly difficult confidently to attribute a particular outcome to a particular reform. There are two main reasons for this. First, major reform programmes of the kind we have been discussing are usually composed of many different actions and tools. Some will work and others will not; some will work in this sector or organisation but not in that one (Pawson, 2013). How, though, can we know which specific actions contributed how much to a given outcome? When customer satisfaction goes up following a reorganisation, was it the new procedures, or the customer service training programme, or the increased resources put into counter services or the refurbishment of public offices, or some combination of these? Second, how can we be confident that the outcome was not partly or wholly caused by something other than the reform? Over the substantial implementation periods frequently involved there may be all sorts of other developments that could influence the same outcome. For example, has an increase in job placements by a reorganised job advisory service been the result of the reorganisation, or of a simultaneous pick-up in the economy (and if the answer is both, then in what proportions)?

Finally, there is often a time problem. Orthodox evaluations seek to compare before and after – to establish a baseline in time, before the relevant interventions are set in motion, against which changes can be measured. The practical circumstances of major reforms frequently make it difficult to follow this design. Often, the reforms begin as soon as they are announced (or in some cases preparatory and anticipatory moves are being made even before the main official announcement, because savvy officials sense the way things are likely to go). So, finding an 'uncontaminated' baseline may be beyond the evaluators. Equally, defining a 'finishing line' can be problematic. The cumulative effects of a major reform may go on for years before they dwindle or cease, but to wait that long for 'answers' is politically and managerially impractical. Indeed, there may be strong temptations to evaluate too soon. For example, one year after launch may still be during a difficult transition period, when the full fruits of reform are not yet apparent but the short-term upheavals and confusions are still in evidence.

Why so little hard evidence? Second reason: lack of sustained interest in specific reforms

> Governments lack a theory of and experience of embedding change coherently, so the people involved and the story lines are dropped/changed too quickly. (ex-Permanent Secretary with extensive experience of reform – email to the author, 12 April 2012)

The minister – let alone the Prime Minister – who is both interested and experienced in large scale organisational change is fairly rare. Most executive politicians are certainly interested in defending and/or expanding their own organisational sphere of action, and most are also willing to take credit for announcements of dynamic new reforms that will, at least in intention, bring benefits to citizens. These two types of interest are, however, inadequate to sustain detailed interest in organisational reforms which often unfold over several years – often beyond the horizon of the next election. Even in a New Labour government officially committed to evidence-based policy making and willing to sponsor evaluations, ministers were often unwilling to wait for the results, rolling out reforms or moving on to the next one before the evidence they themselves had asked for was in (Walker, 2001). Similarly, the original NPM formula, in which politicians were supposed to play the part of strategists setting long-term goals and leaving managers unhindered to manage and make operational choices, never seemed a particularly realistic model for politics (Pollitt and Bouckaert, 2011, ch 6). Politicians often want to intervene in operational matters, and may not be particularly interested in, or skillful at, strategy-making.

Given the technical and methodological problems referred to in the previous section, one can perhaps extend some sympathy to the politicians concerned. They are hardly guilty of ignoring hard evidence that this works better than that. Rather, as one American scholar put it:

> Because Congress and the Presidency simply do not know what does and what does not actually make government work, and because they have no overarching theory of when government and its employees can and cannot be trusted to perform well, they will move back and forth between... reform philosophies almost at random. (Light, 1997, 5)

A UK study reflects a similar sentiment as follows:

> At the level of generalisable, empirically supported causal statements, social science research has been able to contribute little to the normative project of designing governance institutions. (Skelcher, 2008, 41)

Furthermore, the lack of sustained, longer-term political interest in specific management reforms is not the only challenge facing evidence seekers. In some cases evaluations are actually resisted, usually because so much political capital has been invested in a particular reform that finding evidence that it was less than wholly successful would be deeply politically embarassing. That seems to be why, for example, Thatcher's 1989 introduction of an internal market to the NHS was never subject to formal evaluation. Thus a wholly untried organisational form was rather rapidly introduced into one of the largest and most complex organisations in Europe. Some academics did subsequently attempt evaluations, but working *post hoc*, in far from ideal circumstances.

It should be noted, however, that ministers and senior civil servants are not the only groups involved in hatching management reforms. During the early part of our period – up to the early 1980s – 'machinery of government' reforms were usually the business of a very small club – the Prime Minister of the day, the Secretary to the Cabinet and the Head of the Civil Service. A small machinery of government unit in the Civil

Service Department serviced this triumvirate. There were a few exceptions – such as the participation of a few top businessmen in the preparation of Edward Heath's reforms of 1970. But the basic process was both very much in-house and very informal (Pollitt, 1984). This 'path' – a high degree of personal discretion for the Prime Minister of the day – has remained fairly constant throughout the four decades under review.

By the 21st century the cast of what had become the on-going reform drama had grown considerably. Prime Ministers were still central and the civil service continued to play an important part. But gradually management consultants and political advisers also got in on the act - Streeck and Thelen (2005) would call this 'layering'. Public sector management reform became an international business with ideas circulating rapidly through the OECD and consultancy networks (see, for example, OECD, 1995; Sahlin-Andersson and Engwall, 2002; Saint-Martin, 2000; 2005). This somewhat changed the game, because some of the new players brought with them an intense interest in the details of reorganisations. This interest, however, was usually still only short or medium term. Management consultants to some extent reflected the horizons of the politicians and senior civil servants who hired them – the next election (or the next contract) was still an important threshold. Then they would move on to the next client. Political advisers generally wanted reforms which looked good publicly and could be packaged as 'modern'. Neither they nor the consultants usually had future careers in the public services they reformed: they were 'visitors' from outside.

Why so much reform? UK exceptionalism

Much of what has been said so far is widely true across OECD countries. The difficulties of design and method identified above are present in all countries. And there are not many places where we can find politicians who take a deep and sustained interest in organisational matters. A recent analysis of the existing literature on NPM reforms across the EU came to the conclusion that only a very small percentage of studies dealt directly with outcomes, and even in those cases the methodology was sometimes weak, and attribution difficult (Pollitt and Dan, 2011). So in these respects there is nothing uniquely 'wrong' with the UK. Indeed, most of the few good outcome-oriented studies that do exist seem to be of UK examples, mainly because performance measurement systems have flowered here so copiously and for so long (for example, Bevan, 2009; Kelman and Friedman, 2009; Propper et al, 2008 – though even these excellent studies are still substantially concerned with outputs rather than outcomes).

However, there are additional factors which support the proposition that the UK is a special case. To begin with, it is one of the club of Anglophone countries in which an ideology of 'management' itself has taken deepest root. All these countries – Australia, New Zealand, the UK and, to some extent, the USA – have experienced series of large-scale management reform programmes and now have 'modern management tools' firmly in place (OECD, 2011; Pollitt and Bouckaert, 2011). The sheer scale of change and the fervent belief of successive governments that better management is the solution to a wide range of public policy problems have set this group somewhat apart from other major OECD states such as France, Germany or Japan (Lynn, 2006).

Yet there is something that, even in this club of management enthusiasts, makes the UK stand out. It is the sheer ease of major change (rivalled perhaps only by New Zealand, until it acquired proportional representation in 1996; see Pollitt and Bouckaert, 2011, 298–304). For most of the period UK governments have enjoyed a combination of factors which, taken together, lower political costs and reduce veto points for management reformers. The first has been a legal procedure for machinery changes which is very 'light' (Pollitt, 1984; 2007). Consider, for example, the fact that most of the huge 1989–1997 Next Steps programme of agencification was carried out without a single statute being needed – inconceivable in most continental EU member states. Second, most governments have been one-party, so intra-coalition compromises over reform have not been necessary. Third, machinery of government changes traditionally have not even been a matter for the whole of the Cabinet. They lie in the hands of the Prime Minister, who can decide how far to share his/her thoughts with others. Fourth, most parliaments have been submissive. A Prime Minister with a majority in the House of Commons can almost always get his/her way. Parliament has not blocked or substantially amended major management reform programmes. These four factors are not present to the same combined degree in any other OECD country. They mean that, in the UK, the window of opportunity for large-scale management reform is almost always at least half-open. Change itself is cheap, but what does not change so much is the institutional process underlying the 'continuous revolution'.

One might add the observation that, as one moves into the late 1980s and beyond, it is not simply that the political costs of reform are low, but that the political costs of *not* reforming begin to rise. Parties which aspire to government are increasingly *expected* to say something about how they will improve the public sector. This tendency is discussed further in the following section.

Reflections

All this raises the question of why busy, clever people in the civil service, ministerial office and, more recently, management consultancy, have persistently lent their names and efforts to management reforms the final outcomes of which were usually shrouded in uncertainty? How is it that this cycle has endured for so long, despite (or perhaps because of) the many changes in the approaches to public management being espoused?

The motivation for management reform seems to have shifted somewhat over the years. In the 1960s and 70s reforms either stemmed from perceptions of political coordination problems within government, or they were designed to accomodate the rising or falling of particular policy topics or particular individuals (for example, the rise of 'the environment' in 1970, or the need to find a big department for Mr Crossman in 1968; see Pollitt, 1984). They were technical adjustments, or efforts to balance Cabinets. While these kinds of reasons for action continued to manifest themselves in later periods, they were supplemented or even overtaken by a more general perception that management was an important policy issue in itself, and that every new government needed to make its mark by having something to say about better public management (Pollitt and Bouckaert, 2011, 5–11). To govern without some reform platform, complete with popular headlines (joined-up government; open public services) would have been to open oneself to media criticism. It became more or less taken for granted that existing public management was inadequate (though here again, systematic evidence was seldom offered) and that large gains could be had by implementing some kind of 'transformation'. Even in the 2011 white paper, after 30 years of fervid reform, the old spectre of unresponsive, top-down, monolithic public bureaucracy was wheeled out again (Minister for Government Policy, 2011, 7). In short, management became a broad ideology rather than a dusty technical backwater or a matter of the short-term balancing of the personalities in a particular cabinet (Clarke and Newman, 1997; Pollitt, 1993, 1–10). This ideology sported some of the characteristics of an organised religion (Hood, 2005). Interestingly, this managerialism seems to have been capable of embracing, however uncomfortably, both neoliberal *and* post-NPM policy solutions (see Bevir and Gains, 2011, and the associated special issue of *Policy & Politics*). Many factors play into this state of affairs, but in the UK case the most important seem to be this spread of a managerialist 'world view' combined with the unusually unfettered ability of Prime Ministers to move the pieces around the organisational chess board. As management reform has become an ideology, so it has also become a business – a large, thriving, international business in which careers can be made (Saint-Martin, 2000; 2005; Sahlin-

Andersson and Engwall, 2002). For example, in the 2003/4 financial year UK central government spent roughly £2 billion on consultants (but could show no overall result because most departments did not collect information on what had been achieved: National Audit Office, 2006). So, unlike in 1970, there are now substantial organisational interests, both within and without government, with investments in perpetual change and reform. They form an international network or community (Sahlin-Andersson and Engwall, 2002). It is a measure of their success that to even suggest that medium term organisational stability could be attained is to invite the criticism that one is hopelessly out of touch with the complex, fast-moving modern world. The philosophy of the consultancies and the business schools is that we need 'continuous redirection and/or reinvention of the core business without losing momentum' (Doz and Kosonen, 2008, 14). 'Strategic agility' is a key watchword, and has recently been adopted by the OECD public management division, straight out of the business school textbook.

Conclusions

Can this state of affairs be changed? In concrete terms, is it possible that a new government will no longer feel obliged to announce a new programme of management reform or to promise that it will 'transform' the efficiency, effectiveness or citizen responsiveness of British public administration? Or even a government that announces a reform with clear medium-term targets and a robust and independent system for identifying and tracking outcomes? Such developments would indeed represent 'punctuations' or 'critical junctures' in the trajectory documented above.

One line of analysis is that there would need to be a shift in one or more of the factors which have hitherto led a combination of constant upheaval with little longer-term monitoring, evaluation or learning. To put this in terms of path dependency, there would need to be a rupture in the positive feedback that has hitherto encouraged UK Prime Ministers and their advisers to keep on proposing vague, poorly evidenced and largely uncosted programmes of management reform (Pierson, 2004).

However, several contributing factors are unlikely to disappear: the medium- to long-term nature of major organisational change, the reality of redesign and adjustment during implementation, and the difficulties of attributing outcomes to specific techniques, processes or structures. Nevertheless, some of the other factors could, conceivably, change. These include at least the following:

- If the incidence of coalition governments increased so that they became the new norm, rather than a rarity, then management reforms might have to be negotiated between the governing parties. In EU states where coalitions are the standard way of political life large-scale public managment reforms would normally be the subject of negotiations among coalition partners – as in, say, Denmark, Finland or the Netherlands. This process frequently raises the political costs of reform and tends to blunt more radical or puritanical schemes. Some UK political scientists are now predicting a higher frequency of coalition governments than in the past, so this scenario is at least feasible.

- Governments could, as a kind of self-denying ordinance, make the parliamentary and legal procedures for changing the machinery of government more demanding. For example, major machinery change could be defined as requiring statutory action (in Austria, for example, the recent adoption of performance budgeting actually required a change in the constitution). Alternatively (or additionally) an independent evaluation procedure reporting to parliament and public could be mandated. Whilst all this is possible, it is currently hard to see what motivation a government would have for limiting its own prerogatives in this way.

- Governments could become convinced that the short term presentational advantages of announcing major management reforms were no longer present – and, indeed, that further reform announcements would actually fuel public cynicism and resistance. This is not impossible, but there has been little sign of it up to the present. An enthusiast for this possibility might point to the widespread public and professional reaction against the coalition government's NHS reforms as a case in point, but the reforms nevertheless went ahead, as did Mrs Thatcher's equally if not even more unpopular NHS reforms of 1989. Organisational reforms are seldom intended as populist measures anyway – the public may be heavily involved with the NHS as a set of local services, but it is less interested in rearrangements in Whitehall. In this matter governments are, realistically, more focused on the Whitehall/Westminster community. In that narrower forum they can still score political points for 'vision' and political correctness.

It is hard to do brief justice to the actual and potential roles of the social sciences in public management policy making. On the one hand, social scientists frequently play important local parts in implementing particular reforms, but those activities deserve a chapter to themselves. At the level of general policy making one can see ideas that have originally come from the social sciences (and even more from business schools) but these ideas are frequently adapted and used in different – even contradictory – ways by policy makers (for example, Bevir and Gains, 2011; Painter, 2012). Whether social scientists can intervene to insist on a more evidence-based approach to public management reform must be doubted – there has been no sign of that so far. What might be possible, however, would be a more modest strategy of investing more in independent evaluatory research. Academic coverage of previous reforms has been strong in some parts but almost totally absent in others, and overall could not be described as more than patchy. The resulting findings would be one more piece of evidence that could be used to try to persuade political leaders that glib, helter-skelter reform can be costly, counter-productive and even unpopular with portions of the electorate. That last link – with citizens – has been perhaps the most academically neglected aspect of all. It would repay further attention.

We are left, therefore, with an unusual, but apparently quite stable process. Each new government launches big programmes of public management reform. Each claims that they will transform a currently highly unsatisfactory situation – by making the public sector more efficient, more effective, more responsive, more participatory, or all of these. Each then incurs sizeable transaction costs (including disruption effects) as the reforms are implemented. Yet these large efforts are carried out in ways that make them extremely hard to evaluate, and anyway most governments appear to have been strenuously uninterested in attempting any tracking over time, still less in any final reckoning. And so the cycle goes on – little is learned and little is known – at least not by those who are taking the strategic decisions. The promises, however, are plentiful. It is just a pity that they are not cheap.

Acknowledgement

Some elements of the research on which this chapter is based received funding from the European Community's Seventh Framework Programme under grant agreement number 266887 (project COCOPS – see www.cocops.eu).

References

Barber, M, 2007, *Instruction to deliver: Tony Blair, public services and the challenge of achieving targets*, London: Politico's

Bevan, G, 2009, Hitting and missing targets by ambulance services for emergency calls: Effects of different systems of performance measurement in the UK, *Journal of the Royal Statistical Society*, 172, 1, 61–190

Bevir, M, Gains, F, 2011, Ideas into policy: Governance and governmentality, *Policy & Politics*, 39, 4, 451–6

Boyne, G, Farrell, C, Law, J, Powell, M, Walker, R, 2003, *Evaluating public management reforms*, Buckingham: Open University Press

Cabinet Office, 1999, *Professional policy making for the 21st century*, London: Cabinet Office

Clarke, J, Newman, J, 1997, *The managerial state: Power, politics and ideology in the remaking of the social welfare,* London: Sage

Davies, H, Nutley, S, Smith, P, 2000, Learning from the past, prospects for the future, in Davies, H, Nutley, S, Smith, P, *What works? Evidence-based policy and practice in public services*, Bristol: Policy Press, 351–66

Department of Health, Welsh Office, Scottish Home and Health Department, and Northern Ireland Office, 1989, *Working for patients*, Cm 555, London: HMSO

Department of Heath, 1997, *The new NHS: Modern, dependable*, Cmnd 3807, London: The Stationery Office

Dorrell, S, 1993, Public sector change is a world-wide movement, Speech by the Financial Secretary to the Treasury to the Chartered Institute of Public Finance and Accountancy, London, 23 September

Doz, Y, Kosonen, M, 2008, *Fast strategy*, Harlow and New York: Wharton School Publishing

Dunsire, A, Hood, C, 1989, *Cutback management in public bureaucracies*, Cambridge: Cambridge University Press

Edgerton, D, 2007, *The shock of the old: Technology and global history since 1900*, Oxford: Oxford University Press

Hartley, J, 2008, Does innovation lead to improvement in public services? Lessons from the Beacon Scheme in the United Kingdom, in Borins, S (ed), *Innovations in government: Research, recognition and replication,* Washington, DC: Brookings Institute, 159–87

Home Office, 1993, *Police reform: A police service for the twenty-first century*, Cm 2281, London: HMSO

Hood, C, 2005, Public management: The word, the movement, the science, in Ferlie, R, Lynn, L Jr, Pollitt, C (eds), *The Oxford handbook of public management*, Oxford: Oxford University Press, 7–26

Hood, C, Dixon, R, 2013, A model of cost-cutting in government? The great management revolution in UK central government reconsidered, *Public Administration,* 91, 1, 114–34

Johnson, N, 1971, The reorganisation of central government, *Public Administration,* 49, 1, 1–12

Kelman, S, Friedman, J, 2009, Performance improvement and performance dysfunction: An empirical examination of the distortionary impacts of the emergency room wait-time target in the English National Health Service, *Journal of Public Administration Research and Theory*, 19, 4, 917–46

Lewis, D, 1997, *Hidden agendas: Politics, law and disorder*, London: Hamish Hamilton

Light, P, 1997, *The tides of reform; Making government work, 1945–1995*, New Haven, NJ: Yale University Press

Lord President of the Council, 1981, *Efficiency in the civil service*, Cmnd. 8293, London: HMSO, July

Lynn, L Jr, 2006, *Public management: old and new*, New York and London: Routledge and Taylor and Francis

Mahoney, J, Thelen, K (eds), 2010, *Explaining institutional change: Ambiguity, agency and power*, Cambridge: Cambridge University Press

Metcalfe, L, Richards, S, 1987, *Improving public management*, London: Sage

Minister for Government Policy, 2011, *Open public services*, White Paper, Cm 8145, London: The Stationery Office

Moran, M, 2003, *The British regulatory state: High modernism and hyper-innovation*, Oxford: Oxford University Press

National Audit Office, 2006, *Central government's use of consultants*, HC 128, Session 2006–07, London: The Stationery Office

National Audit Office, 2012, *Reorganising central government bodies*, HC 1703, Session 2010–12, London, The Stationery Office

OECD (Organisation for Economic Cooperation and Development), 1995, *Governance in transition: Public management reforms in OECD countries*, Paris: PUMA/OECD

OECD, 2011, *Government at a glance 2011*, Paris: OECD

Painter, C, 2012, The UK coalition government: Constructing public service reform narratives, *Public Policy and Administration*, http://ppa.sagepub.com/content/early/2012/01/25/0952076711427758

Painter, M, Peters, GB (eds), 2010, *Tradition and public administration*, Basingstoke: Palgrave Macmillan

Pawson, R, 2013, *The science of evaluation: A realist manifesto*, Los Angeles and London: Sage

Pierson, P, 2004, *Politics in time: History, institutions and social analysis*, Princeton, NJ: Princeton University Press

Pollitt, C, 1984, *Manipulating the machine: Changing the pattern of ministerial departments, 1960–83*, London: Allen and Unwin

Pollitt, C, 1993, *Managerialism and the public services* (2nd edn), Oxford: Blackwell

Pollitt, C, 2003, *The essential public manager*, Maidenhead/Philadelphia: Open University Press

Pollitt, C, 2007, New Labour's re-disorganisation: Hyper-modernism and the costs of reform – a cautionary tale, *Public Management Review*, 9, 4, 529–43

Pollitt, C, 2008, *Time, policy, management: Governing with the past*, Oxford: Oxford University Press

Pollitt, C, 2009, Structural change and public service performance, *Public Money and Management*, 29, 5, 285–91

Pollitt, C, 2012, The evolving narratives of public management reform: 40 years of reform white papers in the UK, *Public Management Review*, 13, 5, 641–58

Pollitt, C, Bouckaert, G, 2009, *Continuity and change in public policy making and management*, Cheltenham: Edward Elgar

Pollitt, C, Bouckaert, G, 2011, *Public management reform: A comparative analysis* (3rd edn), Oxford: Oxford University Press

Pollitt, C, Dan, S, 2011, *The impacts of the New Public Management in Europe: A meta-analysis*, www.cocops.eu

Prime Minister, 1970, *The reorganisation of central government*, Cmnd 4506, London: HMSO

Prime Minister, 1991, *The citizen's charter: Raising the standard*, Cm 1599, London: HMSO

Prime Minister and the Chancellor of the Duchy of Lancaster, 1995, *The citizen's charter: The facts and figures*, a report to mark four years of the charter programme, Cm 2970, London: HMSO

Prime Minister, 1996, *The citizen's charter: Five years on*, Cm 3370, London: HMSO

Prime Minister and Minister for the Cabinet, 1999, *Modernising government*, Cm 413, London: The Stationery Office

Propper, C, Sutton, M, Whitnall, C, Windmeijer, F, 2008, *Incentives and targets in hospital care: Evidence from a natural experiment*, Bath: CMPO (Centre for Market and Public Organization) Working Paper 9

Public Service Committee, 1997, *The citizen's charter*, third report of the Public Service Committee, Session 1996–97, HC 78-I and II, London: The Stationery Office

Sahlin-Andersson, K and Engwall, L, 2002, *The expansion of management knowledge: Carriers, flows and sources*, Stanford, CA: Stanford University Press

Saint-Martin, D, 2000, *Building the new managerialist state: Consultants and the politics of public sector reform in comparative perspective*, Oxford: Oxford University Press

Saint-Martin, D, 2005, Management consultancy, in Ferlie, E, Lynn, L Jr, Pollitt, C (eds), *The Oxford handbook of public management*, Oxford: Oxford University Press, 671–94

Skelcher, C, 2008, Does governance perform? Concepts, evidence, causalities and research strategies, in Hartley, J, Donaldson, C, Skelcher, C, Wallace, M (eds), *Managing to improve public services*, Cambridge: Cambridge University Press, 27–45

Streeck, W, Thelen, K (eds), 2005, *Beyond continuity: Institutional chnage in advanced political economies*, Oxford: Oxford University Press

Sullivan, H, 2011, Truth junkies: Using evaluation in UK public policy, *Policy & Politics,* 39, 4, 499–512

Tuohy, C, 1999, *Accidental logics: The dynamics of change in the healthcare arena in the United States, Britain and Canada*, Oxford: Oxford University Press

Walker, D, 2001, Great expectations: Can social science evaluate New Labour's policies?, *Evaluation,* 7, 3, 305–30

Wallace, M, Fertig, M, 2008, Orchestrating complex and programmatic change in the public services, in Hartley, J, Donaldson, C, Skelcher, C, Wallace, M (eds), *Managing to improve public services*, Cambridge: Cambridge University Press, 257–78

White, A, Dunleavy, P, 2010, *Making and breaking Whitehall departments: A guide to machinery of government changes*, London: Institute for Government

CHAPTER TWO

Political anthropology and civil service reform: prospects and limits

R.A.W Rhodes

Introduction

A core question for this book, which celebrates 40 years of the *Policy & Politics* journal, is how to use experience to inform future policy. Over the years, *Policy & Politics* has returned frequently to the topic of public sector and public management reform. So, this chapter addresses matters of central concern to the journal in its anniversary year. Specifically, I ask two questions. What lessons about reforming the British civil service can be learnt from using observational methods to study British government departments? What are the strengths and weaknesses of such an approach in the reform of public administration?

Both questions are unusual in political science. First, observation is not a common research tool because of such obstacles as the addiction to secrecy of British government. Thus, Fine et al (2009) cite no studies by political scientists in their survey of organisational ethnography (and see Rhodes, 2013, for citation and discussion). Second, those relatives of observation such as action research and organisational learning (Argyris and Schon, 1996) are said to have limited applicability in civil service reform because these approaches are compromised by the political environment (Common, 2004, 36–8).

As Geertz (1983, 21) points out, 'there has been an enormous amount of genre mixing in intellectual life' as 'social scientists have turned away from a laws and instances ideal of explanation towards a cases and interpretations one' and towards 'analogies drawn from the humanities'. Examples of such analogies include social life as game, as drama, and as text. There is a specific problem for public administration. As we blur genres, we bring 'the social technologist notion of what a social scientist is… into question' (Geertz, 1983, 35). Rather, the task becomes to recover the meaning of games, dramas and texts and to tease out their consequences. So, this chapter blurs genres, combining political science and cultural anthropology to explore civil service reform. Then, confronting the 'social technologist' issue, I ask, what lessons can public administration draw from this research? Can recovering stories provide lessons for the would-be reformer?

The chapter has three sections. The first section provides a brief account of the main characteristics of public sector reform over the past decade; namely, evidence-based policy making, managerialism, and choice. The second section compares the reform proposals with the fieldwork reported in Rhodes (2011) and draws lessons for would-be reformers. I use five axioms for ease of exposition: coping and the appearance of rule, not strategic planning; institutional memory, not internal structures; storytelling, not evidence-based policy; contending traditions and stories, not managerialism; the politics of implementation, not top-down innovation and control. The final section discusses the strengths and weaknesses of my approach both in the study of public administration and for public sector reform. I argue that attempts to impose private sector management beliefs and techniques to increase the economy, efficiency and effectiveness have had at best variable success. I conclude we do not need more managerialism but a different approach to reform that recognises the centrality of organisational traditions and storytelling.

The reforms

This section suggests that the reforms of the civil service proposed by both think tanks and the government over the past decade are pervaded by beliefs in the instrumental rationality of evidence-based policy making, managerialism, and economic choice. These ideas are the shared, almost tacit, knowledge of contributors to the continuing debate about public sector reform. I will be brief because my remarks verge on the obvious.

Evidenced-based policy making

At the heart of the Cabinet Office's (1999) professional policy making model is a belief in evidence-based policy making. For example, their model 'uses the best available evidence from a wide range of sources'; and 'learns from experience of what works and what doesn't' through systematic evaluation (Cabinet Office, 1999, para 2.11). By July 2011, when the Coalition government launched its *Open Public Services White Paper* (Cm 8145, 2011), little had changed. Despite claims that 'something very big and different is happening with this White Paper' (Cameron, 2011), most observers saw only more of the same. The emphasis fell on 'building on evidence of what works'. Phrases like 'sound evidence base' 'what works' and 'robust evidence' abound. Departments would need a 'clearer understanding of what their priorities are' and need 'to ensure administrative resources match Government policy priorities' so the Government can get 'value for taxpayers' money in delivering its

---

objectives' (Cabinet Office, 2012, 14, 16, 20). The instrumental rationality of evidence-based policy making is alive and well and at the heart of the Coalition's reform agenda. Moreover, this view of the policy-making process is widely shared inside and outside government (see, for example, Better Government Initiative (BGI), 2010; Bullock, Mountford and Stanley, 2001; Davies, Nutley and Smith, 2000; Institute for Government, 2010; Lodge and Rogers, 2006; Mulgan, 2009; National Audit Office, 2001; Regulatory Policy Institute, 2009; and Sanderson, 2002).

Managerialism

Managerialism has a long history which cannot be retold here (see Pollitt, 1993). In brief, it is a set of inherited beliefs about how private sector management techniques would increase the economy, efficiency and effectiveness – the three Es – of the public sector. Initially the beliefs focused on managerialism or hands-on, professional management; explicit standards and measures of performance; managing by results; and value for money. Subsequently, it also embraced marketisation or neoliberal beliefs about competition and markets. It introduced ideas about restructuring the incentive structures of public service provision through contracting-out, quasi-markets, and consumer choice. New Labour introduced a third strand to managerialism with its service delivery agenda.

For my purpose, I need to show only that such reform persists (and for a review of the 2000s see Public Administration Select Committee (PASC, 2009). The core concern for decades has been better performance management, whether called accountable management or management-by-objectives. Only the labelling has changed. So, even today, 'effective performance assessment within government helps to identify how well public organisations are meeting their objectives, as well as highlighting where improvements could be made' (PASC, 2009, 3; see also Cabinet Office, 2012, 28–29; PASC, 2003; BGI, 2010, 33).

Delivery and choice

The general principles informing the delivery agenda were outlined by Michael Barber, the Prime Minister's former Chief Adviser on Delivery, in his comments about education:

> Essentially it's about creating different forms of a quasi-market in public services, exploiting the power of choice, competition, transparency and incentives. (interview with Michael Barber, 13 January 2006; see also Barber, 2007, ch 3; PASC, 2005)

Despite the brouhaha about its novelty, the Coalition government also focused on service delivery and customer. Although evidence-based policy making and managerialism remain prominent strands in the Coalition's reform proposals, choice is the first principle of the reforms; 'wherever possible we are increasing choice by giving people direct control over the services they use' (Cameron, 2011). The White Paper claims that 'the old centralised approach to public service delivery is broken', so 'wherever possible we will increase choice' and 'power will be decentralised to the lowest appropriate level'. Such choice will only happen if service delivery is 'opened up to a range of providers of different sizes and different sectors' (Cm 8145, 2011, 8–9). Choice, decentralisation and diversity of providers are three core tenets of the proposed reforms.

All the ideas about evidence-based policy making, managerialism and choice are part of the vocabulary of senior civil servants. For example, O'Donnell (2012), former Head of the Home Civil Service, includes clear objectives, objective evaluation and honouring the evidence among his ten commandments of good policy making. As the Regulatory Policy Institute (2009, para 31) observes, 'every suggestion' in the 'numberless' reports on civil service reform are 'a version of the same, how better to manage an ever more centralised state'. In sum, instrumental rationality, managerialism and choice rule, and it is not OK. It adds up to the 'Civil Service reform syndrome', which comprises:

> ideas like total quality management, red tape bonfires, better consultation, risk management, competency, evidence-based policy, joined-up government, delivery leadership, and now better policy making. Such initiatives come and go, overlap and ignore each other, leaving behind residues of varying size and style. (Hood and Lodge, 2007, 59)

The syndrome persists because the assumptions behind reforms are not fit for public sector purpose.

Lessons

Rhodes (2011) seeks to understand the ways in which the political and administrative elites of British central government departments made sense of their worlds. It provides 'thick descriptions', or my constructions of their constructions of what they are up to (Geertz, 1973), through an analysis of their beliefs and everyday practices. As Law (1994, 263) observes, outsiders studying an organisation 'are no more able to offer a single and coherent account of the way in which it orders itself' than its managers. So, just as civil servants seek to domesticate the everyday life of their minister, I seek to domesticate the many competing beliefs and practices of the departments.

Methods

I draw on three sources of information: 'the pattern of practice, talk, and considered writing' (Oakeshott, 1996, x). On practice, I observed the office of two ministers and three permanent secretaries for two days each. I also shadowed two ministers and three permanent secretaries for five working days each. On talk, I had repeat interviews with: ten permanent secretaries, five secretaries of state, three ministers, and twenty other officials. On considered writing, I had newspaper reports, copies of speeches and public lectures, and committee and other papers relevant to the meetings I observed.

My interviews and fieldwork observations were for citation but not for attribution without the interviewee's permission. I studied three ministries: the Department of Trade and Industry (DTI), the Department for Education and Skills (DfES), and the Department for Environment, Food and Rural Affairs (DEFRA). I conducted the interviews in 2002. The fieldwork was carried out in 2003. There were several repeat interviews and occasional visits in 2004. Following the established practice of latter-day ethnographers, I undertook 'yo-yo fieldwork'. I repeatedly went back and forth, in and out of the field (Wulff, 2002, 117). I also went to more than one fieldwork site because I was 'studying through'; that is, following events through the 'webs and relations between actors, institutions and discourses across time and space' (Shore and Wright, 1997, 14). The research methods and the findings are reported in detail in Rhodes (2011).

Axioms

Political scientists can aspire to 'plausible conjectures'; that is, to making general statements which are plausible because they rest on good reasons, and the reasons are good because they are inferred from relevant information (paraphrased from Boudon, 1993). This section draws out my conjectures or lessons from the fieldwork and asks whether the various reform proposals blend with the everyday beliefs and practices of civil servants and their ministers. I use five axioms for clarity of exposition:

- Coping and the appearance of rule, not strategic planning
- Institutional memory, not internal structures
- Storytelling, not evidence-based policy

- Contending traditions and stories, not just managerialism
- The politics of implementation, not top down innovation and control

I accept that these axioms over-simplify but I want to dramatise the difference between rational and storytelling reforms.

Coping and the appearance of rule, not strategic planning

At the top of government departments we find a class of political administrators, not politicians or administrators. They live in a shared world. Their priority and their skills are about surviving in a world of rude surprises. The goal is willed ordinariness. They do not need more risk. They are adrift in an ocean of storms. Only reformers have the luxury of choosing which challenge they will respond to. Ministers and permanent secretaries have to juggle the contradictory demands posed by recurring dilemmas. They must appear to be in control. I incline to Weiss's (1980) notions of decision accretion and knowledge creep. Thus, policy emerges from routine and builds like a coral reef. Similarly, rational policy analysis creeps into the decision process almost by osmosis, by becoming part of the zeitgeist, rather than overt deliberation. Civil service reform is not, therefore, a matter of solving specific problems but of managing unfolding dilemmas and their inevitable unintended consequences. There is no solution but a succession of solutions to problems which are contested and redefined as they are 'solved'. This analysis is anathema to the would-be reformers of the previous section, but it is the fate of their rational schemes.

Strategic planning is a clumsy add-on to this world. Its timescale is too long; its concerns too far removed from the everyday life concerns of its short-stay incumbents. The demands of political accountability and the media spotlight do not pay attention to strategic priorities. Relatively trivial problems of implementation can threaten a minister's career. Finally, the call for clear roles and responsibilities, for objectives and targets, is an idealised rational model of policy making largely removed from the messy reality of public policy making.

The limits to the rational model of policy making have been spelt out so often, they need no repetition. Crucially, as practiced, rational analysis is retrospective not prospective. It is used to justify decisions already taken by other means and for other reasons. And the other reasons are usually political ones. There is no obvious reason to prioritise economic rationality over political rationality, rather the converse. I agree with Wildavsky, writing back in 1968 about the then fashionable management reform of PPBS (Planning, Programming, and Budgeting System), when he vigorously argued that 'political rationality is the fundamental kind of reason'; it determines 'the decision structures [that] are the source of all decisions (Wildavsky, 1968, 393). So, much government is not about strategy and priorities but the appearance of rule: 'about stability. Keeping things going, preventing anarchy, stopping society falling to bits. Still being here tomorrow' (Lynn and Jay, 1984, 454). I do not seek, as did the authors of the quote, to make people laugh. In this witticism is much wisdom, not cynicism.

Institutional memory, not internal structures

Reform all too frequently involves splitting up existing units, creating new units, redeploying staff, bringing in outsiders, revamping IT systems. A key unintended consequence is the loss of institutional memory. Pollitt (2007, 173) gives his recipe for eroding institutional memory: rotate staff rapidly, change the IT system frequently, restructure every two years, reward management over other skills, and adopt each new management fad. All three departments met most of these criteria. There was a tacit policy of depleting a proven asset for unproven gains. Institutional memory is the source of stories; the department's folk psychology, providing the everyday theory and shared languages for storytelling. These stories involve a retelling of yesterday to make sense of today. They explain past practice and events and justify recommendations for the future. It is crucial if the civil service is to tell accurate and reliable stories.

Of course, there is some awareness of the importance of some everyday routines. The BGI (2010) report, written by senior officials, considers that s and civil servants can move too often between jobs and subject areas. As a result, 'records of previous decisions or past events may no longer exist or be easily available... [and there]... has been a serious weakening of corporate memory with the risk of failure in strategy, policy and delivery'. It calls for 'special attention... to the maintenance, preservation and accessibility of departmental records (BGI, 2010, 35, 36, 41; see also PASC, 2011, 13–14). But such suggestions are the exception not the rule.

Storytelling, not evidence-based policy

Storytelling substitutes plausible conjecture for prediction. It does not exclude rational policy analysis. It treats it simply as another way of telling a story alongside all the other stories in a department. So, stories are modest in their claims. Each story is one set of spectacles for looking at the world (see, for example, Boje, 1991; Czarniawska, 2004; Gabriel, 2000; and Weick, 1995).

How can you tell which story makes the most sense? The short answer is that the civil service has been doing it for years. So, they identify and construct the story line by asking 'what happened and why?' They also ask whether a story is defensible (to both internal and external audiences); accurate (in that it is consistent with known and agreed 'facts'), believable (in that it is consistent with the departmental philosophy). Lying is seen as a worse sin than error, accident, even incompetence. So, they test 'facts' in committee meetings and rehearse story lines or explanations to see what they sound like and whether there is agreement. They judge how a story will play publicly by the reactions of their colleagues. In this way, they can anticipate the reaction of an external audience. They compare stories in the same way.

Contending traditions and stories, not just managerialism

Even today, ministers and civil servants act as if the nineteenth century liberal constitution sets the rules of the political game. The British constitution reminds me of geological strata, a metaphor which captures the longevity of the beliefs and practices. I do not want to suggest that nothing has changed. Obviously much has changed, but much remains. Managerialism and network governance have not replaced earlier beliefs and practices; rather, they coexist with the inherited Westminster tradition. Ministers and civil servants are fluent in all these languages, yet they continue to act as if earlier constitutional beliefs and practices are reliable guides for present-day behaviour. So, my big surprise was that British government was riven with incommensurable traditions and their stories. There was no agreed standard for comparing the stories. Even within a government department, let alone across central government, there was no shared story of how British government worked. Yesterday's story remained an important guide to today's practice. So, the managerial story (in its various forms) and the governance stories have not replaced the Westminster tradition.

Elite actors displayed variable interest or concern in resolving such dilemmas. For example, ministers and civil servants have overlapping roles and responsibilities. Typically, would-be reformers want to clarify the constitutional relationship between ministers and civil servants. They want to spell out roles and relationships. For example, the PASC (2011, 29) argued:

> The conventions of ministerial responsibility... derived from the Haldane Report at the beginning of the last century have, on the whole, stood the test of time. However... it is timely to consider

the development of a new Haldane model to codify the changing accountabilities and organisation of government.

But, typically, ministers and their civil servants have a vested interest in the current arrangements. Its ambiguity protects them from effective scrutiny. Thus, the Government's response to the PASC recommendations was dismissive, brusquely referring the Committee to 'the statutory position of civil servants whose accountability is to s who in turn are accountable to Parliament' (PASC, 2012, 12). Haldane prevails because it serves the interests of both s and their civil servants. And yet the Government proclaims, 'the old idea of a Civil Service "generalist" is dead'. Instead, they say they want 'the right combination of professionalism, expert skills and subject matter expertise' (Cabinet Office, 2012, 23). Where are the political antennae that point out the hole to the minister before he or she falls in? Where are the political skills that pull him or her out of the hole afterwards, and argue that he or she never fell in? Have would-be reformers persuaded ministerial colleagues to forsake the cocoon of willed ordinariness at the top of departments that exists to protect the minister? Private offices exist to domesticate trouble, to defuse problems, and to take the emotion out of a crisis. Protocols are the key to managing this pressurised existence. Everyday routines are unquestioned and unrecognised. The reformers know not what they seek to reform.

Similarly, managerial reform is all too often a secondary concern for s and their civil servants. I agree that effective performance measurement needs more clarity if performance management is what matters. My problem is that, when I imagine myself in a minister's or permanent secretary's shoes, performance management does not seem to matter that much. Useful, but not where the real action is. Ministers are not managers. It is not why they went into politics. A minority of Secretaries of State take an interest, even fewer Ministers of State. These brute facts undermine reform. The civil service exists to give ministers what they want and most do not want anything to do with management reform. At best, it is not a priority. At worst, it is not even on the radar.

The politics of implementation, not top-down innovation and control

Politics and policies do not arise exclusively from the strategies and interactions of elites. Other actors can resist, transform, and thwart the agendas of elites. An anthropological approach draws attention to the diverse traditions and narratives that inform actions at lower levels of the hierarchy, and the actions of citizens. For example, we know street-level bureaucrats shape service delivery in crucial ways. They use local knowledge and local reasoning to decide what policy will be for clients (see Maynard-Moody and Musheno, 2003). In a similar vein, Lindblom (1990) compares professional with lay knowledge to the discomfort of the former. Understandings of how things work around here are embedded not only in the taken for granted routines and rituals of the departmental court but also the beliefs and practices of actors at lower levels of the hierarchy. Not only is such knowledge rarely part of the policy process, it is not valued. Yet it is often crucial to the success of policies, especially in their implementation. Although one strand in the British political tradition asserts that 'leaders know best', the track record of much top-down innovation and control does not inspire confidence.

Moreover, when implementation is part of government thinking, it is strangely divorced from everyday knowledge. Thus, the *Civil Service Reform Plan* (Cabinet Office, 2012, ch 3) adopts the top-down, rational model of implementation with its imperatives for clear objectives, robust management information, and project management. If social science research ever teaches us anything, it tells us that the top-down model is plagued with implementation deficits (see O'Toole, 2000; Pressman and Wildavsky, 1984; Sabatier, 1986). Curiouser and curiouser, the report states that 'much of this failure has been because policy gets announced before implementation has been fully thought through' (Cabinet Office, 2012, 18). From this statement, do we conclude that ministers delay their history-making policy announcements while their civil servants spot snags? Ministers have short tenure. They will not sit around waiting on what they see as mere detail. Probably, they will not be there when the implementation problems arrive. Snag spotting irritates them (Rhodes, 2011, 185). Civil servants are wary of speaking too much truth to power. Even more of a problem, the statement also assumes that civil servants are responsible for implementation when many departments rely on third parties. They have a hands-off, not hands-on, link to policy implementation. As Bovens (1998, 46) puts it, they confront the 'the problem of many hands' where responsibility for policy is shared. Everyday lay knowledge would tell policy makers about the limits to implementation, but no one would be listening.

Dilemmas, languages and storytelling

What would a reform strategy informed by my analysis look like? There are three points of intervention focused on the disconnections between dilemmas, languages and stories.

British government comprises several contending traditions, which have been grafted on to the Westminster tradition. Westminster, managerial and governance traditions coexist side by side with all the attendant dilemmas. Reform should focus on the dilemmas. We need to find out whether different sections of the elite draw on different traditions to construct different narratives about the world, their place within it, and their interests and values. Both the diversity and common ground need to be specified, not taken for granted or ignored. We need to specify the opportunities for, and obstacles to change; otherwise reform will be dogged with misfortune from the moment it starts. Such an approach favours incremental change over more ambitious schemes and gives a distinctive twist to 'what works'.

The several traditions use distinct and distinctive languages. Westminster itself has the classic liberal terminology streaked with the colonialism and class languages of yesteryear, such as chaps and Sherpas. There is the ever-present gobbledygook of acronyms. Managerialism has three main dialects: performance management, marketisation, and delivery. Outsiders import new languages. Think tanks, management consultants and professional experts (inside and outside the civil service) provide specialist advice in their preferred professional language. Special Advisers (SpAds) provide the party political language. When and where are the different languages used? The choice of language is not incidental or neutral. Westminster aspires to be the lingua franca. It is the central stream. Other languages remain in play to the point of ministerial decision; they are the tributaries. The Westminster language symbolises the constitutional verities and sustains the central role of minister and permanent secretary. This primacy means that critics of the civil service for the slow pace of change attack the wrong target. They should look instead to ministers as the main wellspring of change in British government As long as ministers are in the spotlight for civil servants, they will give priority to sustaining the cocoon and willed ordinariness.

Storytelling is not an example of academic whimsy. It is an everyday practice. The challenge is to get the departmental court to wear night vision spectacles to identify and collect the many, relevant and sometimes unheard stories. At the heart of a storytelling approach would be collecting the several voices in the department stories and increasing the voices heard. The second step would be to develop transparent criteria for writing, evaluating and comparing stories. Currently, such criteria are embedded in words like 'sound', 'judgement', 'experience' and 'safe pair of hands'. They communicate understood, shared but tacit meanings.

When collecting the several voices, the focus will be on everyday knowledge, on institutional memory and the limits to implementation. Institutional memory provides the everyday theory and shared languages for storytelling. It is the knowledge base of snag spotting. Ministers are schizophrenic about it. They complain about both the loss of institutional memory and about snag spotting. Both are central to an effective civil service yet I am not aware of any official actions to preserve and enhance institutional memory. Similarly, despite calls by the Coalition for more effective implementation, there is nary a mention of lay knowledge. The beliefs and practices of actors at lower levels of the hierarchy are not deemed important for the policy process. The political-administrative elite know best. The rational model is the favoured way of legitimating decisions. So, lay knowledge is sidelined despite the obvious limits of many top-down reforms. Effective reform hinges on legitimating lay knowledge; on accepting the inevitable influence of folk theories.

Indubitably, the lessons of my fieldwork are not the basis of conventional reform proposals. My portrait of a storytelling political-administrative elite, with beliefs and practices rooted in the Westminster model that uses protocols and rituals to domesticate rude surprises and recurrent dilemmas, is not the conventional portrait, and it is the antithesis of the instrumental rationality of evidence-based policy making, managerialism, and choice. The key task in civil service reform is to steer other actors using storytelling. Storytelling organises dialogues, and fosters meanings, beliefs, and identities among the relevant actors. It seeks to influence what actors think and do, and fosters a shared narrative of change. It is about continuities and preserving the departmental philosophy and its everyday folk theories and shared languages that enable a retelling of yesterday to make sense of today.

Prospects

What are the strengths and weaknesses of the storytelling, ethnographic approach in the study of public administration? What do we know from my story that we don't know from *Yes Minister* and the existing public administration and political science literature? The approach has several strengths.

First, it takes the webs of meaning of actors as its basic building blocks. For example, there is much agreement in the academic literature that the constitution is in disarray (see, for example, Bogdanor, 2003; King, 2007). There is much to agree about in these several critiques of the constitution and constitutional reform. Yet ministers and civil servants act *as if* the old verities are constant; for example, they believe they are accountable to Parliament and act accordingly. My approach provides an actor-centred account of British government. I focus on the social construction of practices through the ability of individuals to create, and act on, meanings. I unpack practices as the disparate and contingent beliefs and actions of individuals.

Second, the approach focuses on diversity. For example, I do not privilege any one tradition but treat them all as *living* and contending traditions. No one account is comprehensive. Each web of inherited beliefs and practices shapes some ministerial and civil servant actions. Each explains some actions by some people some of the time. Similarly, each tradition has its own language, often with dialects. Whitehall is polyglot. Top civil servants are multilingual, combining Westminster, managerial, professional, political, and networking languages. This diversity undermines any reforms that assume one size fits all.

Third, the analysis of the dilemmas posed by the diverse traditions highlights how new ideas produce not only change but also resistance. To twist a familiar saying, 'you can change if you want but this practice is not for changing'. Indeed, it is the embedding of yesterday's beliefs in today's protocols and rituals that makes change such a hazardous enterprise.

Fourth, the ethnographic approach admits of surprises. As with much ethnography, it looks for the hidden and the inaccessible, so there are moments of epiphany that open new research agendas. It accepts serendipity and happenstance. In this chapter, the surprises included the persistence of the nineteenth century liberal constitution and the commonplace use of storytelling.

Fifth, the approach helps to analyse the symbolic dimensions of political action. Most political behaviour has a strong symbolic dimension. Symbols do not simply 'represent' or reflect political 'reality', they actively constitute that reality. By drawing out the negotiated, symbolic and ritual elements of political life, ethnographic analysis draws attention to deeper principles of organisation that are not visible to empiricist or positivist approaches. Thus, ministers are heirs to a royal tradition and it shows in the present-day practices, especially in the appearance of rule.

Finally, this approach does not privilege managerial rationality or the preferences of managers. Rather, it focuses on the manifold stories of government departments. It seeks to give voice to the forgotten in the reform literature. The focus is local, micro and actual (Aronoff and Kubik, 2013, 25).

Limits

What are the limits of such an approach for the reform of public administration? Playing the role of 'social technologists' and using observational fieldwork to produce proposals for civil service reform poses several problems. I consider them under the headings of: roles, relevance, time, evidence, and working with elites (see also Agar, 1996; Kedia and Van Willigen, 2005; Rhodes et al, 2007; Sillitoe 2006; Van Willigen, 2002).

There is no agreement on the role of the anthropologist let alone on whether anthropology should be 'relevant' and how that could be achieved. Van Maanen (1978, 345–6) describes his relationship with the police he was observing as: 'a cop buff, a writer of books, an intruder, a student, a survey researcher, a management specialist, a friend, an ally, an asshole, a historian, a recruit and so on'. He was 'part spy, part voyeur, part fan and part member'. Similarly, Kedia and Van Willigen (2005, 11) distinguish between 'policy researcher or research analyst; evaluator; impact assessor, or needs assessor; cultural broker; public participation specialist; and administrator or manager'. Applied anthropology can serve many masters.

For Van Willigen applied anthropology is about providing information for decision makers so they can make rational decisions. Or, more formally, applied anthropology is a 'complex of related, research-based, instrumental methods which produce change or stability in specific cultural systems through the provision of data, initiation of direct action, and/or the formulation of policy' (Van Willigen, 2002, 150 and ch 10). Not everyone would agree that the task is to help decision makers. For Agar (1996, 27), 'no understanding of a world is valid without representation of those members' voices'. For him, 'ethnography is *populist* to the core' and the task is to be 'sceptical of the distant institutions that control local people's lives'.

Managers are scarcely sympathetic to such aims. They see anthropologists as 'coming forward with awkward observations' and 'as wishing to preserve "traditional" ways' (Sillitoe, 2006, 10). Managers criticise anthropologists because their findings often failed to conform to expectations held by employers about the causes of problems and their solutions. They were dismissed as 'irrelevant or disruptive' (Sillitoe 2006, 14). As Kedia and Van Willigen (2005, 16–20) observe, applied anthropology confronts an acute and recurring moral dilemma 'since the practitioner must negotiate an intricate balance between the interests of the clients who commission the work, and those of the community being studied'. Inevitably, there are issues about whose aims are served by the research, who owns the research results, and individual privacy. Given that observational fieldwork is about decentring an established organisation to identify its several voices, its contending beliefs and practices, and its traditions and stories (Bevir and Rhodes, 2006), then the research is never about privileging any one voice. From the viewpoint of the managers, therefore, there is always the potential for disruption and irrelevance.

Given managerial concerns about such anthropological decentring and disruption, it is ironic that my political science colleagues express concern about its conservative outlook. In effect, they claim that by describing life at the top, I justify it. I am too sympathetic to ministers 'bleating about their world as one of high risk and shock' and I seek to 'make the life of the political administrative class more comfortable'. I agree description can spill over into justification and, therefore, seem conservative but that is not my intention. My aim is to understand, not sympathise. I want would-be reformers to be aware of the likely pitfalls; that is, to know what they are seeking to reform. After all, the reformers have had the field to themselves for decades with, at best, modest success. I am explaining why that success is modest. Reformers who advocate evidence-based policy making need to draw on observational evidence in designing change. It is conspicuous for its absence. Ministers bleat for reforms which they then do little to support. A key part of the inertia is not the civil service but the politicians, and reformers will continue to see their reforms fail because they continue to target the civil service.

The claim to relevance is further compounded by the problem of time. Observation in the field is time consuming and fits uncomfortably if at all with the demands of politicians and administrators alike. The brutal fact is that if you want to understand everyday life you have to stick around, go where you are led, and take what you are given. The minister and the department will not wait on the results from such unstructured soaking. Of course, fieldwork does not have to be the decade-long immersion of the lone researcher. There are shortcuts; for example, by using teams of fieldworkers, collaborative working with the client, snapshots across locations and time, and storytelling circles (Czarniawska, 2004, ch 3). But getting below and behind the surface of official accounts to provide texture, depth and nuance and opening the consciousness of one group of people to another (Geertz, 1988) cannot be done overnight. I was lucky – the civil service agreed to my doing 'curiosity research'.

Finally, there is the delicate issue of managing relationships with the elite. I have considered this at length elsewhere (Rhodes et al 2007, ch 9) but two points bear repetition. I was not studying the powerless. Rather, the research 'subjects' were more powerful than me. They can, and a minority did, refuse interviews, deny access to the organisation, declare documents secret, and insist on anonymity for both themselves and their organisation. All the interviews and periods of observation took place with informed consent but as the work unfolded I had to negotiate constantly to keep that cooperation. Also, it is all too easy to affect the relationship between yourself and the observed, causing them to behave differently. The aim of the so-called 'non-participant' observer is to remain the outsider; 'the professional stranger' (Agar, 1996). However, for lengthy on-site visits and extensive repeat interviews, you have to have a conversation and engage with the people around you. You have to establish rapport. You are sucked into events, even if it is only casual badinage to ease tension. For example, one permanent secretary gave me a copy of his diaries. The analysis of his engagements and committee work showed he was spending about one-third of his time on corporate civil service business outside the department. He was surprised. He had no clear picture of the distribution of his workload. Immediately, he began to reduce his corporate commitments. He could exercise much control over his working life, and he knew it. My example makes it clear that the powerful are different. They can shape your research and change everyday life even as you look at it.

Conclusions

In political science, the dominant tradition is modernist-empiricism with its roots in the natural science model. The argument about blurred genres takes as its starting point the turning away from that model and the idea of law-like generalisations. As Inglis (2000, 112) argues, there has been a lethal attack on modernist empiricism, and the work of philosophers such as Charles Taylor, Peter Winch and Alasdair McIntyre means that using the methods of the natural sciences in the human sciences is 'comically improper'. Richard Bernstein, Clifford Geertz, and Richard Rorty could be added to a long and growing list of such critics, before mentioning the long-standing hermeneutics tradition of Continental Europe. This 'interpretive turn' raises the problem of what counts as evidence. It might seem obvious that 'not everything that counts can be counted, and not everything that can be counted counts' (sign hanging in Albert Einstein's office at Princeton), but not when it comes to civil service reform and policy analysis. It is a world of given facts, positive theory and hypothesis testing. Qualitative data simply does not meet these expectations because it does not count as generalisable evidence. My observational data is evidence as relevant to civil service reform as the evidence conventionally used to support managerialism.

The attempts to impose private sector management beliefs and techniques to increase the economy, efficiency and effectiveness resulted in the civil service reform syndrome. If private sector techniques offer such obvious and available ways to manage, then why is so little implemented across government? It is not because public managers are ill-trained, stupid or venal, but because private sector techniques do not fit the context. Such techniques can be neutered by both bureaucratic and political games, and are subjected to public accountability. Public sector officials also do not share the same risks and rewards. Similarly, rational means-ends analysis is largely removed from the reality of public policy making. Politics, value clashes, interests, cultures, symbolic imperatives, processes and accountability requirements all make the rational actor model untenable in public policy decision making. Internal reorganisation has marginal effects on beliefs, practices and traditions. Chanting the mantras of organisational change and leadership leaves most of the organisation untouched. The choice agenda ignores the political context confronting ministers and senior civil servants. 'Hands off' advice is anathema to the British governing elite that has always known best.

The rational, managerial approach has predominated since 1968, producing little beyond the civil service reform syndrome. We do not need more of the same. We need a different approach to reform. The storytelling approach is a contender. A bottom-up approach to reform rooted in the everyday knowledge of departments is a lone voice in this wilderness, but it can hardly do worse. It holds out the prospect of reforms that command legitimacy at lower levels of the bureaucracy even if they do not directly serve the interests of ministers and permanent secretaries. Therein lies the rub. We must never forget that civil service reform is about the constitutional and political role of public administration in the polity; it is not about better management.

References

Agar, M, 1996, *The professional stranger* (2nd edn), San Diego: Academic Press

Aronoff, MJ, Kubik, J, 2013, *Anthropology and political science: A convergent approach,* New York: Berghahn Books

Argyris, C, Schon, D, 1996, *Organisational learning II: A theory of action perspective,* Reading, MA: Addison-Wesley

Barber, M, 2007, *Instruction to deliver: Tony Blair, public services and the challenge of targets,* London: Politico's

BGI (Better Government Initiative), 2010, *Good government: Reforming Parliament and the executive, recommendations from the executive committee of the Better Government Initiative*, Institute for Government

Bevir, M, Rhodes, RAW, 2006, *Governance stories,* Abingdon: Routledge

Blair, T, 2004, Speech on modernisation of the Civil Service, 24 February, www.number10.gov.uk/Page5399

Bogdanor, V (ed), 2003, *The British constitution in the twentieth century,* Oxford: Oxford University Press for the British Academy

Boje, D, 1991, The storytelling organisation: A story of story performance in an office-supply form, *Administrative Science Quarterly,* 36, 1, 106–26

Boudon, R, 1993, Towards a synthetic theory of rationality, *International Studies in the Philosophy of Science,* 7, 1, 5–19

Bovens, M, 1998, *The quest for responsibility: Accountability and citizenship in complex organisations,* Cambridge: Cambridge University Press

Bullock, H, Mountford, J, Stanley, R, 2001, *Better policy making,* London: Centre for Management and Policy Studies (CMPS)

Cabinet Office, 1999, *Professional policy making for the twenty-first century,* London: Cabinet Office

Cabinet Office, 2012, *The civil service reform plan,* London: Cabinet Office

Cameron, D, 2011, Speech on open public services, 11 July, www.number10.gov.uk/news/speech-on-open-public-services

Cm 8145, 2011, *Open public services White Paper,* London: Stationery Office

Common, R, 2004, Organisational learning in a political environment: Improving policy making in UK Government, *Policy Studies,* 25, 1, 35–49

Czarniawska, B, 2004, *Narratives in social science research,* London: Sage

Davies, HTO, Nutley, SM, Smith, PC (eds), 2000, *What works? evidence-based policy and practice in public services,* Bristol: Policy Press

Fine, GA, Morrill, C, Surianarain, S, 2009, Ethnography in organisational settings, in Buchanan, D, Bryman, A (eds), *Handbook of organisational research methods,* London: Sage 602–19

Gabriel, Y, 2000, *Storytelling in organisations: Facts, fictions and fantasies,* Oxford: Oxford University Press

Geertz, C, 1983, Blurred genres: The refiguration of social thought, in his *Local knowledge: Further essays in interpretive anthropology,* New York: Basic Books, 19–35

Geertz, C, 1988 *Works and lives: The anthropologist as author,* Stanford, CA: Stanford University Press

Geertz, C, 1973, Thick descriptions: Towards an interpretive theory of culture, in his *The interpretation of cultures,* London: Fontana, 1993, 3–30

Hood, C, Lodge, M, 2007, Endpiece: Civil service reform syndrome – are we heading for a cure?, *Transformation,* Spring, 58–9

Inglis, F, 2000, *Clifford Geertz: Culture, custom and ethics,* Oxford: Blackwell

Institute for Government, 2010, *Shaping-up: A Whitehall for the future,* London: Institute for Government

Kedia, S, Van Willigen, J, 2005, Applied anthropology: Context for domains of application, in Kedia, S, Van Willigen, J (eds), *Applied anthropology: Domains of application,* Westport, CT: Praeger, 1–32

King, A, 2007, *The British Constitution,* Oxford: Oxford University Press

Law, J, 1994, Organisation, narrative and strategy, in Hassard, J, Parker, M (eds), *Towards a new theory of organisations,* London: Routledge, 248–68

Lindblom, CE, 1990, *Inquiry and change,* New Haven, CT: Yale University Press

Lodge, G, Rogers, B, 2006, *Whitehall's black box: Accountability and performance in the senior civil service,* London: Institute for Public Policy Research

Lynn, J, Jay, A, 1984, *The complete 'Yes Minister': The diaries of a cabinet minister,* London: BBC Books

Maynard-Moody, S, Musheno, M, 2003, *Cops, teachers, counsellors: Stories from the front lines of public service,* Ann Arbor, MI: University of Michigan Press

Mulgan, G, 2009, *The art of public strategy: mobilising power and knowledge for the common good,* Oxford: Oxford University Press

National Audit Office (NAO), 2001, *Modern policy-making: Ensuring policies deliver value for money,* Report by the Comptroller and Auditor General, HC 289, London: The Stationery Office

Oakeshott, M, 1996, *The politics of faith and the politics of scepticism,* Fuller, T (ed), New Haven, CT: Yale University Press

O'Donnell, G, 2012, Ten commandments of good policy making: A retrospective, http://blogs.lse.ac.uk/politicsandpolicy/2012/05/01/retrospective-sir-gus-odonnell/

O'Toole, L, 2000, Research on policy implementation: Assessment and prospects, *Journal of Public Administration Research and Theory,* 10, 2, 263–88

Pollitt, C, 1993, *Managerialism and the public services,* (2nd edn), Oxford: Blackwell

Pollitt, C, 2007, *Time, policy, management: Governing with the past,* Oxford: Oxford University Press

Pressman, J, Wildavsky, A, 1984, *Implementation: How great expectations in Washington are dashed in Oakland,* (3rd edn), Berkeley, CA: University of California Press

PASC (Public Administration Select Committee), 2003, *On target? Government by Measurement,* HC 62–1, London: Stationery Office

PASC, 2005, *Choice, voice and public services,* HC 49–1, London: Stationery Office

PASC, 2009, *Good Government,* HC 97–1, London: Stationery Office

PASC, 2011, *Change in government: The agenda for leadership,* HC 714, London: Stationery Office

PASC, 2012, *Change in government: The agenda for leadership: Further report,* HC 1746, London: Stationery Office

Regulatory Policy Institute, 2009, *Trust in the system: Restoring trust in our system of government and regulation,* Oxford: Regulatory Policy Institute

Rhodes, RAW, 2011, *Everyday life in British government,* Oxford: Oxford University Press

Rhodes, RAW, 2013, From core executive to court politics, in Strangio, P, 't Hart, P, Walter, J (eds), *Prime Ministerial leadership: Power, party and performance in Westminster systems,* Oxford: Oxford University Press, 318–33

Rhodes, RAW, 't Hart, P, Noordegraaf, M (eds), 2007, *Observing government elites: Up close and personal,* Basingstoke: Palgrave-Macmillan

Sabatier, P, 1986, Top-down and bottom-up approaches to implementation research: A critical analysis and suggested synthesis, *Journal of Public Policy,* 6, 1, 21–48

Sanderson, I, 2002, Evaluation, policy learning and evidence-based policy making, *Public Administration,* 80, 1, 1–22

Shore, C, Wright, S (eds), 1997, *The anthropology of policy critical perspectives on governance and power,* London: Routledge

Sillitoe, P, 2006, The search for relevance: A brief history of applied anthropology, *History and Anthropology,* 17, 1, 1–19

Van Maanen, J, 1978, Epilogue: On watching the watchers, in Manning, PK, Van Maanen, J (eds) *Policing: A view from the street,* Santa Monica, CA: Goodyear, 309–49

Van Willigen, J, 2002, *Applied anthropology: An introduction,* (3rd edn), Westport, CT: Bergin and Garvey

Weick, KE, 1995, *Sensemaking in organisations,* Thousand Oaks, CA: Sage

Weiss, CH, 1980, Knowledge creep and decision accretion, *Science Communication,* 1, 1, 381–404

Wildavsky, A, 1968, The political economy of efficiency: Cost-benefit analysis, systems analysis and program budgeting, in Lyden, FJ, Miller, EG (eds), *Planning programming budgeting: a systems approach to management,* Chicago: Markham, 371–402

Wulff, H, 2002, Yo-Yo fieldwork: Mobility and time in multi-local study of dance in Ireland, *Anthropological Journal of European Cultures,* 11, 117–36

CHAPTER THREE

Just do it differently? Everyday making, Marxism and the struggle against neoliberalism

Jonathan Stephen Davies

Do differently, do very differently, or there is no future for humanity. (Holloway, 2010, 260)

Introduction

Understanding continuity and change is among the greatest challenges for social scientists, rooted in fundamental questions about power, structure and agency. The 2012 anniversary conference of the *Policy & Politics* journal reconsidered the challenge at a perplexing time. Despite a profound and enduring economic crisis, neoliberalism continues to dominate – even extend its hegemony (Crouch, 2011). For critical activists and scholars suffering under neoliberalism, and its durability in the face of economic crisis, only lends urgency to the question of how a different world might be possible.

This chapter explores an increasingly influential theory of change in contemporary policy and politics, that of everyday making (Bang, 2005; Gibson-Graham, 1996); Li and Marsh, 2008). Everyday making seeks to accomplish small-scale, gradual changes by constructing new ways of living and doing politics from the bottom-up. Advocates of everyday making are sceptical that change will ever occur at the systemic scale – the national, international or global levels. They are similarly sceptical about organised resistance to governments and corporations, preferring positive action to direct confrontation (Newman, 2012). However, this chapter argues that although change almost invariably originates in everyday life, strategies and struggles to transform the system remain indispensable. To support this position, it restates the Marxist perspective on capitalism as a fundamentally crisis-prone socioeconomic system. From a Marxist perspective, the challenge is to grasp the relationship between everyday life and systemic trends and struggles. In developing this argument, the chapter touches on each of the three themes of the anniversary conference: what has changed, what endures and how does our understanding of continuity and change inform future strategies for policy and action.

The chapter first discusses the eclectic literatures on everyday making, notably focus on the emancipatory potential in small acts, critique of Marxism and the performative power in networks (our capacity to create and exemplify new worlds by thinking, speaking, acting and associating differently). It then considers the contribution of Marxist analysis to grasping the relationship between everyday life and the system as a whole. Drawing on examples of cooperative enterprise and community organising, it argues that treating capitalism as a deeply crisis-prone system has significant implications. First, it suggests that the activities of everyday makers have boomerang effects. If capitalism must expand, as Marxism maintains, then successfully exploiting gaps also means imposing restrictions on a system that cannot, and does not, abide them (Harvey, 2010, 47). Second, therefore, contesting neoliberalism requires a robustly combative approach to markets. Third, the chapter argues that everyday makers tend to be excessively pessimistic about the role of labour and the workplace, where crises turn cracks into chasms and everyday struggles are potentially scalable. The challenge for policy and politics is not to jettison 'everyday' or 'system' but rather to grasp the enduring relationship in different contexts.

Everyday making and the political economy of 'doing'

Today's preoccupation with everyday making is symptomatic of widespread scepticism about large-scale theories and struggles. Otherwise diverse literatures are rooted in three distinctive ideas. First, they are agent-focused, seeking to deconstruct social structures like capitalism and class (Gibson-Graham, 1996; Nickel, 2007). Second, they emphasise the transformative potential in a multiplicity of small, localised actions in the interstices of power. Third, they tend to downplay 'negative' critique and combative modes of struggle for constructive activity, building practical alternatives in the cracks and fissures of power (Holloway, 2010). Accordingly, everyday makers tend to reject binaries like structure-agency, capital-labour, boom-slump or inside-outside, advancing a theory of change that affirms human agency. The intuition is, as Biesta (2008, 176) commented, that '[w]e can always just begin by doing things differently'.

Beyond these common agendas, however, the literatures diverge. Bang (2005), for example, defined the everyday maker in opposition to the 'expert citizen'. S/he is a 'lay-citizen', sometimes inactive, sometimes active in grass-roots community endeavours and ambivalent towards the state, engaging or opposing as practical needs dictate. According to Bang (2005, 162) everyday makers 'consider knowing as doing', pursuing 'small tactics' rather than macro-strategic projects, thereby exercising 'creative capacities as "ordinary" citizens'. Li and Marsh (2008, 251) summarised the tenets of everyday making thus: do it yourself, do it where you are, do it for fun but also because you find it necessary, do it ad hoc or part-time, do it concretely instead of ideologically, do it with self-confidence and show trust in yourself, and do it with the system if need be. Interestingly, they found that a high proportion of political action fits into this categorisation of everyday making.

Hannah Arendt, on the other hand, distinguished everyday making as 'craft' (an important dimension of 'maker' sub-culture today) from making in the political realm: the public domain where we attain equality, formulating and deliberating the means and ends of our collective lives (see Ranson, 2012). She points towards a hybrid practice where political work takes place in everyday life, but is consciously oriented towards fostering polities and publics (also Newman, 2012). Accordingly, the literature on everyday making also encompasses more overtly politicised practices, where the practitioner is just as concerned with small-scale alternatives and is ambivalent (sometimes hostile) towards the state, but more like Bang's expert citizen insofar as s/he is a committed activist (Mason, 2012). Everyday maker-activists believe 'another world is possible', but that traditional struggles are now neither feasible nor desirable, if ever they were. They see horizontal or networked modes of organising as particularly effective (see further below).

In addition, we can distinguish those who see everyday making as complementing other governance mechanisms, such as by enhancing public participation (Bang and Sørensen, 1999) and others who see it as a form of resistance, a way of contesting and moving beyond neoliberalism and/or capitalism. The latter category is further divided among those contesting the state from within using the tactics of everyday labour (Newman, 2012) and others who reject the state as a terrain of struggle as a matter of principle; where 'doing' is perceived as conflicting with institutional economics and politics (Holloway, 2010). Everyday making is thus claimed and contested among pragmatists, reformists and revolutionaries who see 'doing differently' as a path beyond capitalism. A further variation straddling the categories of expert/non-expert and insider/outsider is the 'everyday fixer' identified by Hendriks and Tops (2005). The fixer is a local activist providing a conduit between state and citizens, often informally, to deal with community problems and complaints. This kind of maker is more of an expert than Bang's and more of an 'insider' than either Bang's or Mason's ideal types.

Newman (2012) identifies yet another mode of everyday making situated within the labour process, offering 'alternative imaginaries of how we might live and work together, not in a fantasised future (when the financial crisis is over) but in the grimly real present'. Newman explored the experiences of women who chose to enter the corridors of power, for example as senior local government executives, a radical agenda. Recognising the limits, compromises and defeats in this endeavour, she nevertheless argues that gendered labour 'in and against the state' challenged institutional sexism and enhanced gender equality. Perhaps because of her commitment to labour in and against the state, Newman eschews the vocabulary of everyday making. However, she echoed a powerful influence among everyday makers who see true communism as that of 'presentism' (Watkins, 2012).

According to Clark (2012), for example, progressives today can only work for small gains. A pragmatic politics should reject all utopianism and be 'transposed into a tragic key', a 'tragic sense of the life possible for the left' (2012, 57). Clark is at the pessimistic end of the 'presentist' continuum, but the spirit of gritty pragmatism and anti-utopianism is strong in literatures on the tasks of everyday makers. Crouch (2011), for example, suggests we are likely to remain trapped in neoliberalism for many years. However, he draws on the intuitions of the everyday maker to find potential checks and balances in the 'quarrelsome voices' of civil society agitating in the 'interstices left among the great erections of political and economic power', 'like little houses springing up busily and untidily' among the corporate skyscrapers (2011, 161).

Against 'capitalocentrism'

One distinguishing feature of everyday making is its scepticism towards the feasibility of universal transformation accomplished through organised resistance to the capitalist system. Gibson-Graham (1996; 2008) is among the most influential theorists and practitioners in this tradition. She argued that Marxists falsely 'essentialise' capitalism. Through 'binary thinking', they represent the profit economy as:

> large, powerful, persistent, active, expansive, progressive, dynamic, transformative; embracing, penetrating, disciplining, colonising, constraining; systemic, self-reproducing, rational, lawful, self-rectifying; organised and organising, centered and centering; originating, creative, protean; victorious and ascendant; self-identical, self-expressive, full, definite, real, positive, and capable of conferring meaning and identity. (Gibson-Graham, 1996, 4)

This 'paranoid stance' means that everything becomes 'large and threatening' (Gibson-Graham, 1996, 618). Marxist preoccupations with the capitalist system therefore make a tangible alternative impossible, inducing political paralysis. Ostensibly critical ideas such as 'neoliberal hegemony' are a form of collusion because by labelling the world as such, we invest it with powers; naming the enemy constitutes its power over us – what Nickel (2007, 215) called 'oppression through ontology'. Interpreted thus, abandoning 'capitalocentrism' for 'doing' is empowering: 'to change our understanding *is* to change the world' (Gibson-Graham, 2008, 615). If we entrench capitalism through discourses about the virtues of markets, competition and accumulation, then the challenge is to substitute non-capitalist discourses and exemplary practices enacting democracy, equality and solidarity.

Interestingly, some within the Marxist tradition itself accept the central tenets of this critique. Holloway (2010) argues that set-piece confrontations between capital and labour are self-defeating, arguing instead for the creation, exploitation and multiplication of everyday cracks and fissures. He argued that such gaps are found not in working class struggles ('abstract labour') but everyday life, where they prefigure (exemplify) alternative ways of living ('concrete labour'). Holloway called for everyday makers to 'do differently, do against labour' (2010, 260), believing that 'power-resistance' struggles (Newman, 2012) re-enact and inadvertently re-institutionalise capitalist rule.

Everyday making and performative agency

Another influence is the claim that the crumbling of structural power – the demise of the institutions and traditions of modernity – enhances 'performative agency', meaning that now is an auspicious time for everyday making. We acquire performative agency when our utterances, discourses and practices invoke the realities they depict (Butler, 2010, 147): an official pronouncing a couple to be married enacts the marriage. Performativity theory asserts that ideas, discourses and practices have much greater transformative power than Marxists recognize. As Swyngedouw (2007, 72) argued, the experimental activities of social movements are performative because they modify 'the map of what can be thought, what can be named and perceived, and therefore also of what is possible'. All manner of 'frictions, cracks, fissures, gaps, and "vacant" spaces arise… These fissures, cracks, and "free" spaces form "quilting" points, nodes for experimentation with new urban possibilities'. Mason's evocative account of the Arab Spring and global resistance to austerity (2012) explained how activists see the network superseding the machineries of power (formal organisations and institutions), unleashing performative agency:

It can achieve those elements of instant community, solidarity, shared space and control that were at the heart of social revolutions in the early industrial age. It can be... a space to form the bonds that would take them through an insurrection... a means absolutely imbued with the nature of ends.... Time and again the impulse to create areas of self-control has led... to an almost mystical determination by protestors to occupy a symbolic physical space and create within it an experimental shared community... liberated spaces... the single most important theme in the global revolt. (Mason, 2012, 84)

Mason here captures an important justification for the political investment in everyday making: we live in a networked society, networks enhance our capacities as agents and networking itself exemplifies an alternative way of living and doing – it is performative. If the network society is a wellspring of performative agency, it adds weight to the transformative potential in everyday making. Not only are there many spaces beyond capitalism if we choose to see them, but the network society better equips us to grow them without becoming ensnared in futile power-resistance struggles.

Marxism, totality and universalism

For Jones (2008, 386), the great strength in these approaches is that they 'move away from economism, capital-centrism, productivism, and essentialism in Marxist analysis'. Fourcade (2012, 402) captured the common premise uniting the diverse literatures:

It is difficult, living in the USA in the second decade of the twenty-first century, to imagine a process of long-term erosion of economic power of capital through interstitial and symbiotic strategies. But it is even more difficult to construct a plausible scenario of a frontal attack on capital resulting in a decisive rupture that breaks the dominance of capitalist class power and ushers in a democratic egalitarian social order. For better or worse, therefore, if we wish to contribute to making such a world possible, the best we can probably do is figure out new interstitial and symbiotic initiatives that build alternatives and solve practical problems, and struggle politically to open up the spaces for these initiatives to be realised.

However, the recent crisis has stimulated renewed interest in Marxism, especially Marx's conception of capitalism as a deeply crisis-prone and aggressively expansionary system (Harman, 2010; Kliman, 2011). The Marxist theory of capitalism is grounded in a critical-realist conception of structure and agency, which begins with the humanist proposition that without people there are no social structures. As Marx (1846) put it:

> History does nothing, it 'possesses no immense wealth', it 'wages no battles'. It is man, real, living man who does all that, who possesses and fights; 'history' is not, as it were, a person apart, using man as a means to achieve its own aims; history is nothing but the activity of man pursuing his aims.

However, the capacity to make history depends not only on determinedly pursuing our goals, but also cultivating the necessary alignments of beliefs, capabilities and resources. Archer (2000) defined social structures as the material and psychological legacies of past action; to paraphrase Marx, the history we make is the pre-condition of what we do in future – we cannot choose the circumstances we inherit. In other words, the distinction between 'structure' and 'agency' is time-dependent; what went before determines what we can do in future and how quickly. To engage successfully in non-capitalist 'doings', we must therefore have or be capable of acquiring the necessary resources and capabilities along with the requisite beliefs and desires (Davies, 2011, 78).

Applying this reasoning to the way capitalism operates introduces additional complications. Marxism posits not only that it is 'real' in Archer's sense, but also that as it is enacted in everyday life it exercises causal power; in Gramsci's vernacular, it has 'propulsive force' (1971, 466). Captalism is not merely a set of background conditions, it is also an active practice which, for Marx, generates unintended consequences that compel capitalists to compete for survival. These rules of reproduction are the conditions of their existence *as* capitalists. As the following discussion of variety highlights, the rules of reproduction give capitalism a strong 'totalising' or expansionary impetus (Callinicos, 2006) explaining why it has enveloped much of the globe and displaced other economic practices. The reason it is 'totalising' is explained by Marx's theory of crisis: an economic system based on competition and accumulation becomes increasingly vulnerable to slump, as it ages.

The theory of crisis has been the source of endless controversy, not least within Marxism. The common premise is, in Kunkel's (2011, 9) words, that the 'existence of bourgeois society itself' is the source of economic crises constituted in the 'fatal schism' between 'profit-seekers… and wage earners'. The schism is fatal because over time, as markets become congested, 'it becomes progressively harder for profit-seekers to generate a return on investment, upon which future rounds of investment, growth and profitability depend' (Davies, 2011, 79). The question of why returns tend to diminish is complicated and controversial but the consequence is that it makes capitalism profoundly unstable and conflictual, and ultimately unsustainable if it cannot expand. According to Marx and Engels (2012, 39), 'the need of a constantly expanding market chases the bourgeoisie over the whole surface of the globe. It must nestle everywhere, settle everywhere, establish connections everywhere'. Expansion, broadly defined, takes many forms. Over and above the geographical spread of markets, it includes the commodification of public services, cuts to pay and welfare entitlements and lengthening working hours; these are all prominent features of European austerity today.

The 'essential' in Marxism, the theoretical 'bottom-line', is therefore that capitalism tends to be both universalising and prone to violent booms and slumps. As it ages, the system becomes increasingly crisis-prone and the compulsion to expand more urgent. However, expansion becomes harder to accomplish because, as more of the globe is subsumed, expansionary space diminishes and older capitalisms stagnate. It is in this sense that capitalism can be understood as a 'system' exercising propulsive and totalising force. And it is this diagnosis that justifies the traditional Marxist preoccupation with comprehensive transformation. Viewing the world through a Marxist lens has significant implications for everyday making, discussed further below.

Varieties of capitalism?

Exploring 'real world utopias' like the Mondragon Cooperative, Erik Olin Wright (2010) underscores what is at stake in the debate through his critique of Marxism. Wright claimed that although crisis is indeed an integral feature of capitalism, there is 'no overall tendency of intensification of disruptions to capital accumulation'. If so, 'we no longer have grounds for the idea that capitalism becomes progressively more fragile over time' (Wright, 2010, 100-101). Wright contends, for example, that Marxists underestimate the degree to which states can counteract the 'business cycle'. Most importantly, he recognises that real utopias can flourish under capitalism *only* if the Marxist theory of crisis is false and markets can be contained behind sustainable economic and political barriers: if, that is, the game is no worse than zero-sum.

The 'varieties of capitalism' literature proceeds from Wright's perspective that the governance and management of capitalism determines the potential for sustainable non-capitalist activity. It occupies an intermediate space between the systemic and everyday, pointing to variations in the institutional configuration of capitalism, such as Esping-Anderson's (1990) 'three worlds' of welfare state: the liberal, social democratic and Christian Democrat models. One of the main preoccupations in the varieties literature is how more egalitarian and solidaristic capitalisms are sustained, and how far systematising trends can be countered by local political and economic practices.

Critics argue that the emphasis on differentiation always underplayed significant commonalities. As Howell put it (2003, 122),

> ... in the absence of an articulation with theorising about the uneven and interdependent development of national capitalisms and the contradictory elements, crisis tendencies, and propensity for perpetual reinvention within capitalist economies, the danger for institutionalist analysis is always that it will become too static, able to explain stability but not rupture, and will render invisible the exercise of class power that underlies coordination and equilibrium in the political economy.

However, many scholars also highlight increasing pressures towards convergence, for example as Southern European economies are forced to implement the Troika's policies; swingeing cuts, the widespread commodification of public goods and the (further) erosion of distinct cultural political economies. According to Streeck (2011), the root of neoliberal convergence lies in the decline in growth rates throughout the West since the 1960s. It occurs not only in the economic domain, but also the social and democratic spheres. Even the Nordic heartlands of the social democratic welfare state are not exempt from convergence pressures(Crouch, 2011, 21). For Streeck, any 'lasting reconciliation between social and economic stability in capitalist democracies is a utopian project' (Streeck, 2011, 24). One question posed by these literatures is for 'real utopians' like Wright whether, as it spreads, capitalism is becoming more or less amenable to political variety. The advantage of Marxist political economy is that it perceives the erosion of variety as characteristic and symptomatic of a malaise rooted in the systemic propensity towards increasingly contagious crises. The remainder of the chapter considers the implications for everyday making, if we work with the Marxist propositions that capitalism is increasingly crisis-prone, depends on expansion for its sustainability, and is tending to erode the space for political variation.

Marxism, everyday life and system transformation

Support for a rapprochement between everyday and systemic thinking is found, somewhat unexpectedly, in the recent work of Judith Butler. Butler was a path-breaking theorist of performative agency, but now reconsiders the relationship between performativity and context. The problem she confronts is the failure of economic performativities in the economic crisis – the web of ideas, discourses and practices anchoring the hegemony of finance capital. How, she asks, did 'theories of finance produce impossible scenarios' that were 'bound to backfire and fail'? She answers that they sought to 'derive endless possibilities from limited resources' (2010,153). In other words, performative 'misfire' arose from the conflict between bubble ideologies and material constraints in the economy: the boomerang effect of structure on agency. Butler continues to resist a systemic reading of capitalism, but edges towards Marxism in arguing that after all, political agency may depend on economic conditions:

> … we might wonder whether the social bond can be thought at all without an understanding of how the basic materials of life are exchanged, how basic needs are addressed or fail to be addressed. One may or may not be a Marxist or indeed a structuralist to say such a thing, and maybe in the end that is much less important than that such a thing should become speakable. (Butler, 2010)

Coming from Butler, the notion that the ideas of Marxism should be at least 'speakable' is a powerful rebuke to the post-structuralist injunction to stop talking about it.

Boomerang effects

Butler's critique of neoliberal performativities draws attention to boomerang effects arising from thwarted intentions and practices; those forms of agency that conflict with but cannot transform the context in which they occur. For instance, if capitalism is real and crisis-prone, then seeking to transform it using the methodologies of deconstruction will result in performative misfire. If they succeed in cultivating non-capitalist practices to a sufficient degree, everyday makers will generate a conflictual relationship with capitalist ones. The following paragraphs explore practical dilemmas highlighted in the literatures on cooperative enterprise.

The cooperative movement, rooted in the Owenite tradition of 'utopian socialism', is often held up as an exemplar of the transformative potential in everyday making, showcasing the potential for equality and solidarity in non-capitalist economic endeavour. The cooperative movement encompasses those envisioning a comprehensively cooperative society beyond capitalism (Ratner, 2013) and, more commonly, those who see mutualism as the third pillar of a mixed economy complementing the state and the market realms (for example, Westall, 2011). In the UK today, both the Liberal Democrat–Tory coalition and the Labour Party see mutualism as a complement to the politics of austerity (The Stationery Office, 2012).

Mondragon in the Basque region, and its international subsidiaries, is among the most widely known and largest of cooperative enterprises. It best exemplifies the complementary economies tradition, working in partnership with both states and profit-making corporations. Mondragon is noted for its (comparatively) egalitarian management structures and equitable distribution of surplus among members. For Gibson-Graham (2003), these practices embody the socialist virtues of solidarity and egalitarianism, and Mondragon is also held up as an example of Wright's (2010) 'real world utopias'. However, to the extent it delivers distributive equality among members (a moot point), it has arguably done so at a cost: exploiting the labour of non-members and pursuing an increasingly market-centred approach as competitive pressures intensify. Nor has operating as a cooperative insulated Mondragon from the crisis, with members accepting large wage cuts and non-member employees being laid off (Durden et al, 2013). Thus, workers may have better conditions and take some decisions collectively, but sustaining itself through the crisis has compelled Mondragon to impose heavy costs on members and non-members alike. As Chomsky commented (interview with Flanders, 2012):

> Worker ownership within a state capitalist, semi-market system is better than private ownership but it has inherent problems.... Take the most advanced case: Mondragon. It's worker owned, it's not worker managed, although the management does come from the workforce often, but it's in a market system and they still exploit workers in South America, and they do things that are harmful to the society as a whole and they have no choice. If you're in a system where you must make profit in order to survive. You are compelled to ignore negative externalities, *effects on others*.

A more radical and adversarial form of cooperative enterprise is found in Argentina, where a major uprising followed economic collapse at the end of the 1990s, including a wave of factory occupations. Initially spontaneous and defensive, preoccupied with economic survival, these struggles had a profound impact on the goals and aspirations of the workers. Some revolutionaries saw the occupations as the basis for a direct challenge to private property and for moving towards nationalisation under workers' control. However, the movement was subjected to violent police attacks and, as the Argentinian state recovered its authority, workers' self-management emerged as the dominant cooperative practice, through the 'recovered factories movement' (Atzeni, 2010).

The movement is a politically diverse alliance of mainly small or medium sized enterprises, which has carved out a small but politically important niche within the Argentinian economy. It highlights a number of dilemmas for cooperative enterprises in a capitalist economy. First, building cooperatives can require high levels of class struggle, when corporations and state actors see them as a threat. The recovered factories movement emerged from a visceral struggle for survival by workers who found themselves confronted by state, market and judiciary. Second, this struggle engendered class-consciousness, lending impetus to the movement for economic and political justice. Ranis (2005, 20) argued that the recovered factories movement 'reinserts the working class as a central ingredient in the pursuit of a just society', posing a performative challenge to the capitalist logics of hierarchical management and private ownership. Third, however, the model of market-based workers' self-management imposes constraints on democracy and solidarity. Atzeni and Ghigliani (2007) found that dealing with the dilemmas of market competition led to the centralisation of power and an increasingly hierarchical internal division between 'productive' and 'directive' labour of the kind also found in Mondragon and other cooperatives. For Ranis (2005), the movement is tolerated and even encouraged because it is relatively small-scale and no longer poses the threat to state and corporations represented by the original factory occupations. Atzeni's dialogues with them showed that factory workers are well aware of the dilemmas. Not to compromise is to contemplate either economic disaster for the workers and their families, or a return to confrontation with the state-market system when the time is right.

The Marxist perspective on this dilemma is that Chomsky is right to argue that workers' self-management is better than corporate management, particularly when the alternative is economic ruin for the workers. However, even a comprehensively self-managed capitalism – welcome as that would be – would remain subject to the crisis tendencies at the heart of market competition. The focal point of critique is not therefore whether self-managed enterprises are a 'pragmatic' alternative to corporations or a 'sell-out', or indeed whether they might gradually recuperate the corporate economy. It is rather whether they insulate workers from and provide a solution to increasingly calamitous market failures. Moreover, because market-based competition produces not equilibrium, but hierarchy, some cooperatives are richer than others. Wage-rates differ between them depending on competitive success. As a vehicle for equality within capitalism, the cooperatives movement depends firstly on Wright's belief that capital accumulation is, at worst, a zero sum game long-term and secondly on the possibility of relative equality among competing and asymmetrically powerful enterprises.

Cooperatives often subsist comfortably within a neoliberal political economy and without posing any challenge to it. More radical and insurgent practices confront boomerang effects; if they resist compromise and attempt to encroach on markets, they risk encountering Argentinian-style coercion and violence. If they do not, they remain trapped in the dynamics of competition and accumulation. The first challenge of bridging everyday and system is therefore the 'recognition' and embrace of dialectical relationships; in Tariq Ali's terms (2013, 74), to 'identify and counter the forces – "the nameable agencies of power and capital, distraction and information" – that continually operated to block or limit any forward move'. As Ratner (2013) argued, naming and speaking this way requires an antagonistic stance towards the market economy – what he calls 'critical social praxis' (2013, 39–55) of the kind witnessed in the earliest days of the recovered factories movement, and which many of its workers still espouse.

From a Marxist point of view, critical social praxis poses (at least) three challenges. The first is whether it is possible to create restraining barriers capable of resisting boomerang effects, such as state and corporate violence. The second is how to ensure that the chill winds of competition do not undermine (relatively) equitable governance arrangements within cooperatives themselves. The third challenge is the forward march; developing propulsive forces capable of not only resisting the incursions of the market, but also rolling it back, as it continues to force working people to pay for the economic crisis.

From cracks to chasms?

In orthodox Marxism the crisis-prone nature of capitalism engenders a structural conflict between capitalists and workers. Diminishing rates of return mean that in addition to expanding geographically, eroding public space and encroaching on leisure time, capitalists have also to drive down costs and increase the surplus value derived from labour – Kunkel's (2011) 'fatal schism'. Capitalism therefore creates an antagonist in the form of the working class, a potential collectivity that Marx and Engels saw as the primary agent of transformation to communism.

Everyday makers are united with mainstream social scientists in dismissing the working class as an agent of social change. This is partly because of the unquestionable decline of Western working class organisation during the neoliberal offensive, particularly in the UK and USA. Anderson (1984, 104) argued that as the 'imaginative proximity of social revolution' retreated, so did faith in the emancipatory potential of labour. The question is whether the decline is reversible, whether the emerging working classes within developing economies have the requisite agency and, if so, whether labour today still has the emancipatory capacity envisaged in classical Marxism: the potentially universal class. It is not possible here to resolve enduring debates about the agency of everyday makers, civil society activists and proletarians, or the extent to which socioeconomic change erodes the potential for class agency. However, the Marxist wager on the working class is justified in the first instance by dire economic need, born of crisis-tendencies: Rosa Luxemburg's stark choice between socialism and barbarism. It is justified secondly by the potential for developing class collectivities; either where affective labour overflows instrumental labour (Hardt and Negri, 2004), or an organised force confronts and dissolves the state-capital nexus. In non-determinist readings of Marxism, transformation is contingent on summoning an organised political response to economic compulsion. In Gramsci (1971), for example, resistance is spurred by asymmetries between the claims of hegemons and the lived experiences of subalterns. However comprehensive hegemonic power might be it is always vulnerable to the instability in capitalist economies and the wedge this drives between expectation and experience. As the discussion of Argentina highlighted, practical struggles for survival can also redefine experience in ways that open up alternative political vistas, including class-consciousness.

This claim is not to overlook the complexity of the human personality, or the deeply ingrained character of identity conflicts cutting against class, such as the enduring cleavage among Catholics and Protestants in Ireland. Nor is it to underestimate the intuitive everyday commitment to capitalist practices engendered through experiences such as formal equality in contract relations, the purchase of commodities or how workers depend for a living on their employers' successes. Ultimately, the efficacy of transformative practices, everyday or systemic, presentist or revolutionary, depends on cultural plasticity and the capacity of political struggles to foster conditions in which solidaristic elements of the human personality flourish. Marx, for example, saw individualisation and atomisation as features specific to capitalist society, not human nature. He argued that the further we look into history 'the more does the individual... appear as dependent, as belonging to a greater whole' (Marx, 1973, 84). Conversely, only in the 18th century did the 'individual' emerge as the 'mere means towards his private purposes'. Given cultural plasticity, political change depends on the potential for conscious and organised agency: the internal and inter-subjective practices of schematisation, hypothesisation and practical judgment through which we change our minds and the world around us (Emirbayer and Mische, 1998).

With respect to the working class, the potential for unity has been demonstrated time and again over the past 150 years, even in unpromising contexts like Ireland where it has on occasion, at least, transcended religious cleavage (for example, Munck, 1985). Blackledge (2012) argued against Holloway's critique of labour that workplace struggles 'point towards a *positive* alternative to capitalism', developing solidarities that tend to 'overflow the confines of alienation'. They prefigure a future socialist society and demonstrate its feasibility in the here and now. Although none have made a decisive breakthrough in the present crisis, class and union-based struggles have been pivotal to the resistance so far, demonstrating the clearest potential for reversing European austerity and, in Greece at least, leading to political resurgence on the left through Syriza. In the Argentinian recovered factories movement, working class agency was feted both by those wanting to get rid of capitalism and those who saw workers' self-management as a pragmatic strategy for surviving in the market. It is also true that struggles originating in everyday life can generalise very quickly. The recent uprising in Turkey began with a local campaign against plans to develop Taksim Gezi Park in Istanbul. Following the brutal police eviction of the campaigners, supporting strikes and protests developed, themselves quickly generalising to encompass a much wider range of issues such as the government's attack on secularism and freedoms of assembly, expression and the press (see www.bbc.co.uk/news/world-europe-23234294). The question is therefore not whether political consciousness changes or is capable of generalising, but rather what kind of political activity is most likely to cultivate and sustain conscious class unity when large-scale, potentially universalising struggles emerge from the everyday campaigns against commodification or oppression.

One way of moving the debate forward is to suggest, following Blackledge, that the everyday maker's investment in 'prefigurative' struggles – how 'doings' showcase the potential for new worlds in the here and now – also operates in the workplace and on the terrain of class struggle, spanning both proximate and large-scale struggles. Newman (2012), discussed earlier, argued that everyday struggles operate in the world of work, where gendered labour in and against the state prefigures gender equality (see also Newman, Chapter Four). Yet, if gendered labour prefigures gender equality, then surely the mass demonstration prefigures, among other things, the right to the city. By extension, the solidarity in Argentina-style strikes and factory occupations prefigures and exemplifies workers' control. In short, Marxism does not take conscious working class unity as its premise. It rather sees myriad socioeconomic struggles at every scale as the grounds for forging it.

The Living Wage Campaign in the UK is perhaps the most successful example of a grass-roots strategy grounded in the combination of community and workplace organising. London Citizens, and its constituent chapter The East London Citizens Organisation (TELCO), led a successful campaign for a living wage for cleaners at Canary Wharf. The campaign also showed how organising in the community can stimulate unionisation, encouraging T & G officials to organise new groups of workers (Wills, 2012). In the 2012 London Olympics, the campaign secured the minimum living wage of £8.30 for all employed staff. For Wills (2013), this success testified to the power of vigorous but pragmatic campaigning among different civil society interest groups, adversarial tactics including strikes, demonstrations and occupations, and bargaining with elites from a position of strength. The underlying philosophy of Citizens UK is that a common interest can be forged among diverse groups around realistic demands (www.citizensuk.org). Accordingly, London Citizens predicated its strategy on the view that opposing the Olympics would be futile and divisive, and that what mattered was how to leverage investments, occurring anyway, for the good of local communities (Wills, 2013). These campaigns are oriented primarily at compelling rich organisations to share their wealth with workers and local people and can be understood as part of what Newman (Chapter Four) calls 'public-making'. Yet, it remains questionable how far they support the everyday-maker's orientation towards small-scale and autonomous 'doings'. On the one hand, as Wills (2012) argued, they are grounded in an adversarial tradition of community organising originating in the 1920s. Wills contends that their success lies in the capacity to institutionalise and root themselves in place, as well as the ability to recognise that they operate at the intersection of power relations configured in and beyond the locale (Wills, 2013, A2). In this sense, the London Citizens model contrasts with the ephemeral and transient modes of network solidarity posited by everyday makers in the post-structuralist and autonomist traditions (for example, Merrifield, 2011). On the other hand, the campaigns stand out for their rarity in achieving victories a the context of dramatically falling wages under austerity. Winning the living wage is a major achievement. However, it remains to be seen whether this model of organising is scalable in the sense of being able to win gains from struggling businesses or public sector organisations slashing wages and services, without mobilising a more fundamental and generalised challenge to neoliberalism. Yet to do this would run counter to the ethos of Citizens UK, which is to fight realistic battles and sustain unity among groups with otherwise widely diverging class, religious and cultural interests, and to avoid taking overtly ideological positions.

Conclusion

As *Policy & Politics* enters its fifth decade, the analytical and political landscape has, in some ways, changed beyond recognition. The purpose of this chapter was to argue that we should also recognise powerful continuities and their implications for political action. In questioning the ethos of everyday making, it argues that the Marxist critique of capitalism remains essential for grasping our predicament and the potential for change. Today, we are arguably confronted by a global 'polycrisis' (Swilling, 2011); the convergence of economic, ecological, resource-depletion and climate-change pathologies, aggravated by rampant economic and geopolitical competition. At such a portentous moment, introducing dualisms between everyday and systemic struggles seems at best unhelpful. At worst it ignores the explosive force of large-scale struggles against neoliberalism. To co-opt a familiar idiom, to be excessively preoccupied with everyday life risks not seeing the chasms for the cracks. The key questions are rather those of scalability and reflexivity: how do we move from one perspective to the other and back again; which cracks can be turned into chasms, and how?

For Gibson-Graham, re-focusing on the systematising nature of capitalism and resistance is politically disastrous, a recipe for paralysis. However, far from being a counsel of despair Marxist 'capitalocentrism' rejects the dualism 'everyday versus system' for a viewpoint that sees small acts posing large questions (for example, Turkey) and vice versa, since large questions also inspire small acts. If, for example, capitalism is seen as the problem rather than public spending, this is not a recipe for paralysis but a *prima facie* reason for mounting practical resistance: to library closures, workfare, wage cuts, the bedroom tax and the commodification of public space. Theorists in the Marxist tradition who focus on the everyday, notably Berman (1984) and Lefebvre (2000), saw that resistance and reconstruction often begins in everyday life but never claimed that the crises of capitalism could be solved locally or outside the labour process.

Some prominent thinkers and activists, with a degree of affinity to the concept of everyday making are now asking questions about the problems of strategy and scale. At the end of his vivid and frightening portrait of the 'new military urbanism', Graham (2010, 384) asked

> 'how might a loose and mobile, yet effectual, totality be forged
> from diverse and multiple countergeographies, to challenge and to
> parallel the multiple sites, circuits and spectacles so characteristic

of the new military urbanism? How, in other words, can we name the enemy'?

After spectacular but fleeting successes in 2011, activists in the Occupy movement consider how to revive and maintain the energy created at the height of the struggle, alongside counterparts in labour movements. In the spirit of a 'politics of asking' (Halvorsen, 2012, 5), they question how movements might find a more strategic footing with greater organisational transparency, without losing the creativity engendered by networks (for example, http://nationalcan.ning.com/page/update-29-03-2012). These are important questions, but an authentic politics of asking does not rule out certain answers as unspeakable. Neither Butler nor Graham wants to name the enemy 'capitalism'. Rather, Graham (2010, 382) echoes the call by Retort for a 'non-nostalgic, non-anathematic, non-regressive, non-fundamental, non-apocalyptic critique of the modern' (Retort, 2005, 185). Yet, strictures of this kind characterise what McGrail (2011) sees as a subtle form of censorship; a regrettable prohibition on utopian thinking, a 'fantasiectomy' undermining qualities that have always inspired struggles for democracy in the face of oppression; the capacity to envision the best of all possible worlds and recognise them when they emerge from struggles in prefigurative form. If so, the presentist, pragmatic and localist dispotif of everyday making risks denying us resources we need to cultivate sustainable new worlds.

Retort was correct that those wanting to escape the confines of neoliberalism cannot ignore the disasters (or mundane failures) of the socialist project in the 20th century. Yet, to 'jettison the legacy of historical materialism would be no advance' either (Watkins, 2012, 102). The Marxist diagnosis and its wager on communism arguably remains as central to that legacy and the possibility of new worlds as it was when *Policy & Politics* was founded.

Acknowledgements

I thank Antònia Casellas, Mike Geddes, Janet Newman and anonymous reviewers for very helpful comments on earlier drafts of this chapter.

References

Ali, T, 2013, Between past and future: A reply to Asef Bayat, *New Left Review*, 80, 61–74

Anderson, P, 1984, Modernity and revolution, *New Left Review*, 1/144, 96–113

Archer, M, 2000, For structure: Its realities, properties and powers: A reply to Anthony King *The Sociological Review*, 48, 3, 464–72

Atzeni, M, 2010, A Marxist perspective on workers collective action, in Atzeni, M, *Workplace conflict: Mobilisation and solidarity in Argentina*, Basingstoke: Palgrave Macmillan, 14–31

Atzeni, M, Ghigliani, P, 2007, Labour process and decision-making in factories under workers self-management: Empirical evidence from Argentina, *Work, Employment and Society*, 21, 4, 653–71

Bang, HP, 2005, Among everyday makers and expert citizens, in Newman, J (ed), *Remaking governance: People, politics and the public sphere*, Bristol: Policy Press, 159–78

Bang, HP, Sørensen, E, 1999, The everyday maker: A new challenge to democratic governance, *Administrative Theory and Praxis*, 21, 3, 325–41

Berman, M, 1984, The signs in the street: A response to Perry Anderson, *New Left* Review, 1/144, 114–23

Biesta, G, 2008, Toward a new 'logic' of emancipation: Foucault and Rancière, in Glass, RD (ed), *Philosophy of Education 2008*, Urbana-Champaign, IL: Philosophy of Education Society, 169–77

Blackledge, P, 2012, In perspective: John Holloway, *International Socialism*, 136, 89–109

Butler, J, 2010, Performative agency, *Journal of Cultural Economy*, 3, 2, 147–61

Callinicos, AT, 2006, *The resources of critique*, Cambridge: Polity Press

Clark, TJ, 2012, For a left with no future, *New Left Review*, 74, 53–75

Crouch, C, 2011, *The strange non-death of neoliberalism*, Cambridge: Polity Press

Davies, JS, 2011, *Challenging governance theory: From networks to hegemony*, Bristol: Policy Press

Durden, S, Haight, M, Hanson, L, Harris, K, Perez, F, Sanchgez, D, Ray, S, Tatum, L, 2013, Working and rebuilding together: Worker cooperatives as an economic development tool, wws.princeton.edu/research/pwreports_f12/591a–Advance–Memphis–Report.pdf

Emirbayer, M, Mische, A, 1998, What is agency?, *American Journal of Sociology*, 103, 4, 962–1023

Esping-Anderson, G, 1990, *The three worlds of welfare capitalism*, Princeton, NJ: Princeton University Press

Flanders, L, 2012, Talking with Chomsky, Counterpunch 30412, www.counterpunch.org/2012/04/30/talking–with–chomsky

Fourcade, M, 2012, On Erik Olin Wright, envisioning real utopias, London and New York, Verso, 2010, *Socioeconomic Review*, 10, 2, 369–402

Gibson-Graham, JK, 1996, *The end of capitalism (as we knew it): A feminist critique of political economy*, Oxford: Blackwell.

Gibson-Graham, JK, 2003, Enabling ethical communities: Cooperativism and class, *Critical Sociology*, 29, 2, 123–61

Gibson-Graham, JK, 2008, Diverse economies: Performative practices for 'other worlds', *Progress in Human Geography*, 35, 2, 613–32

Graham, S, 2010, *Cities under siege: The new military urbanism*, London: Verso

Gramsci, A, 1971, *Selections from prison notebooks*, Hoare, Q, Nowell-Smith, G (trans and ed), London: Lawrence and Wishart

Halvorsen, S, 2012, Beyond the network? Occupy London and the global movement, *Social Movement Studies: Journal of Social, Cultural and Political Protest*, 11, 3/4, 427–33

Hardt, M and Negri, T, 2004, *Multitude*, London: Penguin Books.

Harman, C, 2010, *Zombie capitalism*, London: Haymarket Books

Harvey, D, 2010, *The enigma of capital and the crises of capitalism*, London: Profile Books

Hendriks, F, Tops, P, 2005, Everyday fixers as local heroes: A case study of vital interaction in local governance, *Local Government Studies*, 34, 4, 475–90

Holloway, J, 2010, *Crack capitalism*, London: Pluto Press

Howell, C, 2003, Varieties of capitalism: And then there was one? *Comparative Politics*, 36, 1, 103–24

Jones, M, 2008, Recovering a sense of political economy, *Political Geography*, 27, 4, 377–99

Kliman, A, 2011, *The failure of capitalist production: Underlying causes of the great recession*, London: Pluto Press

Kunkel, B, 2011, How much is too much? *London Review of Books*, 33, 3, 9–14

Lefebvre, H, 1971, *Everyday life in the modern world*, London: Athlone Press, 2000

Li, Y, Marsh, D, 2008, New forms of political participation: Searching for expert citizens and everyday makers, *British Journal of Political Science*, 38, 2, 247–72

Marx, K, 1858 (unfinished), *The Grundrisse: Foundations of the critique of political economy (rough draft)*, Harmondsworth: Penguin, 1973

Marx, K, Engels, F, 1846, *The German Ideology*, New York: Prometheus Books, 1998

Marx, K, Engels, F, 1848, *The Communist Manifesto: A modern edition*, London: Verso, 2012

Mason, P, 2012, *Why it's kicking off everywhere: The new global revolutions*, London: Verso

McGrail, BA, 2011, Owen, Blair and utopian socialism: On the post-apocalyptic reformulation of Marx and Engels, *Critique: Journal of Socialist Theory*, 39, 2, 247–69

Merrifield, A, 2011, Crowd politics: Or, 'here comes everybuddy' *New Left Review*, 71, 103–114

Munck, R, 1985, Class and religion in Belfast: A historical perspective, *Journal of Contemporary History*, 20, 2, 241–59

Newman, J, 2012, *Working the spaces of power: Activism, neoliberalism and gendered labour*, London: Bloomsbury

Nickel, P, 2007, Network governance and the new constitutionalism, *Administrative Theory and Praxis*, 29, 2, 198–224

Ranis, P, 2005, Argentina's worker-occupied factories and enterprises, *Socialism and Democracy*, 19, 3, 1–23

Ranson, S, 2012, Remaking public spaces for civil society, *Critical Studies in Education*, 53, 3, 245–261

Ratner, C, 2013, *Cooperation, community and co-ops in a global era*, New York: Springer

Retort, 2005, *Afflicted powers: Capital and spectacle in a new age of war*, London: Verso

Streeck, W, 2011, The crises of democratic capitalism, *New Left Review*, 71, 5–29

Swilling, M, 2011, Reconceptualising urbanism, ecology and networked infrastructures, *Social Dynamics*, 37, 1, 78–95

Swyngedouw, E, 2007, The post-political city, Urban Politics Now, BAVO (ed), Rotterdam: NAI (Netherlands Architecture Institute), 58–76

The Stationery Office, 2012, Mutual and cooperative approaches to delivering public services, House of Commons Communities and Local Government Committee: Fifth Report of Session 2012–13, www.publications.parliament.uk/pa/cm201213/cmselect/cmcomloc/112/112.pdf

Watkins, S, 2012, Presentism? A reply to Clark, *New Left Review*, 74, 77–102

Westall, A, 2011, Relational economics, *Soundings*, 49, 94–104

Wills, J, 2012, The geography of community and political organisation in London today, *Political Geography*, 31, 2, 114–26

Wills, J, 2013, The London Olympics in 2012: The good, the bad and an organising opportunity, *Political Geography*, 34, A1–A3

Wright, EO, 2010, *Envisioning real utopias*, London: Verso

CHAPTER FOUR

Performing new worlds?
Policy, politics and creative labour in hard times

Janet Newman

Introduction

This chapter addresses the problem of how to engage with the politics of public policy in the current period of cuts, austerity and retrenchment. As Hay and Wincott (2012) argue, the slow pace of economic recovery in Britain and beyond means that hard times are likely to continue, with further pressure on welfare provision and public services. But what does this mean for our understanding of public policy? Can the theoretical frameworks developed for analysing the New Labour years in the UK suffice? The chapter takes up the challenge of this book by offering critical reflections on the implications of austerity governance for the politics of the policy process. But it also argues that critical reflections are insufficient, and goes on to explore the potential of new methods, new actors, and new framings of the policy process to generate new solutions, and to suggest how far actors with 'progressive' social or political commitments are able to enact new worlds within the confines of the present.

The policy reforms traced in this chapter refer to the UK Coalition government in 2011/12, but the chapter traces what I consider to be underlying logics that are likely to be longstanding. These are discussed in a series of short sections whose aim is to provoke ideas and critical dialogue rather than to offer a full account (or critique) of the topic concerned. By bringing them together in a single chapter I hope to suggest both potential synergies and important disjunctures. The chapter then assesses how alternative rationalities and scripts might be performed against this backdrop. As established institutional pathways are fractured there may be some space for 'progressive' interventions to take shape. A final section revisits the vexed question of how far new and emergent performances might be considered as sites of governmentalisation and neoliberal appropriation, and how far they might constitute new terrains of political engagement.

Reframing the policy process

Austerity is not of course a new topic in the political and policy literatures (see for example Clarke and Newman, 2012; Farnsworth, 2011; Jordan and Drakeford, 2012; Lowndes and Pratchett, 2012; Richardson, 2010, Taylor-Gooby and Stoker, 2011; and special issue of *Critical Social Policy*, 2012, 32, 3). But my focus here is the implications of austerity for how the policy *process* is framed in the UK. While others have argued that existing theories of public administration and governance are sufficiently resilient (Kelly and Dodds, 2012) this chapter offers a more sceptical approach. I want to briefly refer to three developments, all conveniently beginning with D, each of which is the focus of multiple enactments of policy and politics. *Divest* involves the stripping away of governing functions – not just service delivery – from the state itself. This is not a new dynamic; previous decades saw extensive academic engagement with processes of marketisation and with the growth of quangos. However, divestment stands as the most visible marker of austerity governance and of wider processes of neoliberalisation. The radical disruptions to both governing and service delivery have generated a new concern with *Design*, and recent years have witnessed an expansion of design from its roots in industry and architecture to an engagement with social and public problems. Design contrasts with an older 'planning' tradition, and draws on forms of expertise beyond the state: in consultancies, think tanks, small-scale enterprises, and in the academy, where academics are encouraged to demonstrate the impact of their research on policy and practice. A third development is *Decentralise*. While this appears to offer a spatial metaphor, bringing governance closer to communities of 'ordinary people', it is primarily concerned with attempts to realise assets beyond the state. Despite the failure of the Big Society as a political slogan, it remains the hope of the UK government that local communities will, if freed from the shackles of the Big State, be enabled and empowered to develop creative responses to the problems they – and others – face. Decentralisation is of course not wholly distinct from either divestment (local community actors are encouraged to take over formerly public assets and to challenge the *public* delivery of local services) or design (most design interventions advocate a localised and decentralised approach to citizen involvement and behaviour change). However I view decentralisation as a paradigm in its own right because it offers a distinct pathway to governance beyond the state.

There is, of course, much more going on that the three Ds can encompass – we might, for example, extend the analysis to include Digitisation and Deregulation. But the three I have focused on suggest some of the ways in which austerity governance is taking shape, and help surface the contradictions at stake as governments struggle to position themselves as efficient and prudent economic managers while retaining electoral support; that is between technocratic and politicised forms of governing. They each also challenge existing narratives of governance established before the financial crisis took shape. The dominant narratives for the last decades have centred on the shifting relationships between state and market, the fate of the New Public Management (NPM) and the rise of network governance. However narratives that looked beyond the NPM to models of network governance, partnerships and participation now seem a little beside the point. In the UK, networks are being torn apart as a product of deliberate processes of 'disintermediation', stripping away layers and returning services to their 'core business'. Inter-organisational partnerships are no longer a desirable norm; rather, new configurations are emerging as organisations establish joint back office functions and call centres, while 'failing' organisations are becoming subject to takeover by those deemed to be successful. The language of partnership has been displaced by that of coproduction, with users and communities invited to be involved in both the design and delivery of services, or taking over formerly public assets and services. And the Conservative Party's hoped for Big Society, which attempted to discursively reframe the policy domain from a state/market binary to a concern with state/society dynamics, proved unsustainable in the context of the stripping away of the infrastructure of voluntary sector, NGOs and local governance that might have sustained it (Alcock, 2012; NEF, no date, 1, 2).

This all presents a fairly grim picture. However in the remainder of this chapter I want to explore what the spaces might be for radical or progressive interventions. Each of the developments I have touched on here – divest, design and devolve – opens up particular questions. For example processes of *divestment* raise the question about how far 'progressive' voices should call for the restoration of what many viewed as deeply flawed state provision, or should look to new models for future public services that offer greater flexibility and diversity. The turn to *design* opens up space for different kinds of expertise – including that of citizens and service users – to help construct possible future pathways. But it might also be viewed as simply the means of delivering greater cost savings. And processes of *devolution* raise questions about how far the localisation of policy and services can offer progressive forms of political renewal in an era of growing spatial inequalities. In what follows, then, I do not want to offer an overly optimistic picture, and the examples I refer to are unlikely to be longstanding. But my aim is to turn some attention (empirical as well as political) to sources of creative labour and to new sites and forms of political agency which might help to configure prefigurative pathways towards a post-austerity politics.

Performing new worlds?

Reframings of the policy landscape, from network governance to coproduction, from partnership to participation, tend to become the focus both of enthusiasm (about opening up the field to new actors and ideas) and of profound pessimism (reducing all to yet another example of neoliberal governance). In an attempt to open out a terrain of productive critique, I want to raise two questions about how innovations (including those associated with the three Ds) might be assessed. One concerns the relationship between ideas and policy enactments, while the second explores the wider political implications of what appear to be politically neutral or normatively desirable interventions. In developing the first of these arguments, I want to draw attention to the ways in which policy may be considered as a form of performance. Performances may be spontaneous (a practice made up to deal with a tricky situation or new challenge) or rehearsed (developed through dialogue with others or perhaps shaped by a director). They may follow a script (the policy text) but may offer new interpretations and translations, or may abandon the script altogether. They may deliberately rupture expectations, or may follow established traditions. They are, however, embodied and affective rather than simply discursive; performance offers a conception of policy as lived and enacted, albeit within cultural and material constraints.

The chapter, then, is influenced in part by performance studies: a growing field that encompasses the study of cultural forms (texts, the visual arts, architecture and so on) but also draws on studies of embodiment, action, behaviour and agency (Schechner, 1985). Performance studies look back to Goffman (1959/93), but current developments encompass work on aesthetic labour (Jackson, 2011) and post-structuralist theories of performativity (Butler, 1990; 2010). The latter are particularly relevant for my argument since they show how new policy models, theories and texts may be constitutive in their effect: that is, they have a capacity to bring into being, to enact and embody, the worlds they describe. This resonates with academic work on the role of social science in enacting, rather than simply describing, the social (Law and Urry, 2004). Of particular note is the contribution of Gibson-Graham (1996; 2006; Gibson-Graham and Roelvink, 2011) whose studies of alternative economic forms and experiments show how new worlds can be enacted within the confines of apparently hegemonic economic systems. They propose a model of collective action in which 'collective' is not the massing together of like subjects but a broad and distributed entity that includes those engaged in theory building alongside, and in collaboration with, participants in particular projects. And their 'action' is viewed as having a performative force, surfacing tacit knowledge and bringing it to bear on what they term 'world changing experiments' (2006, 166).

Here I am concerned with forms of collective action that help generate new performances within the constraints of the present, and how those with a commitment to progressive politics might engage with the policy process in hard times. My use of 'progressive' here denotes those with a commitment to social and political change who do not stop short at criticising what already exists but who also attempt to create alternatives (see also Roseneil, 2012). This interest comes out of my own recent research, which explored the experiences of women who had taken activist commitments into their working lives, developing new rationalities through community projects, in local government, the civil service, think tanks, political parties, trades unions, the academy and the creative industries (Newman, 2012a). I used the title *Working the Spaces of Power* to show how women had worked the borders between government policy and personal commitments in a period spanning the 1950s to 2012 (extended into 2013 though a series of informal workshops[1]). This multi-generational research showed how older generations had helped bring the politics of feminism and other social movements into the professions of the expanding welfare state. Some of those confronting the adversarial politics of the 1980s recalled an ethos of working 'in and against' the state, creating pockets of radicalism and resistance where they could. In the Blair years of the 1990s participants in the research had helped shape the focus on joined up government, partnership and participation, while others used the 'invited spaces' these had created to expand the scope for progressive interventions. In the present many younger – and older – women are opening up new forms of activism, mobilising against the cuts, taking part in the Occupy movement, feminist and antiracist struggles, global social justice campaigns and/or environmental politics. Some are becoming social entrepreneurs within the diverse marketplace for public goods, while those still occupying governance or service roles are seeking to mitigate the impact of austerity, trying to make policy less bad than it might otherwise have been. And some are using the developments discussed above – divest, design and decentralise – to create new platforms for their own work and to attempt to appropriate these governmental discourses for more progressive ends.

However the scope for progressive politics to be performed within the constraints of austerity governance is limited. In what follows I assess the scope for such adaptive or disruptive performances and tease out the wider implications of austerity governance.

75

Divest: the politics of 'diversity'

As noted earlier, austerity governance is characterised by the divestment of services and governance functions away from the state.[2] This is not a new process, but in conditions of austerity the market dynamics of the NPM are traversed by a divestment of policy and governance functions. For example the UK government is not just commissioning private sector suppliers to deliver major new programmes, but is turning to venture capital bodies to invest in the possibility of future profits by managing the risks of commissioning on its behalf. In local government, outsourcing to the private sector is intensifying as a result of stringent budget cuts, and is increasingly concerned with governing and planning functions. And the commissioning role is itself increasingly shared with service providers. There are many other examples of divestment, from the sale of public assets to non-state providers to the proliferation of new models of hybrid organisation in health, schooling and other services. As well as reducing accountability and opening up new forms of marketisation, such developments introduce greater fragmentation of services (see for example Toynbee's analysis of the effects of the opening out of the NHS to 'any provider', Guardian 12 October 2012, 33). But they also disrupt governance and policy making: for example in June 2012 the UK Cabinet Secretary proposed that policy making itself should become more open and 'contestable' by commissioning non-government actors – for example think tanks or academics – to take on policy tasks formerly limited to civil servants. The compound effect of such developments, we might argue, is to make it increasingly difficult to 'steer' policy from the centre.

As was the case under New Labour, divestment is framed within an ideological politics that blurs diversification (of suppliers) and the expansion of diversity (of organisational forms and of consumer choice). Certainly new organisational forms are proliferating: mutuals, cooperatives, so-called 'free' schools, foundation trusts, social enterprises and so on. Divestment is also enabling voluntary and civil society organisations, faith groups and charities to take on more extensive service delivery roles. However it has generated a range of different responses and experiments that are not easily evaluated. The Birmingham Policy Commission notes a number of challenges raised by the diversification agenda in local government (University of Birmingham, 2011). One is the development of a more segmented approach to service provision. This may be user driven but tends to overlook wider social and economic questions of cohesion and economic or environmental wellbeing. A second is the subordination of democratic concerns resulting from the increased complexity of commissioning arrangements and delivery networks. A third is the shift of risks to those least able to bear them, whether small service suppliers or users themselves.

Diversity, then, is an ambiguous goal. It is certainly the case that new actors are entering the marketplace. However, rather than divestment leading to greater diversity and choice, a dominant dynamic is that of enabling established players (Circo, Capita, Price Waterhouse and others) to consolidate and expand their market position as public service providers. For example a majority of the GP consortia have decided to pursue the voluntary outsourcing of the management of NHS commissioning bodies, further expanding the remit of large corporate players rather than increasing diversity. This process has not gone uncontested: several radical outsourcing programmes in local government have met with widespread opposition, and some chief executives and council leaders have either reversed earlier policies or stepped down from their roles as a means of registering their opposition (Guardian, 17 October 2012, 15). This suggests some possible gap between governmental programmes and local responses, and highlights the significance of local authorities as creative and innovative actors (see also Lowndes et al, 2013).

Divestment, it is clear, is not a single process but opens up an unstable field of interests, actors and strategies with unpredictable outcomes. This in turn generates the possibility of creative responses to austerity, albeit at the margins. For example new provisions for public bodies to raise capital from bond markets to fund large projects has enabled some local authorities to secure capital funding for green energy projects (with resistance, however, from a distrusting central government). Some not-for-profit and community organisations have taken up market opportunities in an attempt to secure their (no doubt temporary) survival in the face of the withdrawal of public funding. Some former state workers are becoming (or attempting to become) social entrepreneurs, freed from some of the performance requirements of the institutions they used to work for (but facing a much more precarious working life). Alternative economic experiments, including local trading and cooperative enterprises, are flourishing. And the closure of some public services has generated new public mobilisations (for example over threatened library closures) but also radical interventions (the reopening of Friern Barnet library in north London by a group of squatters in September 2012). Some of the participants in my own research are involved in policy oriented, political or campaigning bodies (the Family and Parenting Institute, Compass, UNISON, the Women's Budget Group, and a range of think tanks), from which they can not only make the effects of cuts visible, but also can develop and enact alternatives.

These emerging performances and enactments (both political and economic) are likely to be short-lived, and all are highly contested. But I want to draw out two points from the discussion. First, divestment strategies lead to an expansion of what Durose, Justice and Skelcher (2012) term 'governing beyond the state'. They argue that, as well as privatising the public realm, this can also serve to publicise the private, opening up the political and governing systems to actors excluded from elite governing networks. This opens up the possibility of appropriations 'from below' of new legislative and policy provisions: forms of appropriation which many of those I interviewed were engaged in. What happens to such actors in the increasingly disorganised marketplace for public goods is of course another matter: new market opportunities opened up by small entrepreneurs and local non-profit providers tend to be readily gobbled up by corporate players, and the risks associated with new forms of 'precarious labour' (Standing, 2011) are high. But second, the analysis shows how neoliberal governance, even in conditions of austerity, has to reach accommodations with other forces and fields (Clarke, 2008). The diversity of actors and spaces that emerge do not, however, necessarily foster greater social and political diversity; the dynamics of neoliberalism not only serve to expand the scope and reach of corporate capital but also deepen the economisation of social life.

Design: the politics of expertise

My focus on design is intended to mark the significance of new forms of expertise in the development and enactment of policy (marked, for example, by the Redesigning Public Services report generated by a recent Parliamentary Inquiry: www.policyconnect.org.uk/apdig/ design-commission). The traditional planning model of public policy is now traversed by design professionals expanding the remit of design from industry and architecture to policy work, and by a proliferation of interventions by think tanks, consultancies, entrepreneurs, university research centres, policy commissions and NGOs, all part of a post-welfare economy based on the knowledge-intensive and creative industries.

Good design (whether of projects, services or social dynamics) is of course a public good in its own right. However, design is an ambiguous commodity: it encompasses a range of different purposes and applications. Its methods cover crowd-sourcing (Mindlab, 2011), the use of web 2.0 (Leadbeater and Cottam, 2007); experimental methods (Stoker, 2010; Stoker and John, 2009); the development of 'nudge' strategies for changing individual behaviour (John et al, 2011), and numerous forms of coproduction. These offer different conceptions of the person, from affective to deliberative subjects, or from individualised economic actors to collective agents. It follows that design also supports a range of different purposes. The dominant claim is that design can deliver both better outcomes and substantial cost savings (see for example NESTA's chapter on securing 'radical efficiency' in local government: Gillinson et al, 2010). Design is frequently utilised to remodel universal or high cost benefits, or to enable local authorities and health services to secure efficiencies by re-engineering or streamlining services. However the relationship between costs and outcomes tends not to be addressed.

But design also has strong activist roots. For example Actant argue for design to be viewed as a social or public good rather than simply as a means of finding ways to change individual behaviour. They elaborate the affinities between the design paradigm and the Big Society agenda but go on to

> … wonder whether this seemingly happy union brushes over something important, specifically how particular issues become social problems in the first place….We argue that Design has to reclaim the value that it places on making social problems visible, understandable and graspable, reminiscent of the stance of earlier designers … who saw their work as a kind of social activism. (Blyth and Kimbell, 2011)

Implicit here is the concept of design as a progressive political methodology that can be performed within the constraints of austerity governance. The ambiguities of design, then, depend not only on the market positioning of the designers but also on their closeness to or distance from government as purchaser of their skills, and on their approach to citizen involvement. Although design is dominated by corporate players, several of the participants in my own research (cited earlier) had moved from voluntary organisations or the public sector to work on the redesign of services, either as social entrepreneurs or as members of think tanks (such as the New Economics Foundaton (NEF)). Others, working as academics and researchers, were attempting to enable public policy and public service staff to draw on the results of their research to help design better outcomes.

In assessing the capacity of design to open up progressive policy alternatives, we might want to dig beneath the apparent neutrality of its methodologies, rather than being attracted to what appears to be a series of post-political policy interventions. To the extent to which it draws on citizen experience and expertise, design is likely to produce better outcomes. But one is left wondering *which* citizens benefit in practice, and which are left to suffer from the reduction of resources and imposition of austerity measures. While good design can be viewed as a normative requirement for progressive public services and the development of public goods, the policy worlds that are constituted through its diverse methodologies are highly diverse and ambiguously public.

Decentralise: the politics of locality

Governmental rhetoric paints an attractive picture of local involvement, action and enterprise flourishing if the state gets out of the way – the Big State is depicted as a handicap and barrier rather than enabler and resource provider. The localism agenda has spawned a range of policies, including the promotion of market mechanisms through the community 'right to buy', the attempt to give local people direct control over neighbourhood services, and the promotion of local action and local self improvement through the work of 'community mobilisers'.[3]

The dominant critiques of the localism agenda in the UK tend to circulate around the effects of continued – and intensified – control from central government, the stripping away of the supporting institutional architecture of local government and voluntary sector (NEF, no date 2), the opening up of local spaces and services to the private sector, and the weakening of a wider public framework for resource distribution, regulation and control. But my focus is not (only) on critique, but on the diverse ways in which local may be imagined and performed, and by whom. There is a rich body of literature which centres on the local as a site of solidarities and which offers strategies for mobilising and empowering local actors to participate in solving local problems, in enhancing local capacities, and in contributing to the wider polity. Current policies on community mobilisation can be viewed as enactments of such an approach. However austerity may change the conditions in which local connective labour is possible, closing many of the spaces from which it was conducted and shifting the political climate itself to one more closely characterised by political disaffection and dismay.

Furthermore in conditions of austerity the local may be performed as a defensive space, turned in upon itself to protect its particular cultural or physical resources from the incursion of its 'others'. The 'others' may of course be highly diverse. Historic patterns of closure against migrants may be overlaid with attempted closure against those made homeless, jobless or sick as a result of the economic downturn and benefit cuts. Alternatively the 'other' of defensive strategies may be the supermarket chain seeking to encroach on local space in return for the promise of delivering much needed housing or other public goods. Such differences and specificities suggest the poverty of policy narratives that suggest that if the state retreats, local involvement and action will proliferate in its stead – an imagined relationship widely critiqued (Alcock, 2012; Durose, 2012; Sullivan, 2012).

However, while the rolling back of the state may not itself be a catalyst for the development of civic action, the current political landscape is generating a resurgence of local mobilisations. Many of the women I interviewed are engaged in promoting such mobilisations, supporting a range of community based and civil society projects, some attempting to rework the Big Society agenda, others fostering alternative pathways. The possibilities and limits of these forms of engagement have been highlighted elsewhere: see for example Durose (2012) on the expansion of 'civic entrepreneurialism' in Salford. Durose analyses the work of local brokers: those who form coalitions of people who are able to get things done and keep things going in and around the neighbourhood. She concludes that:

> In part, local brokering reflects the aspirations of the Big Society but does so through strategies shaped through local knowledge and also begins to provide means of community resilience, if not resistance. (201, 28)

Such studies point to some of the ways in which the localism agenda is performed in specific places by actors who are adapting their 'front line' public sector, faith based or community development roles to respond to the changing needs and conditions of the communities they serve.

But the specificity of place matters; localities and local authorities vary in the cultural and political resources on which they can draw. In viewing the local as something that is performed in different ways, then, I do not want to imply that such performances take place in isolation from a wider material and cultural context. The resources and capacities that enable or constrain particular enactments of the local are significant. So too are the discursive scripts through which new kinds of enactment are summoned. The dominant policy model assumes that solutions are to flow from civil society action, from collaborative redesign, from private sector innovation, from new forms of social entrepreneurship, and from the restoration of the traditional ties of interdependence based on family, faith and community. These are of course not necessarily compatible: modern economic individualism sits rather uneasily with the imaginary solidarities of community, and traditional ties may hinder, rather than enable, the possibility of forging the kinds of connectivity that underpin civic action. The next section, then, moves beyond my three Ds to address a wider politics of public-making.

Connect: the politics of public-making

Austerity governance does not only concern a politics of debt and retrenchment but also has affective, cultural and psychic consequences. It brings a possible retreat into individualism and defensive localism, and deepens tendencies towards political alienation and disaffection. Within each of the above discussions of the three Ds, I have shown how some actors and interventions are attempting to counter these effects by making new connections, juxtaposing different things to create new relationships between them, and generating new forms of thinking and action. Many of those I interviewed, who worked in the public or voluntary sectors, offer an image of an expansive form of leadership that looks beyond organisational boundaries. Here I want to expand this analysis by focusing on the connective work of public-making: the process of fostering attachments, relationships and a wider public culture, and of surfacing – and acting on – public issues that transcend the boundaries of the local or particular. This is both a means of mitigating the material effects of austerity by fostering protest and dissent against cuts, but is also a route towards addressing the affective consequences of austerity – disaffection, powerlessness and disconnection.

The notion of public-making has roots in the work of Michael Warner (2002), Clive Barnett (2008) and others who have drawn attention to the processes through which publics come into being, and to their fluid, impermanent character. It was developed in an AHRC/ESRC seminar series on Emergent Publics that focused on three questions: how new publics might emerge; how new objects of public action arise; and how both are mediated by new dynamics of public governance (Mahony et al, 2010). Publics, it is argued, have to be convened: they are discursively summoned up, addressed, hailed as such. That is they are *constituted* through different performative repertoires: through forms of public leadership, through social and political action and through representational practices.

Elsewhere I have discussed public leadership as a form of public-making (Newman, 2011). This is concerned with summoning (addressing citizens as publics rather than simply as consumers or communities); mobilising (fostering dialogue and action around public issues); and mediating (paying attention to the ways in which institutional practice may constrain or enable different kinds of public to emerge). As the long-term assault on public institutions – the state, the public sector, public regulation and so on – intensifies, so such forms of leadership become more significant in local government, the academy and the professions. It may also take place within the architecture of the state itself. For example, in response to the government initiative to make policy making more 'contestable', in October 2012 the Public Administration Select Committee launched a consultation chapter on how policy making could be adapted to offer greater opportunities for public engagement.

Public-making is also a product of the work of emerging political groupings and movements such as Compass, Open Democracy, UK UNCUT, Occupy, the World Social Forum, and other gatherings. Many of those I interviewed were participating in such movements, or were engaged in experiments to re-imagine work and the local economy, from creative uses of land to cooperative shops and food production enterprises, or to local LETS schemes and time banks. Others were involved in charities or cooperative enterprises promoting education, health, housing or care as common goods. All such mobilisations were enabled – in part – by representational practices.[4] Much attention has been paid to the development of new social media: citizen journalism, blogs, exhibitions, events, participative documentary production, and the use of social media to convene and orchestrate new performances of politics. This continues a long tradition of the use of documentary arts and other visual methods to highlight issues of inequality and injustice, as well as enabling groups to research and take action on the conditions in which they live or work (for example, Bredin, 2012; Rose, 2012; Stephansen, 2012).[5] They can, then, be integral to the processes of public-making, but can also foster wider political engagement and action.

These and other forms of public-making, I want to suggest, take on particular significance in the current conditions of austerity. They can be contrasted with a governmental approach that requires individuals to become active citizens distanced from, and substituting for, a wider public sphere of state action, public deliberation and public judgments (Mahony and Clarke, 2013). But processes of public-making also generate political ambiguities. London Citizens, for example, has been highly effective in mobilising a predominantly faith-based public which has challenged local and national political leaders, promoted the London living wage and brought other benefits; however faith-based publics can also be viewed as socially conservative (especially on issues of sexuality and gender equality: Kettel, 2012; Dhaliwal, 2012). Community mobilisers can be viewed as significant new resources and as opening up forms of development and careers for local actors, but also as displacing more political forms of activism (Wills, 2012). Publics, like localities, can be defensive, or can be expansive in their orientation. They can traverse the boundaries of the local or national public spheres and can assemble new forms of collective actor, while disrupting what have traditionally been considered legitimate forms of democratic public. But an engagement with public-making suggests the potential of new methods of engagement to address the affective and cultural, as well as material, consequences of austerity (see also Gilbert, 2012).

Creative labour: the politics of border work

Each of the alternative pathways discussed so far is generated through different forms of border work. Many actors with public and political commitments necessarily have to face in multiple directions, work between conflicting allegiances (personal, professional and political), and try to reconcile governmental and counter-governmental power: see for example studies of how workers perform their own active/activist citizenship in and through their public service roles (Barnes and Prior, 2010; Van Hulst et al, 2011; Newman, 2005; 2012a). These studies suggest something of the ways in which the borders between government policy and personal/political commitments are worked. Such work – which I argue is a form of creative labour – can lever governmental resources and capacities for 'other' purposes and/or bring alternative perspectives and skill sets into the policy process.

Like the civic entrepreneurs in the Durose study (discussed earlier), the work of participants in my own research showed the significance of brokering and coalition formation, but not necessarily bounded by locality. Their capacity to perform new worlds within the constraints of the material and political conditions of the present flowed from creative engagements across borders, facing in multiple directions and negotiating between different rationales and commitments in order to create something new or different (Newman, 2012b). Of particular interest was the ways in which actors negotiated the 'contact zones' (Askins and Pain, 2011; Pratt, 1992) in which progressive personal and political commitments confronted governmental power, and how they mediated, appropriated – and sometimes bent – government policy.[6] The research was completed in 2011, but I have since been returning to the data, conducting new interviews and engaging with individuals and groups to explore how far their activist commitments and enactments can be sustained in the present, and what new spaces of power may be emerging (see Note 1).

The analysis shows how activism continues, and how it is unevenly aligned with many of the policy innovations discussed in previous sections. But it also highlights the ambiguities and dilemmas associated with creative labour in these perilous times: how the very words one speaks can rebound as they become taken up in government discourse (Newman, 2013c). Those working with and for communities debated how far they could appropriate the Big Society discourse to generate new connections and possibilities, but also wondered whether, in doing so, they were complicit with the rolling back of the state. Those still in public sector jobs described how they were attempting to mitigate the effects of cuts in order to protect the most vulnerable, but also – in some cases – how they were using the imperative of budget reductions to redesign services in ways that they hoped would generate better outcomes. Those who had moved into consultancy, design or research roles were promoting new ways of working that were progressive in their intention, but they also highlighted both the constraints they worked under and their own economic vulnerability. Some were members of groups bidding to take over formerly public assets or to run local public services. These found themselves struggling to secure sufficient resources but also spoke of how the process of bidding was helping to foster new capacities, networks and political alliances. Some were engaged in more adversarial forms of politics than had been possible in their state-work in the past, but others were continuing to work across the governmental/activist boundary as policy actors sought out allies to support new government strategies. Some were taking on work as (paid or unpaid) policy entrepreneurs trying to do some of the 'joining up' between a stripped down state, malfunctioning market and impoverished civil society.

Their experience offers important theoretical and methodological resources for studying the performance of policy in conditions of austerity: how the effects of cuts are mediated, how new actors take the stage, how policy is translated, how activists seek to use the opportunity of radical change in creative ways. The analysis offers a more nuanced picture of how far the withdrawal of the state is likely to enable new energies to be released and new experiments to emerge. But it also points to ambiguities and dilemmas. Those filling gaps in state services felt they were doing important work to provide local resources and to foster new forms of civic action, while also being highly ambiguous about how far this supported the climate of cuts. Many were engaging in projects that they hoped would prefigure wider developments, while noting the potential problems of cooption by private enterprise or government policy (Newman 2012a, ch 9, postscript). This takes me to the final section of the chapter.

Political appropriations, political possibilities

The experiments and performances traced in the previous sections offer creative routes towards the performance of 'new words'. But they do so within the constraints of the present policy terrain. Such constraints are of course rooted in the current economic climate, but also reference constraints of theory (how we imagine and understand the world) and embedded institutional pathways.

In terms of theory, I want to offer three different contributions. The first concerns the framing of policy as performance. This suggests a lived and embodied conception of 'doing' rather than interpreting or implementing policy. It challenges rational linear conceptions of the policy process (see also Cropper and Carter, 2013) and draws attention to the diverse and particular ways in which policy is enacted. It also points to the significance of human agency, offering a more peopled, relational conception of governance (Jupp, 2013). The place of agency in the policy process has tended to be conceptualised through notions of the street level bureaucrat, operating at the front line of service delivery organisations and using their discretion. Alternatively agency has been inherent to the role of the 'everyday makers' working in the spaces of community and civil society (Bang, 2005). Both, however, tend to be conceptualised as individualised and/or highly localised actors, detached from wider political and cultural forces. By drawing on Gibson-Graham's concept of *collective* action I have tried to go beyond an individual agent-centred approach.

A focus on policy as performance also suggests how the current policy repertoire draws on, borrows, and often reconfigures already existing performances beyond the state. This is not equivalent to government seeking to *animate* such performances, in order, for example, to constitute responsible citizens, to change behaviours or to foster new organisational forms. Rather, it points to how policy draws on a range of *already existing* prefigurative practices or emergent capacities. These may be of long standing, for example the governmental appropriation of cooperative forms of organising with its roots in the 18th and 19th centuries to promote alternative models of organising. Or they may be relatively recent: for example progressive practices initiated within a coproduced design experiment, or within a particular local authority, that are taken up by government as beacons or pathways for others to follow (what might be conceptualised as 'policy by vignette'.) They may draw on differently spatialised experiments and acts, from the highly localised mobilisations that prefigure wider shifts to a more general cultural or political repertoire that enables new political performances to emerge. They may emerge from oppositional forms of politics such as the Occupy movement (not simply concerned with protest but attempting to configure the new through disruptive performance of politics, education, care and living). But they may also arise from state and non-state actors using 'spaces of power' within governance regimes to open up alternative practices. Such actors do not fall neatly into the specific categories of performance discussed in this chapter, but tend to work across them. It is not the case that some are compromised and others engaged in a more authentic politics; what is at stake are multiple spaces of power and resistance with which actors engage – pragmatically as well as politically. Forms of public-making may emerge from or be constituted by design and localisation strategies. Creative enactments may arise in local activist projects and the work of front-line staff. But performance is a concept that helps illuminate how actors work *across* governmental and alternative projects in order to mobilise capacities and resources that might mitigate the effects of austerity.

This takes me to a second contribution: one that points to the tension between normativity and critique. Here the chapter addresses the question of how to assess policy ideas and experiments that appear to offer new approaches to solving the social problems of the day. The discourses of better design, of local involvement, of coproduction, of empowerment, of community mobilisation and active citizenship are all highly normative. And like the discourses of choice and partnership before them, they are difficult to critique, not least since those working for positive or progressive change tend to see their benefits as well as the ideological difficulties they present (see for example Needham, 2011). Much critical academic work in the New Labour years centred around revealing the hidden structures of power and authority inherent in so called 'network' governance. The 'governmentality' literature flourished as a means of showing the ways in which power at a distance was exercised by summoning up new forms of governable subject. However such critical work tended to hinder productive conversations across the academic/practitioner divide. It also often paid insufficient attention to how new governmentalities were mediated and translated by state actors, or how they were refused, inhabited or reworked by those they summoned (Barnett et al, 2011; Clarke et al, 2007).

The third and final contribution is towards the opening up of apparently totalising narratives, especially those of neoliberalism, to critical analysis. While a useful political slogan, neoliberalism tends to fold everything into one seamless narrative: that of an overwhelming force, able to appropriate all forms of resistance and all alternative rationalities. This squeezes the space of politics and political action, leaving us with what Ferguson describes as 'a politics largely defined by negation and disdain' (Ferguson, 2010, 166). However, privileging agency or resistance may mean paying insufficient attention to the significance of the neoliberal project. Within the scope of this chapter it is not possible to offer a full analysis of neoliberalism (but see Clarke, 2008; Ferguson, 2010; Larner, 2000). In other work neoliberalism is depicted as multiple – and often highly divergent – discourses, actors, practices and forms of political engagement. These may be aligned in relationships of dominance and subordination, and crosscut by emergent forces and tendencies (see Newman and Clarke, 2009; Newman 2012a; 2013a, b). Such an approach enabled me to use empirical research to depict how progressive features of new policy scripts and ideas may be unevenly aligned or coupled to neoliberal rationalities, and where spaces or cracks might open up or reconfigurations emerge. Rather than a singular narrative, of a post-political world heralded by the triumph of neoliberalism, this points to the need (political as well as theoretical) to understand the simultaneous dynamics of retreat and proliferation, creativity and constraint, activism and incorporation.

Conclusion

This chapter began by offering critical reflections on current developments in public policy, then has moved through a series of discussions about what forms of 'progressive' intervention are possible within the current reconfiguration of the policy landscape. These, I suggest, generate interventions that open up possible futures for public policy and public service. However, neoliberal inclined governments tend to seize on such interventions and bend them to their own purposes. I want, then, to end by widening the analytical framework to ask rather more political questions concerning how far new and emergent performances might be considered as new sites of governmentalisation and neoliberal appropriation. In the process of being taken up in public policy, design experiments and local projects are vulnerable to becoming detached from the politics that generated them, or translated in ways that strip them of their radicalism. But more importantly for my argument here, they each open up prefigurative pathways to a *post-public* domain of policy enactment. This domain is peopled by the consultancy and research industries (elements of the neoliberal knowledge-based economy) as well as by activist groupings, faith-based organisations and commercial enterprises, all engaging with the new commissioning agenda. This institutional evacuation of the public domain is accompanied by post-public conceptions of citizenship. For example the focus on behaviour change in many design projects enables responsibility (and blame) to be relocated beyond the state itself. A focus on the local as the source of problem solving offers a more collective conception of citizenship, but similarly tends to shift blame away from the incumbent government; hardship and inequality are thus presented as a product of local decision-making. In addition decentralisation prefigures new patterns of spatial inequality, leading to potential resentments, political disaffections and social divisions. Such critiques are however difficult to voice: good design and local involvement appear as inherently normatively desirable, and established state-based designs and interventions were, in any case, often highly flawed. Academic nitpicking, then, is often received unsympathetically by practitioners working for progressive change.

Each of the different performative repertoires I have discussed offers a break with – or perhaps helps reconfigure – dominant templates. Each brings into view particular actors, and privileges particular methods; as such they help constitute the field of action in ways that close down some possibilities and open up others. Each may be aligned – or not – with neoliberal rationalities, while also opening up alternative spaces and possibilities. I do not, then, want to draw an optimistic picture in which new media practices, new forms of public, and the expansion of sites of creative labour will necessarily generate solutions to the policy problems generated by state retrenchment. But the specificities of scripts, actors, places, temporalities and performances matter in terms of what forms of prefigurative pathways might be generated, and what might happens to them as they are aligned with dominant forces. As a result the chapter has not attempted to offer normative recommendations about how to do policy differently. Rather, it has been about how to offer an alternative to the politics of negation and disdain by 'performing new worlds' in ways that transcend the institutional and imaginative constraints of the present.

Notes

[1] For example through the Feminist Policy, Politics and Practice forum, jointly convened by myself and Sasha Roseneil, which met three times in 2012-13 at Birkbeck.

[2] See for example the provision of the Open Public Services White Paper (Cabinet Office, 2011, Cm 8145). This had the explicit aim of promoting greater diversity of public service provision, and the Modernising Commissioning Green Paper (Cabinet Office, 2010), which sought to open up existing markets to new providers, including civil society organizations.

[3] See the provisions of the Localism Act (Department for Communities and Local Government, 2011) which included Community Rights (to challenge existing providers of local public services) and Neighbourhood Planning, as well as reforms to housing and local government.

[4] I refer here to forms of cultural representation (symbols, narratives, images and so on) rather than democratic practice, though these are not completely distinct.

[5] All contributing to a Creating Publics, Creating Democracies workshop, a collaboration between the Publics Research Programme at the Open University, Westminster University and Goldsmiths College in June 2012.

[6] Elsewhere I have described something of the difficulties associated with performing across multiple borders and boundaries, and the self-work and emotional labour at stake (Newman, 2012b).

References

Alcock, P, 2012, The Big Society: A new policy environment for the third sector? *Voluntary Sector Review*, 1, 3, 379–90

Askins, K, Pain, R, 2011, Contact zones: Participation, materiality and the messiness of interaction, *Environment and Planning D: Society and Space*, 29, 803–21

Bang, H, 2005, Among everyday makers and expert citizens, in Newman, J (ed), *Remaking governance: Peoples, politics and the public sphere*, Bristol: Policy Press, 159–78

Barnes, M, Prior, D, 2010, *Subversive citizens: Power, agency and resistance in public services*, Bristol: Policy Press

Barnett, C, 2008, Convening publics: the parasitical spaces of public action, in Cox, K, Low, M, Robinson, J (eds), *The Sage handbook of political geography*, London: Sage

Barnett, C, Cloke, P, Clark, N, Malpass, A, 2011, *Globalising responsibility: The political rationalities of ethical consumption*, Chichester: Wiley-Blackwell

Blyth, S, Kimbell, L, 2011, *Design thinking and the Big Society: From solving personal troubles to designing social problems*, London: Actant and Taylor Haig

Bredin, M, 2012, Transmedia flows and assembling publics for Aboriginal rights in Canadian democracy, chapter presented to Creating Publics, Creating Democracies conference, Westminster University, June

Butler, J, 1990, *Gender trouble: Feminism and the subversion of identity*, London: Routledge

Butler, J, 2010, Performative agency, *Journal of Cultural Economy*, 3, 2, 147–61

Clarke, J, 2008, Living with/in and without neoliberalism, *Focaal: European Journal of Anthropology*, 51, 135–47

Clarke, J, Newman, J, 2012, The alchemy of austerity, *Critical Social Policy*, 32, 3, 299–319

Clarke, J, Newman, J, Smith, N, Vidler, E, Westmarland, L, 2007, *Creating citizen-consumers: Changing publics and changing public services*, London: Sage

Cropper, S, Carter, P, 2013, Narratives of progress: A historiography of policy analysis, chapter presented to *Policy & Politics* 40th anniversary conference, Bristol, September

Dhaliwal, S, 2012, *Religion, moral hegemony and local cartographies of power*, PhD thesis, Dept of Sociology, Goldsmiths, University of London

Durose, C, 2012, Front-line workers as local brokers: Neighbourhood working in austerity, chapter presented to the 7th International Conference in Interpretive Policy Analysis, University of Tilburg, July

Durose, C Justice, J, Skelcher, C, 2012, Governing at arms length: Privatising the public or publicising the private? chapter presented to *Policy & Politics* 40th anniversary conference, Bristol, September

Farnsworth, K, 2011, From economic cuts to a new age of austerity, in Farnsworth, K, Irving, Z (eds), *Social policy in challenging times,* Bristol: Policy Press

Ferguson, J, 2010, The uses of neoliberalism, *Antipode,* 41, 166–84

Gibson-Graham, JK, 1996, *The end of capitalism, as we knew it,* Minneapolis, MN: University of Minnesota Press

Gibson-Graham JK, 2006, *A postcapitalist politics,* Minneapolis, MN: University of Minnesota Press

Gibson-Graham JK, Roelvink, G, 2011, The nitty-gritty of creating alternative economies, *Social Alternatives,* 30, 1, 29–33

Gilbert, J, 2012, Moving on from the market society: Culture, and cultural studies, in a post-democratic age, presentation to Crossroads in Cultural Studies conference, Paris, July, www.open-democracy.net/ourkingdom/jeremy-gilbert/moving-on-from-market-society

Gillinson, S, Horne, M, Baeck, P, 2010, *Radical efficiency: Different better, lower cost public services,* London: National Endowment for Science, Technology and the Arts, www.nesta.org.uk/publications/assets/features/radical_efficiency)

Goffman, E, 1959, *The presentation of self in everyday life,* New York: Anchor Books, 1993

Hay, C, Wincott, D, 2012, *European welfare capitalism in hard times,* Basingstoke: Palgrave

Jackson, S, 2011, *Social works: Performing art, supporting publics,* London: Routledge

John, P, Cotterill, S, Moseley, A, Richardson, L, Smith, G, Stoker, G, Wales, C, 2011, *Nudge nudge, think think: Experimenting with ways to change civic behaviour,* London: Bloomsbury Academic

Jordan, B, Drakeford, M, 2012, *Social work and social policy under austerity,* Basingstoke: Palgrave Macmillan

Jupp, E, 2013, I feel more at home here than in my own community: Approaching the emotional geographies of neighbourhood policy, *Critical Social Policy,* http://csp.sagepub.com/content/early/2013

Kelly, J, Dodds, A, 2012, Public administration in an age of austerity: The future of the discipline, *Public Policy and Administration,* 27, 3, 199–211

Kettell, S, 2012, Religion and the rise of the Big Society: A mismatch made in heaven?, *Policy & Politics,* 40, 2, 281–96

Larner, W, 2000, Neoliberalism: Policy, ideology, governmentality, *Studies in Political Economy,* 63, 5–25

Law, J, Urry, J, 2004, Enacting the social, *Economy and Society,* 33, 3, 390–410

Leadbeater, C, Cottam, H, 2007, The user-generated state: Public services 2.0, in Diamond, P (ed), *Public matters: The renewal of the public realm,* London: Methuen

Lowndes, V, Pratchett, L, 2012, Local governance under the coalition government: Austerity, localism and the Big Society, *Local Government Studies,* 38, 1, 1–20

Lowndes, V, McCaughie, K, Roberts, S, Stafford, B, 2012, Cuts, costs and creativity: Prospects for local public services under austerity, *Policy & Politics,* 41, 4, 533–49

Mahony, N, Clarke, J, 2013, Public crises, public futures, *Cultural Studies,* 27, 4

Mahony, N, Newman, J, Barnett, C (eds), 2010, *Rethinking the public: Innovations in research, theory and methods,* Bristol: Policy Press

Mindlab, 2011, *How public design?,* Copenhagen: Danish Ministries of Business Affairs, Employment and Taxation

Needham, C, 2011, *Personalising public services: Understanding the personalisation narrative,* Bristol: Policy Press

NEF (New Economics Foundation), no date, 1, Austerity and the Big Society: Interim briefing, www.neweconomics.org/files/new-austerity-and-big-society

NEF, no date, 2, Cutting in Birmingham: Why the grass roots aren't growing any more, www.neweconomics.org/files/cutting-in-birmingham

Newman, J, 2005, Enter the transformational leader: Network governance and the micropolitics of modernisation, *Sociology,* 39, 4, 717–34

Newman, J, 2011, Public leadership as public-making, *Public Money and Management,* 31, 5, 315–22

Newman, J, 2012a, *Working the spaces of power: Activism, neoliberalism and gendered labour,* London: Bloomsbury Academic

Newman, J, 2012b, Beyond the deliberative subject? Problems of theory, method and critique in the turn to emotion and affect, *Critical Policy Studies* 6, 4, 465–79

Newman, J, 2013a, Diagnosing the contemporary: Activism, neoliberalism and the problem of power and consent, *Critical Policy Studies,* 148, in press

Newman, J, 2013b, Landscapes of antagonism: Local governance, neoliberalism and austerity, *Urban Studies,* in press

Newman, J, 2013c, But we didn't mean *that:* Feminist projects, governmental appropriations and spaces of politics, in Roseneil, S (ed), *Beyond citizenship: Feminism and the transformation of belonging,* Basingstoke: Palgrave Macmillan

Newman, J, Clarke, J, 2009, *Publics, politics and power: Remaking the public in public services,* London: Sage

Pratt, ML, 1992, *Imperial eyes: Travel writing and transculturalism,* London: Routledge

Richardson, J (ed), 2010, *From recession to renewal: The impact of the financial crisis on public services and local government,* Bristol: Policy Press

Rose, M, 2012, Making meaning, making publics: Collaborative documentary as DIY citizenship, chapter presented to Creating Publics, Creating Democracies conference, Westminster University, June

Roseneil, S, 2012, Doing feminist research after the cultural turn: Research with practical intension, in Roseneil, S, Frosh, S (eds), *Social research after the cultural turn,* Basingstoke: Palgrave Macmillan

Schechner, R, 1985, *Between theatre and anthropology,* Philadelphia, PA: University of Pennsylvania Press

Standing, G, 2011, *The Precariat: The new dangerous class,* London: Bloomsbury

Stephansen, H, 2012, Communicate to mobilise to communicate: Creating publics through media activism in the World Social Forum process, chapter presented to Creating Publics, Creating Democracies conference, Westminster University, June

Stoker, G, 2010, Exploring the promise of experimentation in political science: Micro-foundational insights and policy relevance, *Political Studies* 58, 300–19

Stoker, G, John, P, 2009, Design experiments: Engaging policy makers in the search for evidence about what works, *Political Studies,* 57, 356–73

Sullivan, H, 2012, Debate: A Big Society needs an active state, *Policy & Politics,* 40, 1, 145–8

Taylor-Gooby, P, Stoker, G, 2011, The coalition programme, *Political Quarterly,* 82, 1, 4–15

University of Birmingham Policy Commission with Demos, 2011, *When Tomorrow Comes: the future of local public services,* Birmingham: University of Birmingham www.birmingham.ac.uk/policycommissions

Van Hulst, M, de Graaf, L, van den Brink, G, 2011, Exemplary practitioners: A review of actors who make a difference in governing, *Administrative Theory and Praxis,* 33, 1, 120–42

Warner, M, 2002, *Publics and counterpublics,* New York, NY: Zone Books

Wills, J, 2012, The geography of community and political organisation in London today, *Political Geography,* 31, 2, 114–26

Weathering the perfect storm? Austerity and institutional resilience in local government

Vivien Lowndes and Kerry McCaughie

Introduction

Across much of Europe local government is facing a dramatic decrease in resources alongside a sharp increase in citizen demand. In England, the 2010 Comprehensive Spending Review proposed a 27% cut in local government budgets, alongside major reductions in other funding streams that impact local communities. The cuts are being experienced in the context of the wider costs of recession, notably declining incomes and rising prices for food and fuel, which are leading to rising demand for many local authority services. At the same time, demographic changes are increasing further the pressure on local services, most significantly in relation to the needs of an ageing population.

This chapter asks how English local authorities are weathering what amounts to a 'perfect storm'. Are they merely trimming their sails to accommodate the buffeting as best they can, or have they decisively changed course? Gerry Stoker (2012) proposes two scenarios for local government in 2020. The 'life after the cuts' scenario sees budget cuts as driving innovation in public service delivery, while the 'sustained recession' scenario sees a long term depression characterised by *ad hoc* rather than strategic responses to the cuts. The scenarios approach, while providing a useful heuristic, runs the risk of overdrawing the choice between action and inaction. The aim of this chapter is to analyse the balance between 'trimming' and 'transformation' on the ground, and to examine those practices which fall between these extremes.

Reflecting the unprecedented scale of the cuts at hand and the early point in their implementation, we start with open questions rather than specific research hypotheses. We employ a case study methodology, using interviews and observations. We contextualise our data with reference to national surveys on the early impact of the cuts, and in relation to research on previous periods of austerity, notably in the 1980s. The chapter draws upon, and contributes to, the literature on institutional change and austerity, in general and in respect to local government. The first section looks at the nature and scale of the cuts; the second section specifies our research questions and explains our methodology; while the third and fourth sections present research findings and analysis respectively. We conclude by arguing that, while cost-cutting and efficiency measures dominate, creative approaches to service redesign are also emerging, based upon pragmatic politics and processes of 'institutional bricolage'. While the absence of radical new ideas and overt political conflict is surprising, local government reveals a remarkable capacity to reinvent its institutional forms to weather the storm.

The extent of the cuts

The Comprehensive Spending Review, covering the period 2011/12 to 2014/15, singled out local government for dramatic budget reductions. A £5.5bn reduction in the budget for local government was proposed; a fall of 27% from £29.7bn in 2010/11 to £24.2bn in 2014/15 (HM Treasury, 2010, 81). In addition, by 2014/15 total local authority capital expenditure was expected to fall by 30% (HM Treasury, 2010, 50). Other cuts are having, or will have, a significant knock-on effect for local government, for example the abolition of the Working Neighbourhood Fund, the Educational Maintenance Allowance, cuts in Decent Homes funding, reductions in subsidies paid to bus operators, the freezing and effective means testing of child benefits, and the £7bn cut in welfare expenditure that will be achieved via the introduction of Universal Credit.

At the time of our research, the IFS (2012) reported that only 6% of proposed cuts in public service spending (overall) had actually been made. The rate of decline of local government budgets has been three times greater than that during the recession of the late 1970s and early 80s (Talbot and Talbot, 2011, 69). The OBR report has argued that current policy amounts to no more than a 'five year fiscal repair job'. Yet more severe cuts are expected after 2017, particularly as the percentage of the population over 65 rises to above 20%. National debt looks set to hit 90% of GDP by 2016, which is more than twice pre-crisis levels (OBR, 2012). The LGA estimates that the costs of adult social care will absorb 90% of council expenditure by 2020, suggesting the services most popular with the public (libraries and leisure facilities) could effectively wither on the vine (LGA, 2012).

Learning from the experience of previous recessions, we can expect the impact of the cuts to be greatest among groups disadvantaged in the labour market and most dependent upon state services, notably those with low skills and educational qualifications, young people, disabled people and members of ethnic minorities (Stafford and Duffy, 2009; Browne, 2010; Equality and Human Rights Commission, the Department for Work and

Pensions and the Government Equalities Office, 2009). Moreover, there is already evidence that women are bearing a disproportionate burden of the cuts in public expenditure (Women's Budget Group, 2010), and that over the medium term the typical family with children is at risk of a fall in real income (Browne, 2010). Indeed, the Government's own statistics revealed 2.3 million children in poverty in June 2012 (DWP, 2012).

Under the Coalition's policy to promote 'localism', local authorities have gained greater 'freedom' to manage their finances, with the end of central government ringfencing, a simplification of the grant regime, and a partial devolution of the business rate. As the Treasury put it, this 'will require tough choices on how services are delivered within reduced allocations' (HM Treasury, 2010, 8).

Researching the cuts

Reflecting the unprecedented scale of the cuts, and the early point in their implementation, our primary research was based on open questions rather than specific hypotheses. Our research questions were as follows:

- How are the cuts being experienced by local authorities and their partners?
- What responses are emerging?
- What is the balance between incremental and strategic cuts?
- What scope, if any, is there for the creative redesign of local services?

Using a case study method, data collection involved: 11 semi structured interviews with city-level service managers in the local authority and its partners (including police, employment, housing and public health); two interviews with leading councillors; a focus group of front-line council workers in a disadvantaged neighbourhood within the city (covering housing, environmental services and community safety); and an interview with a neighbourhood based social enterprise involved in local service delivery. Informal discussions, documentary analysis and observation were also used. Data collection took place between September 2011 and February 2012. The small sample size means that the responses cannot be taken as typical or representative in any strict sense. Rather, this is exploratory research in which the data serves to generate theoretical propositions for further investigation, both in England and across Europe. We use secondary data to contextualise our case study findings, including national surveys on the current cuts and evidence from previous periods of austerity. The chapter looks specifically at responses to the cuts from public servants and councillors, but this research is part of a larger project which also considers the experience of service users and citizens (see Lowndes et al, 2012).

To protect the anonymity of the city in question, at an acutely sensitive time, we cannot provide extensive contextual details. Suffice to say, the city is a unitary authority and the lead partner in the Local Strategic Partnership, with a local economy that is heavily dependent upon business and financial services and the public sector (all adversely affected by the economic crisis). While the city has areas of high deprivation it is not, in comparative terms, an extreme case.

Responses to the cuts

Interviews with service managers and front-line staff revealed a high level of awareness, and concern, about spending cuts and their effects on residents. Large budget reductions had already made a significant impact upon the city council and its key partners, with many interviewees agreeing that the full effects of the expenditure cuts will not be felt for another two or three years: 'You ain't seen nothing yet', was a common refrain. As one interviewee summed up: 'It's probably the single biggest change with regards to the city council in history, the cuts are absolutely unprecedented… the simple answer is nothing is going to be the same again from top to bottom'.

Efficiency savings had been the main strategy to date, referred to most commonly as 'salami slicing'. One interviewee noted evocatively that: 'we've been nibbled away at and nibbled away at'. Studies of local authority responses to austerity in 1970s and 1980s show a similar pattern, with incremental budget reductions twice as common as strategic cuts (Talbot and Talbot, 2011; see also Mouritzen, 1992). In our case study authority, 'back office' functions had taken the biggest hit, but all services had been affected, for instance through reduced staff hours and the number of staff employed. The council staff we interviewed claimed they were expected to work longer days for no extra pay and to pick up the work of colleagues who had been made redundant or not had their contract renewed. This was alongside the pressures of working in an environment of growing social need. Our focus group of front-line staff put their weight behind a comment from one participant that, 'We have had the stuffing knocked out of us so many times… we are struggling to get back up'.

Interviewees highlighted the compound effect of budget reductions – that is, the way in which the spending decisions of different services could combine to produce a more serious impact for a particular group of citizens (or a specific locality). As an example, changes in services related to domestic violence had produced a seriously negative compound impact, when budget decisions were made for 2010/2011. Interviewees linked this to poor communication between different services which were making cuts, and the lack of a coordinated approach to the mitigation of risk. And these changes took place at a time when incidents of domestic violence were rising dramatically, in the context of the increasing economic pressures faced by already vulnerable families. In general terms, there was a danger that different agencies (for example, health, police and local government) all 'decommissioned' services relating to a particular group of users, or a particular locality, at the same time.

Interviewees and focus group members felt strongly that urban areas, which already faced significant levels of poverty and disadvantage, were facing the most severe cuts. The scrapping of special grants, which had been heavily targeted on deprived areas, was augmenting the effect of generic budget cuts. These observations are supported by a national survey which found that the biggest reductions in government support as a share of revenue spending have been in urban areas in the north, midlands and inner London (Audit Commission, 2012, 16). In our case study, staff pointed to the intertwined effects of spending reductions and the wider costs of recession, which were impacting particularly upon food and fuel prices. Evidence from our case study neighbourhood is backed up by a national study of 2,000 families which found that 70% of families were close to 'financial meltdown', with one in five mothers regularly missing meals so that their children could eat. And, in this study, 16% of respondents were being treated for a stress-related illness (Netmums, 2012; Netmums' online members' survey does not control for socioeconomic variables, but the organisation claims its 1.2 million membership has a broad social base and draws attention to the size of the sample).

A senior manager explained how this situation was affecting young people living on outer city housing estates: 'There is a feeling of no hope, desperation, that they've got nothing, can't get anything, have nowhere to go and at an age when they want their independence'. A local councillor identified the scrapping of the Educational Maintenance Allowance and pre-employment training schemes as major contributors to this situation. A community police officer noted an increase in theft of food from local shops, and the growth in illegal money-making activities, notably indoor cannabis cultivation. Working as part of a multi-service neighbourhood team, a housing officer observed that: 'the worse the financial situation out there gets, the more desperate our tenants get, the more time they spend doing stuff we don't want them to do, so the more work that raises for us'. The cuts are generating increased pressure on other services that are themselves also facing cuts (for example, community anti-drugs teams and youth services).

The council's strategy to date reflects what Hastings et al (2012) call the 'universalist' option in their national survey of local authority responses to the cuts. Such an approach implies 'a focus on service sustainability and equity', which in practice involved either applying 'proportional cuts' to all services, or 'deleting entire services'. Our case study had seen reduced opening hours for services like libraries and the phasing out of 'extra' provision, like support services to social housing tenants. But, recognising the gravity of problems faced by residents, as well as the pressures on its own resources, there had also been moves to consider a more fundamental redesign of local services. For instance, youth services had – in the words of a youth worker – been moved away from an emphasis on 'entertaining youths' towards a focus on preparing young people for employment, which involved building new relationships with schools, colleges and employers, and a reduced emphasis on sports and arts. At the same time, staff interviewees confirmed that they were being asked to focus their services on citizens considered to be the most vulnerable. Indeed, many interviewees felt that such targeting was the only way to deal with the reduction of budgets, and spoke matter-of-factly about moving the threshold for services (for example, within adult social services).

Looking across a range of services, attempts at service redesign were focusing upon collaboration, commissioning, and citizen involvement. We look at these in turn:

Collaboration

The Coalition abolished the requirement for Local Strategic Partnerships (LSPs), but most cities have sought to adapt these structures, with a view to coordinating cuts, leveraging resources and generating capacity (and ideas) from across the public, private and third sectors. But, despite the rhetoric of 'shrinking together', interviewees agreed that the city's LSP could do more to coordinate decision making. There was agreement that the commitment of partners was present and that good relationships existed. But many interviewees felt that partnership working was not achieving its potential. As one interviewee put it, partnership meetings could be no more than 'sitting around a table and being nice to each other... it's not clear what we're leading and what is the vision'. There was a feeling that the basic function of coordination could be improved, particularly in relation to sharing information on the scale and focus of each partner's budget cuts. It was agreed that the rushed nature of 'in year' budget cuts (imposed by government) had undermined collaborative working.

More ambitiously, there was an appetite for building a new style of 'collaborative civic leadership' aimed at achieving broad outcomes (like health and wellbeing, or educational achievement) rather than chasing targets, as was often the case in the past. This would require partnership members to act more as city leaders and less as representatives of their sector, alongside a greater focus on 'delivery', possibly through neighbourhood-level partnerships. With the end of New Labour's special funding pots ('funny money', as interviewees put it), partnerships would survive only if they were seen to add value. Some interviewees had actually discovered a greater capacity for creative thinking within the constraints of the current context. As one partner put it:

> I think the most positive thing is around using all your resources, when resources are tighter and you have to think better, you have to think quicker. I'm hoping it will reduce bureaucracy because this crisis way of working to me actually should be the normal way of working. You shouldn't need a crisis to make simple decisions in simple ways... Things are simpler now, there's less egos and logos in the sense that a lot of the problems were about different funding streams that different people had to lead... with tighter resources you have to get there quicker and realise it's about outcomes. You're there to do a job.

Partnership working in the city was also being up-scaled, with the introduction at the city-region level of Local Enterprise Partnerships and subsequently City Deals, which devolve to new 'combined authorities' economic development funds and powers related to a locally specific City Ask or bid. Our case study city was also exploring down-scaling via a stronger emphasis on cross-service neighbourhood level. Building on New Labour's 'total place' initiatives, and anticipating the roll-out of the Coalition's 'community budgets', the aim was to bring together public sector budgets being spent in one locality, and to get different professionals working together in a more holistic and outcome-oriented manner. Interviewees felt that neighbourhood working was 'absolutely vital' to managing the process of cuts in a context of rising demand, with advantages including information sharing, asset pooling, and the reduction of duplication. The council had already reorganised in relation to key 'themes', linked to, for instance, environmental improvement or community safety, with each requiring joint working between specific departments (for example, police and housing, or environmental services and leisure). Paradoxically, 'themes' were now themselves in danger of becoming sedimented into new 'silos'. As one front-line officer put it: 'there's a lot of cost saving to be had through proper coordination; but when you're funded and performance-managed on one theme, its only goodwill that's going to get these guys across their themes'.

Mobilising this goodwill was seen to require a new type of manager or leader: 'You have to have creative officers that think outside the box... it's not always about money.' Or, as someone else put it: 'To roll this out, you do need to have special people'. The particular qualities required included 'seeing the gaps and the links' (particularly from the viewpoint of citizens), creativity and risk-taking, networking and deal-brokering, a passion for the area, a capacity to build trusting relationships and make difficult decisions, and a sense of humour! While it was recognised that it wasn't possible to 'produce' such people, we did discuss with interviewees the potential for incentivising and supporting this type of behaviour, which may not be captured by conventional recruitment and promotion criteria (or underlying performance measures) (Lowndes and Squires, 2012; Mulgan, 2012).

A recent national review of 'the emergence of one-stop shops' highlights the benefits of having a single entrance to a wide range of services, with a close proximity to the citizens they serve, alongside potential efficiency gains (Askim et al, 2011). Multi-service, accessible neighbourhood offices appealed across our research, although there was a low awareness of the council's plans to re-divide the city into new sub-areas. The neighbourhood ideal was well exemplified by this plea from the chief executive of a local social enterprise:

> If you had this little office, it doesn't need to be big or posh, and we were all there – we were names and people – then, if you were with a family and you didn't know how this bit worked, you could pop over the road and sort it out.

Commissioning

The government's *Open Public Services* White Paper (2011) calls for 'a vibrant public service market' comprising not only the big commercial players (like Capita and Onyx) but also small businesses, mutuals, social enterprises and the voluntary and community sectors. Commissioning is seen as a way for local authorities (and other partners) to clarify the purpose of services they pay for, and to establish who the most appropriate providers may be. Our research found new approaches to commissioning underway, notably through the introduction of 'zero-based budgeting', which started with the identification of need, rather than a commitment to maintain any particular service configuration (or provider). This provided an alternative to simply requiring a specific cut in each of a range of traditionally designed services without considering options for service redesign, in order both to save money and respond to (changing, and sharply increasing) needs in new ways. 'Impact Boards' had been set up, bringing together existing providers and user groups, to share information about emerging needs and seek to anticipate (and mitigate) the compound effects of cuts or decommissioning decisions. A senior manager explained the principles thus:

> Cuts over the last year have followed a needs-led approach rather than a service-led approach: assume there are no services, here are people with needs, so what services do we need to provide? This is rather than chipping away at current services. And we're having stakeholder events. We want a very inclusive coproductive approach where options are worked out together.

It was recognised that 'commissioning for innovation' required active 'market making', in the sense of stimulating and supporting new providers (for instance, micro enterprises in social care). A Commissioning Review had been instigated to engage the voluntary and community sector. But there was concern that support and coordination for this sector implied major investment, which would not be forthcoming. Interviewees reported anger among social enterprises about new government schemes based on 'payment by results', which they felt were systematically undermining their opportunities to provide commissioned services (despite government rhetoric). Indeed, at a national level, a survey of 100 third sector organisations involved with the Work Programme (to take an example) found that 79% of charities said their prime contractor was not 'shielding them from risk' (NCVO, 2012).

Interestingly, while commissioning was gaining ground, the city council had a strong tradition of keeping services in-house, minimising outsourcing and privatisation. A topic that elicited strong views, some respondents felt that this had placed the council in an advantageous position, with 'greater control over the choice of whether you maintain the quality or you cheapen the cost' of public services. Respondents noted a clear view among residents that any privatisation of the bus service (for instance) would lead to a reduction in routes and a rise in prices, deepening existing problems of social exclusion on the outer estates. Another view was that the possession of valuable assets provided the potential to free up cash, or put resources to new or extended uses to achieve social benefit. For example, a council incinerator was able to produce cheaper energy for homes and businesses in the city, and to act as a platform for exploring new commissioning arrangements with private energy companies to extend capacity still further. The opposing opinion was that many of the council's assets actually presented a serious financial burden, especially given their poor state of repair. Some interviewees welcomed the fact that the council was not tied into long-term contracts with private providers, arguing that this provided greater scope to realign budgets across services. But, on the other hand, it was noted that the council could not walk away from service commitments by cancelling, or failing to renew, contracts. Put simply, stopping doing things was a harder option when more services and assets were in-house.

Citizen engagement

Many of our interviewees supported elements of the Government's Big Society agenda, relating specifically to volunteering, personal responsibility and citizens taking control of decisions which affect them. However, there was frustration that the new policies did not acknowledge existing good practice and, either tacitly or overtly, linked more engagement to less state provision. It was also agreed that it was rare to find local people who wanted to bring forward a development brief for a particular neighbourhood and see it through from start to finish, particularly in the most disadvantaged areas where need is also most acute, and in the absence of council funding or support. As a senior manager explained:

> I do think that local government has already done a lot in terms of using volunteers where that is appropriate, but I think the difficulty with this latest policy is that people are struggling to see how, with all the cuts to the voluntary community sector and local groups, you are building capacity for them to do more. Actually the opposite is true. And for volunteers to run services like a library or a post office or a museum or a swimming pool calls into question liability, social responsibility, corporate responsibility and the quality of the service.

A national survey of 2000 people, commissioned by Forresters UK, found that 43% of people would like to volunteer on an ongoing basis – such as at a charity shop or hospice (Municipal Journal, 2012). However, in our research, neighbourhood-level staff observed that, as residents increasingly felt the pinch of the economic downturn, 'the harder it gets, the more despondent people get, and the less they actually want to be active'. Evoking a similar distinction to that between bridging and bonding social capital, interviewees argued that residents were more likely to 'hunker down', preferring to focus on their own and their families' wellbeing. They also reported concern that local organisations could no longer expect the necessary support to recruit, train and supervise volunteers. An exception to this trend was provided by new resources associated with the transfer of public health responsibilities to local government, although there was a low level of awareness about these opportunities among other neighbourhood staff.

We did learn about some small projects that were using volunteering (sometimes with an honorarium) to fill gaps left by service cuts, in one case providing pre-employment training to youths involved in antisocial behaviour, at the same time improving the very environment that they had damaged. The scheme was supervised through the multi-service neighbourhood team (police, housing, youth work and environmental services), and had the active involvement of a local councillor who was also a resident of the estate. She explained that:

> There's a gang of about 12 kids, they've been causing all sorts of hassle, now we've been paying them seven quid an hour – massive wage, right – and they've been doing up fencing, clearing back alley ways. We're moving on to other streets now. It's changed the whole atmosphere of that street.

While we encountered a generalised commitment to volunteering to support local communities, there was hostility towards substituting volunteers for professional service providers (relating to potential job losses and to uncertainties regarding legal liabilities and guarantees of service quality). At the same time, Big Society was in danger of becoming a toxic brand, largely because of its assumption of a zero-sum relationship between community provision and state action (Lowndes and Pratchett, 2012; Sullivan, 2012).

There was widespread acceptance, however, among council staff (and partners) that the voluntary and community sectors were important because of their ability to access 'hard to reach' individuals, and their history of spotting new community needs and responding in a flexible manner. Nationally, research for the Joseph Rowntree Foundation has established the increasing importance of non-state action and mutual support in the context of austerity (Hossain et al, 2011). Moral support, and help with meals and transport, was highlighted particularly: needs that may not even be visible to policy makers. In our research, it was agreed that locally based third sector organisations had the potential ability to 'join up' the citizen experience in the context of fragmented spending cuts, and to engage in early intervention and preventative work. The council was looking to build new partnerships with community and faith-based organisations in anticipation of the need to support 'non standard claimants' under the Universal Credit scheme. There was concern that the new online system, which involves monthly payments into bank accounts, could cause difficulties for vulnerable claimants, in terms of accessing payments and budgeting over longer periods (and many people will simply receive less money). Novel approaches were also developing bottom-up. For example, a local social enterprise was considering establishing a citizen advocates programme, to enable local volunteers – who were trusted and understood local mores – to act as neighbourhood-based intermediaries between vulnerable families and statutory services. Such a project had the potential to translate several redesign principles into action at the same time: neighbourhood working, cross-sectoral collaboration and citizen engagement.

So what's going on?

Any theoretical assessment is necessarily provisional, given both the complexity and volatility of the situation. But it is worthwhile in so far as it generates concepts with analytical leverage that are also able to suggest directions for policy development, and questions for further research. Working with policy makers and practitioners at the present time is a salutary exercise, given their coexisting tendencies to seek both light and shade. There is undoubtedly an appetite for new heuristics and evidence to drive innovation, but this exists alongside a race for the shadows, as policy makers seek to defend themselves against grim stories of the cuts' impact and the still grimmer predictions embedded in 'the graph of doom' (as it has become commonly known) which shows that, by 2020, council budgets will be insufficient even to meet the costs of adult social care and children's services (LGA, 2012).

As researchers, our reactions in the field were similarly contradictory. Was there a crisis or wasn't there? Our overwhelming impression was one of institutional resilience. Borrowing from the wider literature on resilience, we can define this as the 'capacity to absorb disturbance and reorganise into a functioning system' (Cutter et al, 2008, 599). Resilience can also be described as an unexpected positive outcome achieved in the context of adversity (Batty and Cole, 2010, 8). Indeed, a national survey found councils coping 'better than expected', with 71% seeing the impact of the cuts as neutral or even positive (RSA, 2012). At the same time, there has been a steady rise in the percentage of people saying they trust local councillors 'a great deal' or a 'fair amount' (YouGov, 2012a). More surprising still, 23% of people claim not to be aware of any cuts to local services (in addition to 8% 'don't knows') – figures that have actually risen since 2011 (YouGov, 2012b). Drawing on our case study findings, we now consider what underpins local government's apparent resilience in the face of deepening cuts.

New ideas or new practices?

In his work on crises of the British state, Colin Hay (1996; 2012) points to the significance of competing 'narrations', which offer discursive constructions of what's gone wrong and what the way out should be. A coherent and convincing narration provides a platform for political interests seeking to influence long term change, as happened when 'new right' ideas came to the fore as economic crisis gripped the British state in the late 1970s. And, as the contradictions of Thatcherism deepened two decades later, local government became an incubator for 'third way' ideas (like the networks and partnerships of 'community governance'), which came to underpin the Labour Party's 1997 manifesto and subsequent election victory. In a similar vein, Mark Blyth (2002) argues that existing institutions become delegitimised during times of crisis, at which point new ideas become the raw material for political contestation over future directions.

Kevin Orr (2009) compares the 'crisis surfacing' tactics of the Thatcher governments (as in the abolition of the metropolitan counties and the imposition of the poll tax) with the 'crisis suppressing' approach of New Labour as it sought to 'modernise' local government from 1997 onwards. Our research suggests that the Coalition prefers a third approach, that of 'crisis indifference', in relation to the challenges facing local government. Unlike its Conservative predecessors, the Coalition government seems determined to avoid a debate with local government over ideas. Cooke and Muir (2012, 3) note the failure of the Coalition 'to develop an animating philosophy for Conservative public service reform'. Our research has shown the limitations of localism and the Big Society in this respect. Substantively, these policies keep close to New Labour themes of devolution, volunteering and business engagement – although with massively reduced resources. Interviewees saw the policies as an attempted cover for cuts: localism would shift the blame for reduced services from central to local government, while Big Society made a virtue out of communities picking up the pieces. Ideational continuity seems to dominate within local government too, witnessed in salami slicing tactics (less of the same) rather than bold new visions. Despite fiscal battering from above and escalating demands from below, English local government currently sees a surprising lack of new ideas, or indeed any serious questioning of what went before.

But this is not to say that nothing creative is happening. With a more practical than ideational bent, our case study saw novel institutional arrangements being fashioned from an existing stock of alternatives:

- Commissioning was being combined with pre-Thatcherite needs-based planning (via zero-based budgeting), offering the possibility that commissioning could become more than simply another word for procurement and market diversification. New commissioning arrangements with private sector energy suppliers recalled the utility-providing city corporations of the late Victorian era.
- Local Strategic Partnerships were being remodelled away from target delivery and towards collaborative city leadership. An infusion of 1980s local economic development orthodoxy was strengthening Local Enterprise Partnerships (Heseltine, 2012). Indeed, institutions at the metropolitan level, abolished nearly thirty years ago, were being rehabilitated (without elected members) in the form of new combined authorities to deliver City Deals which aim to boost regional growth.
- The dusting-off and reinvigoration of neighbourhood institutions suggested a 'remembering' of lessons from local cross-service working and citizen engagement which dated back to the 1980s at least (Lowndes and Stoker, 1992). One-stop shops and civic voluntarism made for another novel combination, inflected also by a new paternalism of 'early intervention' which resonates with ideas from postwar social work about family dysfunction and the benefits of home-based, hands-on support and instruction.

What we are seeing in our case study, and local government more generally, is the active work of institutional bricoleurs in fashioning new forms of what Colin Crouch (2005) has called, in another context, 'recombinant governance'. Institutional bricolage involves 'the recombination and reshuffling of pre-existing components or other institutional materials that happen to be at hand and that, even when depleted, can serve new purposes' (Lanzara, 1998, 27). Such strategies appear to be particularly important in times of acute resource constraint, where bricolage may be the only opportunity to shore up institutional configurations or effect change in response to new challenges (Lowndes and Roberts, 2013, 180). As Howard Elcock (1984) observed in the 1980s, cuts may be managed through strategies of 'creative defence'. Institutional bricolage takes place in distinctive local contexts, bounded as it is by specific institutional legacies (for instance, the decision to keep services in-house in our case study). As Coleman et al (2010, 290) put it, processes of 'local sensemaking' are 'required to reconcile old assumptions and identities with new realities'.

The public servants we interviewed described their strategies as 'keeping it together', 'keeping heads above water' or 'hanging on in there'. Interestingly, these images mirror those used by vulnerable families coping with the impact of cuts and the recession (Batty and Cole, 2012, 10–11). These are descriptors that, at first glance, suggest nothing much is happening. But our research reveals the real creative work that underpins such strategies. Keeping our heads above water requires, after all, that we pump our arms and legs vigorously, that we breathe deeply, and that we look for things to hold on to, or even craft together to produce a raft or platform. Heads are not being kept above the waters of the perfect storm through inertia or panic, but through creative and context-dependent processes of institutional bricolage. Our interviewees used active verbs to describe their responses, referring specifically to their efforts to 'mitigate', 'ameliorate' and 'compensate for' the effect of the cuts.

As well as the 'institutional remembering' and recombining of elements within local government's existing repertoire, we also see attempts at 'institutional sharing' whereby the repertoire itself is expanded (Lowndes, 2005; Lowndes and Roberts, 2013, 183). There is a continuing transfer of private sector management techniques into local government (witness Barnet's easyCouncil, modelled on easyJet), and an ongoing softening of the public/private boundary (for example, new commissioning arrangements for public access to energy in our case study council). But, as our research showed, institutional boundary crossing increasingly involves civil society as its rules and practices are stitched into new modes of local service delivery, whether through commissioning social enterprises as care providers or developing new forms of volunteering (as in the plan for citizen advocates). Hence actors seek to harness what Janet Newman (2012, 172) calls, albeit in another context, 'the generative potential of border work'.

A politics of the present

While austerity has deep political significance, it has yet to manifest itself in terms of an overt political crisis. In local government, it is pretty much business as usual. No council has yet to challenge the government in any fundamental way (apart from judicial reviews on the cancellation of specific programmes, like Building Schools for the Future). The lack of public support for the Coalition's scheme to re-boost New Labour's policy of directly elected city mayors (Fenwick, 2013) has ensured that local political institutions remain largely intact, reflecting Jon Pierre's (2009, 595) wider observation of a 'conspicuous institutional stability' in the political as opposed to administrative domains of public service. There have been no significant strikes or industrial action among staff, and public protest has been marginal or, like the August 2011 disturbances or the Occupy movement, insufficiently focused to produce major disruption or clarion calls for change. That there is a resource crisis, however, is clear not just from the graph of doom but from the reduced availability of services on the ground, via restricted hours, more aggressive targeting, and straightforward deletion (as evidenced in our case study). The resource crisis is apparent too in the physical deterioration of neighbourhoods and community facilities, even in relatively well-off areas.

And yet, life goes on. As we have seen, the real engine of change appears to be not ideas but *practice*, which 'connects knowing with doing' (Denis et al, 2007, 19). While there is a dearth of new ideas, there are new forms of practice that are enabling local government to meet what Hupe and Hill (2007) call the 'action imperative'. An amazing array of complex services continues to be delivered (from child protection to traffic management), vast numbers continue to be employed (and paid), and citizens continue to access the essentials of schools, social housing and health facilities. Our research findings resonate with a definition of resilience as 'the ability to take intentional action to enhance the personal and collective capacity' to respond to and influence change (CCE, 2000).

But, underneath it all, people are deeply anxious – if not actively angry. Anxiety is as much about what is to come as what is currently being experienced – and this goes for staff and managers as well as ordinary service users. As our case study showed, the compound effects of the cuts alongside the wider costs of recession are becoming clear, especially for the most vulnerable families. Growing numbers of poor people quite simply do not have enough to eat and food banks and feeding projects have made their appearance on the local stage. And public servants are worried about their jobs as they sit on their at-risk (of redundancy) letters, issued in most councils to entire workforces at one time, and ponder the graph of doom.

Our research points to the need for a materialist analysis of the challenges facing local government, and a recognition of what we can call the 'politics of the present' (adapting the work of Clark, 2012). The current crisis is a material not an ideational one. For local government, it is a crisis of hungry bodies, broken things, shut doors, and stuck people. Demographic shifts, environmental pressures and fiscal crisis are fundamentally material phenomena, as are their effects. The current context sees no decisive break with past ideational regimes, and no new narrations of alternatives ahead. The big idea, if there is one, is to act. As Clark (2012, 54, 57) puts it, this avoids turning over the 'entrails of the present for signs of catastrophe and salvation'. Instead, it is a 'present-centred' and 'non-prophetic' politics that proceeds by 'small steps', focusing on 'what can'. The politics of local government has become 'transposed in a tragic key' (rather than a heroic register).

Our research also suggests that we need to take the embodied and particular character of this action, these small steps, more seriously. Our case study revealed the importance of 'special people' in undertaking the work of institutional bricolage, but we have very few conceptual tools to deal with this finding. Despite our academic obsession with the structure/ agency relationship, we are actually not very good at analysing agency, particularly in its embodied form. There is a tendency for academics and practitioners alike to feel embarrassed when confronted with the truism that personality and passion and individual qualities matter. Our research shows that *how* agents think is as important as *what* they think, in addressing current challenges. As Stoker and Moseley (2013) have noted: 'A capacity to see like a citizen rather than seeing like a state is a considerable challenge for the effective development of new tools of intervention'. Our case study confirmed the importance of an ability to 'see the gaps and the links' and to combine creativity and risk-taking with a capacity to build trusting relationships. In a similar vein, Geoff Mulgan (2012) has compared the skills needed in a new form of 'relational state' with those of the 'delivery state', arguing that 'relational performance' should be rewarded alongside more conventional outputs. As an interviewee in a related research project put it: 'You can't create special people, but you can create the environments for them to flourish' (Lowndes and Squires, 2012).

To recognise the materiality of the current crisis is also to ponder the quality of the resources that local government has to hand in confronting it. Such a recognition is reflected in Gerry Stoker's (2011, 27-28) reappraisal of his championing of 'soft power' in the context of 'network governance' – that is, 'the power to get other people to share your ideas and vision' via framing, influencing, bargaining and diplomacy. The danger, he feels, is that such a focus may mean that local government is 'able to do little directly for its citizens to save them from harm or promote their development'. Arguing for the transfer of more substantive powers to local government, and the development of a new 'social productivity' model, Stoker (2012) argues that 'governing on thin air' will not be enough to meet the material realities of the current context. This view resonates with emerging moves by local councils to explore their investment role in local infrastructure (following changes in the rules on local government pension funds), their potential as commissioners or providers of local utilities (notably energy and broadband), their scope for supporting local business development (through investing in peer-to-peer lending schemes that bypass banks), and their opportunity to act as stewards of 'the local commons' (that is, resources held in common by, and accessible to, local people).

Conclusion

Looking at the scale of cuts, and the extent of rising demand, we have argued that local government has an impressive capacity to act, and to reinvent its institutional forms to weather what amounts to a perfect storm. We have argued for a materialist analysis that studies not just the institutions of local government but also the 'embodied cognitive capacities' (Schatzki, 2001, 8) of those who act to sustain or adapt them. As Cooke and Muir (2012, 10) point out, 'Rather than being seen as units to deliver goals or plans... the people working in public services (along with citizens themselves) are the fundamental source of agency'. While institutional bricolage won't fix the graph of doom, resourceful and reflexive actors are stitching together a new institutional fabric from what they have to hand. They are reassembling, in Janet Newman's words (2012, 187) 'dominant, residual and emergent practices'. The temporal trajectory is not 'from-to', but involves backward, forward and outward movements as actors search their own and others' repertoires for institutional resources. At the same time, spatial scales are bent and boundaries blurred, as actors hurl grappling hooks into unfamiliar institutional matter, hoping to secure some productive new attachment or articulation. Such sorties may yet serve to expand what Gamble (2000) calls 'the space of the political'. This is not transformation, but it isn't inertia either. And, while we lack heroic politics or big ideas, we are witnessing an active politics of the present. Out of this politics, there may yet emerge a Plan B for local government which is focused less on implementing austerity and more on stimulating growth and building socially productive relationships. A rich agenda for policy, practice and research lies ahead.

Acknowledgements

The authors would like to thank the interviewees and focus group members for their time and commitment to the research. Thanks are due also to Professor Bruce Stafford and Dr Simon Roberts, who contributed to the wider action research programme.

References

Askim, J, Fimreite, AL, Moseley, A, Pederson, LH, 2011, One-stop shops for social welfare: The adaptation of an organisational form in three countries, *Public Administration*, 89, 4, 1451–68

Audit Commission, 2012, *Tough times: Councils' financial health in challenging times*, London: Audit Commission

Batty, E, Cole, I, 2010, *Resilience and the recession in six deprived communities*, York: Joseph Rowntree Foundation

Blyth, M, 2002, *Great transformations: Economic ideas and political change in the twentieth century*, Cambridge: Cambridge University Press

Browne, J, 2010, *Distributional analysis of tax and benefit changes*, Institute for Fiscal Studies, www.ifs.org.uk/publications/5313

CCE (Centre for Community Enterprise), 2000, *The community resilience manual*, Port Alberni, BC, Canada: CCE

Clark, TJ, 2012, For a left with no future, *New Left Review*, 74, 53–75

Coleman, A, Checkland, K, Harrison, S, Hiroeh, U, 2010, Local histories and local sensemaking: A case of policy implementation in the English National Health Service, *Policy & Politics*, 38, 2, 289–306

Cooke, G, Muir, R, 2012, The possibilities and politics of the relational state, in Cooke, G, Muir, R (eds), *The relational state*, London: Institute for Public Policy Research

Crouch, C, 2005, *Capitalist diversity and change*, Oxford: Oxford University Press

Cutter, SL, Barnes, L, Berry, M, Burton, C, Evans, E, Tate, E, Webb, J, 2008, A place-based model for understanding community resilience to natural disasters, *Global Environmental Change*, 18, 598–606

Denis, J, Langley, A, Rouleau, L, 2007, Strategising in pluralistic contexts: Rethinking theoretical frames, *Human Relations*, 60, 179–215

DWP (Department of Work and Pensions), 2012, *Households below average income*, London: DWP, http://research.dwp.gov.uk/asd/index.php?page=hbai

Elcock, H, 1984, *Local government: Policy and management in local authorities*, London: Routledge

Equality and Human Rights Commission, Department for Work and Pensions and Government Equalities Office, 2009, *Monitoring update on the impact of the recession on various demographic groups*, London: Government Equalities Office

Fenwick, J, 2013, Elected mayors: Slumbering deeply, *Policy & Politics*, 41, 1, 123–4

Gamble, A, 2000, *Politics and fate*, Cambridge: Polity

Hastings, A, Bramley, G, Bailey, N, Watkins, D, 2012, *Serving deprived communities in a recession*, York: Joseph Rowntree Foundation

Hay, C, 1996, Narrating crisis: The discursive construction of the 'winter of discontent', *Sociology*, 30, 2, **253–77**

Hay, C, 2012, Treating the symptom not the condition: Crisis definition, deficit reduction and the search for a new British growth model, *British Journal of Politics and International Relations*, http://onlinelibrary.wiley.com/doi/10.1111/j.1467-856X.2012.00515.x/full

Heseltine, M, 2012, *No stone unturned: In pursuit of growth*, London: Department for Business Innovation and Skills

HM Government, 2011, *Open public services 2011*, London: The Stationery Office

HM Treasury, 2010, *Spending review 2010*, Cm 7942, London: The Stationery Office

Hossain, N, Byrne, B, Campbell, A, Harrison, E, McKinley, B, Shah, P, 2011, *How people in poverty experienced recent global economic crises: Findings*, York: Joseph Rowntree Foundation

Hupe, P, Hill, M, 2007, Street-level bureaucracy and public accountability, *Public Administration*, 82, 2, 279–99

IFS (Institute of Fiscal Studies), 2012, *Green budget 2012*, London: IFS, www.ifs.org.uk/budgets/gb2012/gb2012.pdf

Lanzara, G, 1998, Self-destructive processes in institutional building and some modest countervailing mechanisms, *European Journal of Political Research*, 33, 1–39

LGA (Local Government Association), 2012, Popular council services under threat, London: LGA, www.local.gov.uk/web/guest/media-releases/-/journal_content/56/10171/3624637/NEWS-TEMPLATE

Lowndes, V, 2005, Something old, something new, something borrowed… How institutions change, and stay the same, in local governance, *Policy Studies*, 26, 3, 291–309

Lowndes, V, Stoker, G, 1992, An evaluation of neighbourhood decentralisation: Staff and councillor perspectives, *Policy & Politics*, 20, 2, 143–52

Lowndes, V, Pratchett, L, 2012, Local governance under the Coalition government: Austerity, localism and the Big Society, *Local Government Studies*, 38, 1, 21–40

Lowndes, V, Squires, S, 2012, Cuts, collaboration and creativity, *Public Money and Management*, 32, 6, 401–08

Lowndes, V, McCaughie, K, Roberts, S, Stafford, B, 2012, Cuts, costs and creativity: Prospects for local public services under austerity, chapter presented at *Policy & Politics* Conference, Bristol, September

Lowndes, V, Roberts, M, 2013, *Why institutions matter*, Basingstoke: Palgrave

Mouritzen, P (ed), 1992, *Managing cities in austerity: Urban fiscal stress in ten western countries*, London: Sage

Mulgan, G, 2012, Government with the people, in Cooke, G, Muir, R (eds), *The relational state*, London: Institute for Public Policy Research

Municipal Journal, 2012, People keen to do their bit for society, *Municipal Journal*, www.themj.co.uk

NCVO (National Council for Voluntary Organisations), 2012, *Work Programme Special Interest Group Survey 2012*, London: NCVO, www.ncvo-vol.org.uk/sites/default/files/work_programme_survey.pdf

Netmums, 2012, *Feeling the squeeze*, www.netmums.com/home/netmums-campaigns/families-in-crisis

Newman, J, 2012, *Working the spaces of power,* London: Bloomsbury Academic

OBR (Office for Budget Responsibility), 2012, *Commentary on the public sector finances June 2012*, London: OBR, http://budgetresponsibility.independent.gov.uk/wordpress/docs/July-2012-PSF-

Orr, K, 2009, Local government and structural crisis: An interpretive approach, *Policy & Politics*, 37, 1, 39–55

Pierre, J, 2009, Reinventing governance, reinventing democracy?, *Policy & Politics*, 37, 4, 591–609

RSA (Royal Society of the Arts), 2012, *Councils cut the fat but cracks are beginning to show*, London: RSA, www.thersa.org/about-us/media/press-releases/councils-cut-the-fat-but-cracks-are-beginning-to-show

Schatzki, T, 'Introduction: practice theory' in Schatzki, T, Knorr-Cetina, K, Von Savigny, E (eds), *The practice turn in contemporary theory*, London: RoutledgeStafford, B, Duffy, D, 2009, *Review of evidence on the impact of economic downturn on disadvantaged groups*, Department of Work and Pensions Working Paper No 68, London: DWP

Stoker, G, 2011, Was local governance such a good idea? A global comparative perspective', *Public Administration*, 89, 1, 15–31

Stoker, G, 2012, The political environment and localism: What future?, in Graham, S (ed), *Housing 2020: Six views of the future for housing associations,* Coventry: Orbit Group, 7–22

Stoker, G, Moseley, A, 2013, Motivation, behaviour and the microfoundations of public services, in Griffiths, S, Kippin, H, Stoker, G (eds), *Public services: A new reform agenda*, London: Bloomsbury Academic

Sullivan, H, 2012, A Big Society needs an active state, *Policy & Politics,* 40, 1, 145–8

Talbot, CR, Talbot, CL, 2011, Local government strategies in an age of austerity, in Oyarce, C (ed), *Redefining local government*, London: Accenture

WBG (Women's Budget Group), 2010, The impact on women of the Coalition spending review 2010, www.wbg.org.uk/RRB_Reports_4_1653541019.pdf

YouGov, 2012a, *YouGov trust tracker*, London: YouGov

YouGov, 2012b, *YouGov economy tracker*, London: YouGov

Complex causality in improving underperforming schools: a complex adaptive systems approach

Martijn van der Steen, Mark van Twist, Menno Fenger
and Sara Le Cointre

Introduction

In most welfare states, the quality of education greatly determines the future opportunities of children and of society in general. Therefore, high quality education is considered an important public service and schools that are underperforming are considered a policy problem. In the Netherlands, the government has developed policies and interventions that deal with underperforming schools – referred to as 'very weak schools'. These schools are included in a black list that is published online annually and then they become subject to increased supervision by the Inspectorate for Education. However, the results are diverse. In some schools, the approach has led to major improvements in quality and positively surprising results, whereas in other schools the situation has spiralled out of control in a series of undesired policy effects. Similar interventions have had different effects; some intended, others unintended; some desired, others undesired. This empirical observation is the starting point of this chapter: what causes the differences in outcomes of similar policies in similar contexts? Can patterns and causation be found in what seem to be unpredictable, unstable, and chaotic systems?

In general, policy is constructed along the lines of intentions and expectations of policy makers. Policy makers often assume, or desire, a 'magic button' that they can push to achieve intended outcomes. However, for decades, social scientists, historians, and economists have all been fascinated by the ubiquity of the so-called 'unintended', 'unanticipated', or 'unexpected' consequences of policies; policy plays out differently, sometimes positive, but often tragic. How can such 'surprises' be explained and understood? What mechanisms underlie the intentions and anticipation – or lack thereof – of public policy? Why are 'great expectations dashed' (Pressman and Wildavsky, 1984)?

Throughout its 40-year history, the *Policy & Politics* journal has devoted much attention to explaining the – often unexpected – outcomes of policy interventions. From the first volume in 1972 (see Sigsworth and

Wilkinson, 1972) to the current volume (see Lindsay and Dutton, 2013) many articles have tried to open the 'black box' of the mechanisms through which policy interventions reach their impacts, and to identify conditions that affect the transfer of policy interventions into policy outcomes. In browsing through 40 years of *Policy & Politics*, we can observe that we are confronted with the complexity and unpredictability of causality in the public domain, on the one hand (see, for example, Monagan, 2008; Bate and Robert, 2006). On the other hand, in its recent history, the journal is also closely witnessing the scientific progress that has been reached in explaining the complex causal relations between policies and outcomes. Firstly, this progress is made through deconstructing different configurations of conditions that lead to specific outcomes (see Mackie, 1988). Secondly, the dissemination of national and international comparative policy research has significantly contributed to the progress of the conceptual models of conditions affecting policy outcomes (see Lewis and Ross, 2011; Carson and Kerr, 2010). Thirdly, and more recently, methodological breakthroughs have also been reached through the developments of advanced methods for configuration analysis or qualitative comparative analysis (QCA) (see Rihoux, 2006). This chapter takes the debate about the topic of complex causality one step further by building upon the ideas of the complex adaptive systems approach to improve the understanding of causation in public policy. Rather than attempting to deconstruct complex causality as such, the chapter focuses on the process dynamics behind complex causality that can enrich the analysis and understanding of causality of public policy. It adds new viability to this long-running topic in *Policy & Politics* and the academic work and practices behind it.

In recent decades, much attention has been paid to explaining – and for some solving – the issue of the unintended and unanticipated consequences of policy. Scholarly work on unintended and unanticipated consequences is abundant and the questions, explanations, and hypotheses posed are manifold. However, the focus on the typologies of surprises and categorisations of causes leaves a remarkable gap in our knowledge. Little attention is paid to cause and effect; there is little debate about the causal mechanisms at work in policy implementation processes (Leeuw 2008; see, for exceptions, Margetts, 6, and Hood, 2010). Or, to state it more precisely, work about outcomes – either intended or unintended – of policy largely pre-assumes linear conceptions of causality (Merton, 1936; Sieber, 1981; Pawson, 2006),, whereas empirical evidence suggests looking at a more diverse concept of causality in policy. The lack of attention for concepts of causality in policy is remarkable because more complex concepts of causality are abundant in growing fields such as complexity theory (Gell-Mann, 1994; Brown and Eisenhardt, 1997; Anderson, 1999;

McMillan, 2004) and system dynamics (Forrester, 1994; Roberts, 1978; Saeed, 1994). Although work on complex adaptive systems (CAS) is increasingly integrated in public management research, policy researchers have not ventured deeply into the realm of causal mechanisms, mutual causality, and causal ambiguity.

The aim of this chapter is to explore the contribution of a CAS approach to the analysis of the unintended consequences of public policy; that may enhance the methodology of policy research, but also improve practitioners' take on policy design. We use an explorative design to illustrate the use of an alternative perspective of mutual causality in the study of unintended consequences of policy. We develop a conceptual lens based on a CAS approach and test it on four cases of policy-intervention in complex systems – in our case, underperforming primary schools in the Netherlands. Despite the widespread evidence of unanticipated and unintended consequences of public policies, many policy makers and scholars draft programme theories from a simple model of causality; they suggest direct links between causes and consequences, without attention being paid to the complex nature of the systems that policy intervenes in. Our approach starts from the perspective of complexity and highlights the importance of mutual causality, feedback mechanisms, and cyclical loops in the production of policy outcomes. Instead of identifying the unanticipated consequences of policy we take these as inherent elements of causation in policy and use that to look at policy and consequences. That offers an alternative for policy professionals and scholars who wish to better study or anticipate the often complex relation between causes and consequences in policy.

The chapter is structured as follows. We start by exploring the existing literature about unintended consequences, policy interventions, and unexpected outcomes. From this we argue that linear conceptions of causality obstruct the understanding of the complexity of issues such as policy for very weak schools. Concepts derived from CAS, such as mutual causality, feedback loops, and non-linearity provide us with alternative perspectives on causal mechanisms. We then apply this loop perspective to four empirical examples in which we demonstrate the power of a loop perspective for understanding and explaining the consequences of policy. In the final section, we discuss the implications of our conceptual framework for policy makers and policy analysts.

Unintended and unanticipated consequences

The notion of unintended and unanticipated consequences goes back for centuries. Early philosophers have pondered the unintended consequences of human action (David Hume) and the matter of social benefits resulting from individual profit-seeking behaviour (Adam Smith). However, it was not until Robert Merton drew attention to the issue that it became an object of sociological analysis. In this section, we will briefly review the literature on unintended consequences to identify the different explanations provided by different authors regarding diverse and variable outcomes. Merton (1936) recognises four factors that limit the ability to correctly anticipate the consequences of social action. These factors are (1) ignorance of facts; (2) erroneously assessing the situation and/or execution of action; (3) misplaced interests or tunnel vision; and (4) self-defeating prophecy (Fine, 2006). Incorrect anticipation and prediction as a result of these factors creates unintended and unexpected consequences. Merton calls for amending public policy to 'reduce ignorance and error, better to guide interest and to manipulate the mechanisms and probabilities of self-defeating prophecy' (6, 2010, 46).

A fairly large body of literature on the unexpected consequences of interventions does not come from the field of policy studies but rather from organisational analysis and the studies of government reform. It deals with the question of why and how reform processes often fail to achieve the stated results or why they often take unexpected turns and produce many 'side-effects'. An early example of this type of study is that of Hirschman (1991) who extends the understanding of the types of unanticipated and unintended consequences of reform into a trichotomy of types. Negative relations between intentions and outcomes of the attempted reform of public sector organisations can be classified as (1) futility (the intervention has no effect on the problem situation), (2) perversity (the intervention undermines the very thing policy makers tend to promote) or (3) jeopardy (the intervention undermines some other thing that policy makers care about). The trichotomy was initially developed to analyse the unintended outcomes of policy reform but was widely used in the analysis of policy consequences (6, 2010).

Rather than in the ill-understanding or flawed anticipation that revolves around organisational processes, Sieber (1981) sees the cause of unintended consequences in the reverse effects of policies, which are also referred to as fatal remedies (Sieber, 1981) or perverse effects (Boudon, 1982). Policy suffers from so-called 'conversion mechanisms': 'policy converts the intentions of agents into the opposite outcomes' (Sieber, 1981, 56). There are seven such mechanisms, namely functional disruption, exploitation, goal displacement, provocation, classification, over-commitment, and placation. Unexpectedness is not the result of flawed judgment, it is a product of mechanisms that are set in motion 'ex post' by the policy itself. Sieber does not consider these effects to be 'unexpected' or a side effect. On the contrary, they are part of the normality of policy dynamics and are in that sense predictable (Sieber, 1981, 10). The dilemma of reverse effects can be resolved, by 'recognising and coping with reverse effects especially before they are allowed to occur' (Sieber, 1981, 203). Here, Sieber refers to the reflexive character of social systems as explanations for the unintended and unanticipated outcomes of public policies. The complex systems approach, as discussed in the next section, further analyses the impact of the adaptive character of social systems on external interventions.

A missing link in the study of consequences: concepts of causality

From the previous section it appears that we need to move beyond singular mechanisms of cause and effect in order to explain the unintended and unpredicted outcomes of public policies. In the case of the very weak schools policy in the Netherlands the same intervention generated dissimilar outcomes in similar circumstances. To study not only the unintended and seemingly unanticipated consequences but also their dissimilar nature, we need to widen our perspective and look for explanations that take causality into account. Existing studies may show different typologies and categorisations of types of consequences and causes, yet provide little understanding of the process of causation. More specifically: to analyse the unintended consequences of public policy it is necessary to look for more diverse, multiple and circular concepts of causality and perceive policy intervention as a system of interactions (Pawson, 2006; Tilley, 2010).

   System dynamics and cybernetic studies have a long tradition in the study of causality mechanisms in complex environments (for example, Forrester, 1961; Perrow, 1984; Wildavsky, 1988; Senge, 1990; Haraldsson, 2000; Cavana and Mares, 2004). Central to systems thinking is the interconnectedness of elements in a system and the feedback mechanisms that shape the interactions between them. Outcomes and effects of inputs are considered the effect of complex, interrelated interactions between many different elements of the system, in relations that are often instable, emergent, varying and can, therefore, hardly be predicted – or only very limitedly. Crucial to systems thinking is the notion of feedback: actions in the system generate interactions and feedback that either reinforce or balance out the primary action. System thinking defines causal relations as reciprocal and interactive. It was the cybernetic movement that mainly contributed to this way of thinking about regulating mechanisms in a system. Feedback loops regulate systems' performance by a 'circular arrangement of causally connected components' (Merali and Allen, 2011). When there is an odd number of negative links between components in a system, it will show self-balancing behaviour (Haraldsson, 2000; Lane, 2008; Merali and

Allen, 2011). Different terms are used to describe these loops in systems, such as an equilibrating system (Maruyama, 1963), self-balancing system (Senge, 1990; Haraldsson, 2000), negative feedback loop polarity (Lane 2008), or negative loop (Richardson, 1986; Toole, 2005). When there is an even number of negative links the system will 'display a self-reinforcing exponential runaway behaviour' (Merali and Allen, 2011). A change in one factor enforces a loop that leads to a magnification of the original effect (Lane, 2008). These developing loops are referred to as deviation-amplifying loops (Maruyama, 1963), self-reinforcing systems (Senge, 1990; Haraldsson, 2000), positive feedback loop polarity (Lane, 2008), or positive loops (Richardson, 1986; Toole, 2005). Systems characterised by self-reinforcing loops will be more volatile and prone to rapid downward or upward spirals (Toole, 2005) because small and seemingly insignificant changes will set spirals in motion that can lead to highly magnified outcomes. The nature of self-balancing and self-reinforcing loops can be visualised as follows (see Figure 6.1). Note that these loops are non-linear, and that self-reinforcing loops can have a negative and positive character.

Figure 6.1: Visualisation of the nature of loops

Self-reinforcing loop   Self-balancing loop

Causality in complex adaptive systems

The original system dynamics perspective (Roberts, 1978; Randers, 1980) assumes a stable set of design principles in complex multi-actor systems that, for instance, allow for management and some extent of control of them. However, that assumption was criticised when the centralised, hierarchical notions of management and control that underlie these principles came under fire in the later part of the 20th century (Simon, 1957; Mintzberg, 1978). This initiated a new wave of theory on complexity: the complex adaptive systems approach (CAS). This approach followed from a 'growing concern about the unintended and unforeseen consequences of planned management interventions' (Merali and Allen, 2011). It focuses on the dynamics of interaction, on learning and evolution, and on the emerging nature of complex systems. Complex adaptive systems are understood as 'systems that adapt and evolve in the process of interacting with dynamic environments' (Merali and Allen, 2011).

As we have shown in the literature review in this section, the notion of interactions is missing in most studies of unintended consequences. Studies focus on factors instead of the processes that develop within the system due to interactions and feedback loops. It is this underlying movement that can have explanatory value in analysing the causal mechanisms of policy interventions. Theories and concepts from system dynamics and cybernetics provide us with the tools to use a more elaborate concept of causality that is hardly used in policy analysis and theory, or in policy practice. Policy analysis seems stuck in the review of monocausal mechanisms as drivers of interventions and causes and effects. However, insights from complexity theory, CAS, and cybernetics suggest that mutual causality helps make sense of unintended and dissimilar outcomes of policy interventions (Roberts et al, 1983; Richardson 1986; 1991; Richmond, 1993; Toole, 2005; Klijn, 2008).

Mutual causality refers to the circular patterns of interaction in a system where cause and effect may be co-defined. As opposed to mechanical and singular causality, it takes into account the second order effects (or second cybernetics): change happens in loops rather than lines (Forrester, 1991; Maruyama, 1963; 1982). Instead of linear relations, where a small stimulus will produce a small response, non-linear relations explain how even the smallest stimulus in one part can have major, sometimes catastrophic, effects in another part of the system (Juarrero, 2011) and, more important to the central question of this chapter, how similar stimuli lead to dissimilar effects.

This chapter takes the concept of non-linear and possibly circular causal relations as the main object of study. The insights of system dynamics and cybernetics show that the environmental conditions play a major role in the development of systems and the causal connections that interact in that system. This can explain the causal ambiguity often found in policy systems and help to understand how and why similar interventions lead to dissimilar effects. In the remainder of this chapter, we will use the lens of causal loops to review our empirical cases of policy interventions in very weak schools in the Netherlands. By engaging this loop perspective to our empirical cases we hope to make sense of the dissimilar effects of similar interventions.

Explaining dissimilar results of policy for 'very weak schools'

Research method

The purpose of our empirical study is to apply the lens of mutual causality to the dissimilar effects of policy interventions in Dutch, very weak schools. We studied four different primary schools in the Netherlands that were at the time of the study recently characterised as 'very weak' by the Inspectorate of Education and had been put under increased supervision. The increased supervision implies that schools are required to participate in a standardised programme of measures that should improve the schools' performance. Each school that is put in the programme is to improve its performance within two years to a particular pre-defined standard. If not, the school is permanently closed. However, schools in the system usually manage to improve their performance in time and meet the standard after the two-year programme.

What makes the cases suitable for testing our conceptual lens of linear causality is the fact that although each school eventually improves to standard, the Inspectorate is unable to explain how and why they do so. While schools start in the same position and receive similar 'treatment', the outcomes are highly dissimilar and – from the perspective of the Inspectorate's policy theory – unanticipated. We apply our conceptual lens of mutual causality to the puzzle of dissimilar and unexpected outcomes of policy interventions for very weak schools and explore the alternative explanations that it produces.

Our case studies are explorative in nature, and the cases were selected for their contribution to understanding the varied and complex reality of this particular problem (Weiss 1994; Rhodes, 't Hart, and Noordegraaf, 2007). Therefore, we selected two cases that showed effects beyond the formal policy programmes' expectation (very quick recoveries and continued improvement after termination of the programme) and two cases that showed effects below the programmes' stated goals (slow or absent recovery, or a fall back to poor performance shortly after the programme). We also wanted our cases to at least partly represent the variety of scale of schools that is a typical characteristic of the primary schools system in the Netherlands. Therefore, we selected a larger and smaller school, within a rural and urban area. We used these contextual factors for the selection of the two 'positive' and 'negative' cases. For our research design, it does not matter how the positive and negative cases are spread over the rural or urban, smaller or larger school categories. This case selection is represented in Table 6.1.

Table 6.1: Case selection

	Large urban schools	Small rural schools
Miraculous recovery	School D	School B
Disastrous demise	School C	School A

The schools in our case sample can be briefly characterised as follows:

1. School A is a small, public primary school that is in the countryside in northern Netherlands, in a small town, with two other schools in close proximity. The three schools compete for students in an economically and socially deprived area. Public schools, contrary to private schools, have to accept all students. This means school A takes in relatively more students lagging behind, such as immigrant children with serious language and other problems, and 'special needs' children[1].
2. School B is a small private Christian school in northern Netherlands in a small village. Classes at different levels are combined because of size and the student population comprises a large number of special needs children. They require extra attention, which pressures the day-to-day teaching process, and they lower the average performance of the school in annual national performance scores that are important elements of the assessment of the quality of the school
3. School C is a large public school in a medium-sized city in the south. In the 1980s it was one of the biggest schools in the Netherlands but since then has suffered a dramatic drop in student population. The decline of enrolment impacts the school in many different ways, but has also led to the school innovating and reforming drastically in the past decade.
4. School D is a large private Steiner school in a large Dutch city. It has an anthroposophist philosophy in teaching, which is why most parents choose this school for their children. Personal development of the child, rather than test results, is the leading principle. There is little competition with other schools and parents are less likely to opt for an exit. However, the school cannot comply with the required annual tests, because the tests are not taken in the school.

We used a variety of methods to gather our data. First, we conducted a desk review to map the policies with regard to under-performing schools, the design of the system and to analyse the contextual background to understand the policy interventions in 'very weak' schools (included were legal and policy documents, inspection frameworks, working methods and local improvement plans). The desk research allowed us to construct a factual account of the history and development of the schools, of the regulatory and procedural environment they operated in, and a detailed account of the often long history of the Inspectorate with the school. Secondly, we conducted semi-structured interviews, with topic lists derived from the desk research (context of the school, interventions and measures taken, relations between relevant stakeholders), with key stakeholders at the school; at each school, we talked to teachers, parents, school directors, members of the school board and inspectors involved with that particular school. The interviews were conducted on site, during one or two-day visits at the schools. In total, we conducted 20 interviews at the four schools. Thirdly, after the document analysis and interviews, we issued a report with preliminary findings and discussed this in a focus group with a broad selection of representatives from all stakeholder groups in the different cases.

The intervention repertoire of the Inspectorate

The 'very weak school intervention' is founded in the education quality policy of the Dutch national government. This policy considers under-performing primary schools as an important and urgent problem that should be solved by a public policy solution. Over the past decade, various tools have been developed that allow the Minister of Education to deal with this issue more directly, such as ceasing funding to very weak schools or closing schools that under-perform long term. However, the core of the policy is that these measures are tools of last resort that are preceded by a system that allows schools to recover on their own and that supports the efforts of school boards, managers, teachers, and staff to do so.

The policies for underperforming schools are enacted by the Inspectorate of Education. It supervises primary schools based on a system of risk-based inspection: when a school is at risk of under-performing, the Inspectorate initiates a further investigation. This requires schools to provide additional information on quality and performance. When the Inspectorate determines increased, new or persistent shortcomings, it publishes its findings in a report. This report includes a so-called 'Inspection Chart', showing performance in the categories sufficient, weak, or very weak. This report is published online, as a form of a 'naming and shaming' strategy of enforcement. Schools classified as very weak enrol in a mandatory two-year improvement period. During this period schools are required to improve their performance through operational plans. The Inspectorate engages with school boards and monitors the implementation of its recommendations. They remain in this programme until the Inspectorate assesses the quality as sufficient. If the quality is not sufficient by the end of the programme, the Minister will close the school.

The policy strategy and intervention strategy of the Inspectorate are based on certain causal assumptions, as outlined by the Ministry itself (Van Twist et al, 2011). The Inspectorate expects the intervention to play out as represented in Figure 6.2.

Figure 6.2: Policy assumptions in the 'very weak school' programme

The overall results of the policy appear to be positive: the number of 'very weak' schools dropped below 1%, which exceeded the objective for 2012. Moreover, every year more 'very weak' schools return to the basic inspection arrangement. Therefore, since 2009 the number of small schools is decreasing (De Wolf and Verkroost, 2011). The Netherlands is acclaimed as a 'best practice' in reducing the number and relative weakness of the so-called 'very weak schools'.

However, the relative success of this policy has some uncomfortable sides to it as well. Firstly, even though the policy is successful in restoring quality in the schools classified as 'weak' or 'very weak', it has not been able to prevent new schools from entering these categories. Secondly, some schools do not make it out of the 'weak' or 'very weak' category within two years, and are closed in spite of the programme and policy. Although the 'Dutch approach' works for many schools, it does not do so for all of them. And thirdly, it remains ill understood why the same interventions work in one case and not in another. Some schools improve dramatically and never fall back into poor quality again, even if the increased pressure of the inspection is long gone. Other schools do not improve at all, or quickly drop back into failing quality.

Using a loops perspective we try to explain these different outcomes. In the next section, we present the processes we observed in our four cases. That provides insight into what actually happens when the Inspectorate intervenes with its 'very weak classification' tool, and what dynamics are set in motion in and around the school systems that help us understand the dissimilar outcomes of this policy programme.

Mutual causal processes in practice: vicious and virtuous cycles in schools

In this section, we present the causal mechanisms that emerged from the analysis of the four cases (see Figure 6.3; for the full case studies see Van Twist al, 2011). These causal mechanisms show how some schools ended up in a vicious cycle of decline after the Inspectorate had classified them as very weak, whereas other schools propelled themselves into a virtuous cycle of self-reinforcing positive loops.

Figure 6.3: Overview of loops occurring in the four cases

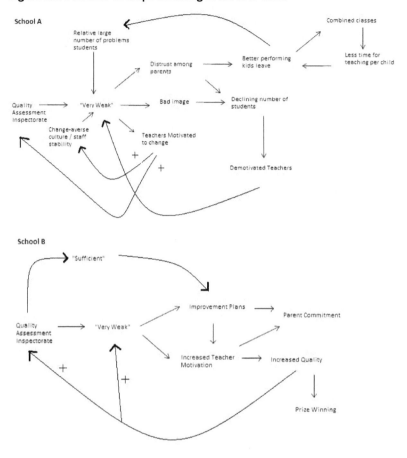

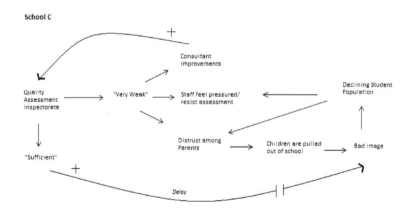

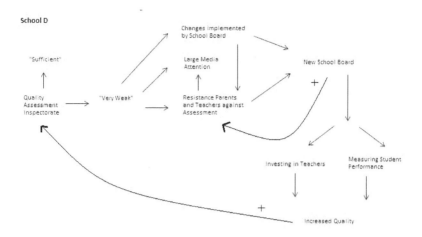

School D

"Sufficient"

Quality Assessment Inspectorate

"Very Weak"

Changes implemented by School Board

Large Media Attention

Resistance Parents and Teachers against Assessment

New School Board

+

Investing in Teachers

Measuring Student Performance

+

Increased Quality

School A

The very weak qualification by the Inspectorate came as an unexpected blow to the parents of the school. The Inspectorate and Board informed the parents in a special meeting, but this did not end their concerns. Instead, with many schools to choose from, several parents immediately transferred their children to other schools. More importantly, the better performing students were transferred, which decreased the average quality of the student population and test scores. 'It weakened our student population', stated a teacher. However, after the initial transfers, things became worse. Signalled by the departure of some of the students, more parents opted out of the school. Parent after parent followed suit and in the new school year there were not enough students to sustain separate classes for different levels and age groups. Classes were combined, which meant extra effort from teachers and students was required, and less time could be spent on individual students. This again sparked a wave of transfers from the school. It became a cascading effect of children leaving. Eventually, this meant the relative number of 'problem' students increased even more vis-à-vis 'regular' students: its negative consequences fed back into the system and reinforced its vicious cycle to almost unsustainable levels.

Furthermore, issuing the label 'very weak' to the school created a bad image for the school. The image of the under-performing school where teachers lack the time to provide a good quality education, and too many underperforming kids in the classroom, became real: not because it was all that bad at the start of the process, but because the policy interventions set events in motion that led to the implosion of the school. To make matters worse, the increased pressure on teachers became too much for many of them. Some lost motivation, others went off sick. As one teacher told us: 'two teachers left, we had a lot of substitutes, and then another colleague left as well because it was unbearable.' The distrust of parents towards the school overpowered the positive changes that were supposed to be happening after the intervention by the Inspectorate. Eventually the interactions of other elements spiralled the school into a vicious, negative cycle from which it did not recover.

School B

At first, the teachers in school B were defensive and in denial about the very weak qualification. Yet they soon realised changes needed to be made and they pulled together to lift up the school's quality. Improvement plans were made, and morale and team spirit flourished: 'everyone agreed to put their best effort in', as the school manager told us. This not only increased the quality of their teaching, it also showed parents they were committed to their children. Parents in turn became committed to the teachers and school and not a single child was transferred. The increased quality of the school was recognised by the Inspectorate and within two years the school was qualified as 'sufficient'. The school kept on improving itself and its teachers and went on to win several prizes for excellent education. It shows that the dynamics in school B created a virtuous cycle of positive, self-reinforcing loops. Once teachers started to pick up the process of improvement, they went on – even beyond the level of sufficient quality. Once set in motion, the process of improvement did not stop – even after the external pressure from the Inspectorate was long gone and the school was already doing more than well. The effects of the policy intervention remained, even while the 'causes' for it were long gone.

School C

When the qualification of very weak came through, the school board hired an external consultant to help analyse the problems in the school and propose the necessary changes. The consultant successfully assisted the school in tackling its problems regarding the quality of education, a period which is described by the people involved as 'hard but necessary'. After two years, the school was no longer considered very weak and was again qualified as 'sufficient'.

However, some other developments were far stronger in the dynamics of this intervention process. The initial qualification led to huge distrust among parents: the school and its teachers were unable to redeem themselves. Even though quality had improved, parents transferred their children and discouraged others to enter their child into school C. The bad image of the school led to a decline in the student population: not only were children taken out of school, hardly any new children enrolled in the following years. The school struggled to reach the required number of 23 students to stay open. Even though the quality of education had increased and the school had improved, the imprint of 'very weak' never really left and this eventually put the school out of business. The school remains, but it is not likely to recover from the blow of policy intervention, as the image does not seem to fade and successful attempts to improve have been overtaken by a downward spiral.

School D

In school D the fact that its teaching philosophy does not focus on – or believe in – test results is important. The Inspectorate, however, considers test results as one of the main indicators for quality. When the school was qualified as very weak, the parents and teachers were the ones who specifically resisted this. They distrusted the Inspectorate's assessment. However, the school board could not dismiss its judgement and started implementing changes, which further angered parents and teachers. In this hectic period, where some parents presumably threatened the school board, the national media paid much attention to the school. Eventually a new school board was installed, which appointed a new director.

Around that time, the Inspectorate returned to assess improvements. Given the short time that a new director was in place, they decided to give the school a second chance. Both parents and teachers believed in the changes of the new school board and relaxed: it invested in the teachers and started measuring students' progress that suited both the philosophy of the school and the Inspectorate's demands. Eventually this increased the quality of education and the school was judged 'sufficient'. In the dynamics of this school, the new school board and new director functioned as a catalyst for positive developments that created a virtuous loop, even though negative loops had also developed.

In the previous paragraphs we have briefly described the loops that have occurred in each of the cases. Figure 6.3 shows an overview of these loops, indicating clearly how the simple causal relation between intervention and outcome – as presented in Figure 6.2 – in real life consists of different patterns of actions and interactions. These patterns include the motivation of teachers, the commitment of parents, the development of the student population and school leadership. In each school, these patterns interact differently with other elements of the system, resulting in different consequences. This figure shows how a 'loops' or 'complex system analysis' perspective does not focus on causes and consequences, but rather on patterns of actions and interactions. Process tracing these different patterns contributes to the understanding of the outcomes. In the next section we analyse the importance of these dynamics and their implications for future research and practice.

Conclusion and implications

Looking back at our four cases, we clearly see how different dynamics emerge in similar intervention processes. Schools A and B showed an initial increase in teacher motivation. In school B a small increase in teacher motivation reinforced several other elements in the intervention system, such as parent commitment, the implementation of improvement plans and the quality of their teaching performance. In school A the small increase did not have a major effect on the overall quality and remained a positive yet isolated effect.

Furthermore, in schools C and D the staff reacted fiercely and negatively to the very weak classification. Both schools enforced programmes to support the teachers with new skills and methods to improve the quality of their in-class performance. However, in school C the staff were demotivated by the 'ever-changing teaching methods' and 'new things that were tried out on them'. In school D, however, after initial resistance from staff and parents, which even received national media attention, a strong sense of urgency for change set in, partly by the instalment of a new board. The positive developments eventually reinforced a rapid recovery and caused the disturbed parents to relax and give the school a chance. These two examples show that the mutual causality within the system generates different dynamics with different outcomes.

Another factor that becomes evident in the causal loops of the intervention processes is the importance of whether children stay or leave the school when it is classified as very weak. In school B and D, parents' distrust of the situation did not lead them to leave the school. This was one of the reasons the schools pulled through. Contrary, the parents in school A and C started to transfer their children to other schools, and this led to a disastrous decline in the number of students. In school C the transfer of children resulted in an ever worse image. Although the school's quality of education increased, it was still perceived as under-performing and as a school where sensible parents would not send their children. Hence, despite improved performance and the acknowledgement thereof by the Inspectorate, the school is now more than ever threatened by complete closure. The intervention by the Inspectorate did not have the desired effect: the school still had problems. Solving one problem – quality – led to a more dramatic new one, the absence of students to keep the school afloat.

The dynamics of the intervention processes that we have shown in our case studies demonstrate that circumstances, context, and factors interact with each other. The Inspectorate often did not expect these interactions. The value of the loop perspective is that it enables us to discover these mechanisms and relations between different causes and effects, and tells us how they emerge. The causal loops also show the disproportionality of the process. Not all elements in the process are of equal size. Small causes can turn into major effects with consequences far beyond the initially 'targeted' domain. For instance, from our cases we have learnt that it is important which parents pull their children out of school. The decisions of parents who play an important role in the local community to stay and help improve the school, or to remove their children, may trigger a circular loop. Another important insight from the causal loops is the role of time delays. Even if a school returns to a sufficient classification, this does not feed back into the system immediately and the bad image that was created might be irrefutable. Positive feedback comes too late to change crucial factors in the system.

In addition, the cases show how local knowledge matters for understanding the loops that emerge. Parents do not respond to 'one child' who leaves a school, but rather to who leaves; they do not look at impersonal numbers or statistics, they have highly interpretive, normative and often intuitive judgments about what they consider relevant indicators of progress or decline in the school. They look for clues to how the school is developing, and many of those indicators cannot be brought down to simple statistics of objective parameters. However, that does not imply that they cannot be predicted or monitored. On the contrary, many of the inspectors and school directors we interviewed told us that – in hindsight – they could have predicted the impact of certain children leaving schools, specific teachers going off sick, courses coming at the right or wrong time, and of many other highly variable impacts of extremely specific interventions. This suggests that loops can be predicted, but only with use of the intimate and local knowledge of actors close by or 'in' the system.

The case studies teach us that understanding the effects is not so much about studying causes, but about understanding the loops that emerge out of initial policy interventions. Understanding policy effects requires actors to look for causal mechanisms, understand how they interact, and see how relations influence each other. We have shown how the use of concepts and language of circular causality – for example, loops, feedback, catalyst, delays – can improve the understanding of otherwise unanticipated effects of policy interventions. There are several implications connected to this. The first is related to the academic understanding of unanticipated consequences. Policy theory seems to be caught in a language deficit that forces a static and linear perspective on the study of policy effects that is inappropriate for the complex systems that are studied. The use of a dynamic perspective and the language of circularity to policy analysis may improve our understanding of the consequences and interventions. Our current attempt needs further elaboration, for example developing reasons for amplification and dissipation, and the local elements that matter. Our analysis suggests that factors such as leadership, resources, governance and community involvement matter. But how and in what way do they affect the system and its feedback loops? There are still many challenges that need to be faced in capturing the components of mutual causality in complex policy systems. In this chapter, we have explored the contribution of a 'loops' or mutual causality perspective in linking policy interventions and outcomes. By bringing the complex systems perspective into the realm of *Policy & Politics*, we have showed a fruitful future direction for taking up these challenges.

A second implication is related to practice. Understanding policy intervention as loops can help policy makers 'looking for the right button to push' to build smarter arrangements for intervention. Reflexivity and recognition of emergent processes are key elements, as is monitoring: it is the process that matters in implementation, not the plan or evaluation at the end. Interventions should be designed to be adaptive and flexible, local and emergent. This moves the attention of policy makers from analysis *ex ante* towards the local knowledge of the process as it emerges. To increase the understanding of local and emergent knowledge in relation to policy making we can build on existing theories such as those from Yanow (1996; 2004) and Durose (2009). Local knowledge is understood as 'the mundane, yet expert, understanding front-line workers develop from their own contextual experiences' (Durose, 2009). Local adaptability and divergent implementation imply knowing what happens when it happens, require space for local professional judgment and, therefore, imply variety at the system level.

Note
[1] Special needs children have a physical or mental disability or severe behavioural or learning problems. Although they are often entitled to special needs education based on a medical indication, parents often choose a 'regular' school with extra supervision (*rugzakje*).

References
6, P, 2010, When forethought and outturn part, in Margetts, H, 6, P, Hood, CC (eds), *Paradoxes of modernisation: Unintended consequences of public policy reform*, Oxford: Oxford University Press, 44–60

Anderson, P, 1999, Complexity theory and organization science, *Organization Science*, 10, 3, 216–32

Bate, P, Robert, G, 2006, 'Build it and they will come' – or will they? Choice, policy paradoxes and the building of NHS treatment centres, *Policy & Politics*, 34, 4, 651–72

Boudon, R, 1982, *The unintended consequences of social action*, New York: St Martin's Press

Brown, SL, Eisenhardt, KM, 1997, The art of continuous change: Linking complexity theory and time-paced evolution in relentlessly shifting organizations, *Administrative Science Quarterly*, 42, 1–34

Carson, E, Kerr, L, 2010, Contractualism and social inclusion: Strands of policy emulation in UK and Australian local employment services, *Policy & Politics*, 38, 1, 41–55

Cavana, RY, Mares, ED, 2004, Integrating critical thinking and systems thinking:

From premises to causal loops, *System Dynamics Review*, 20, 3, 223–35

De Wolf, IF, Verkroost, JJH, 2011, Evaluation of the theory and practice of the new education supervision, *Journal for Supervision*, 2, 2, 7–24

Durose, C, 2009, Frontline workers and 'local knowledge': Neighbourhood stories in contemporary UK local governance, *Public Administration*, 87, 1, 35–49

Fine, GA, 2006, The chaining of social problems : Solutions and unintended consequences in the age of betrayal, *Social Problems*, 53, 1, 3–17

Forrester, JW, 1961, *Industrial dynamics*, Cambridge, MA: MIT Press

Forrester, JW, 1991, System dynamics and the lessons of 35 Years, in De Greene, KB, (ed), The systematic basis of policy making in the 1990's, 1–35

Forrester, JW, 1994, System dynamics, systems thinking, and soft OR, *System Dynamics Review*, 10, 2/3, 245–56

Gell-Mann, M, 1994, *The quark and the jaguar: Adventures in the simple and the complex*, New York: WH Freeman

Haraldsson, HV, 2000, *Introduction to systems and causal loop diagrams*, System Analysis course, Lund University (January), 1–33

Hirschman, AO, 1991, *The rhetoric of reaction*, Cambridge, MA: Belknap Press, Harvard University Press

Juarrero, A, 2011, Causality and explanation, in Allen, P, Maguire, S, McKelvey, B (eds), *The Sage handbook of complexity and management*, London: Sage, 155–63

Klijn, EH, 2008, Policy and implementation networks. Managing complex interactions. in Cropper, S, Ebers, M, Huxham, C, Smith Ring P (eds), *The Oxford handbook of inter-organizational relations*, Oxford: Oxford University Press, 118–146

Lane, DC, 2008, The emergence and use of diagramming in system dynamics: a critical account, *Systems Research and Behavioral Science*, 25, 3–23

Leeuw, FL, 2008, *Behavioural mechanisms behind government intervention and rules of law*, Inaugural speech: University of Maastricht, www.maastrichtuniversity.nl/web/file?uuid=a8d20b49-221a-4ffe-83e3-47028a0d1e99&owner=4a641a32-dbe5-494a-9d0c-8b10afd66169

Lewis, JM, Ross, S, 2011, Research funding systems in Australia, New Zealand and the UK: Policy settings and perceived effects, *Policy & Politics*, 39, 3, 379–98

Lindsay, C, Dutton, M, 2013, Promoting healthy pathways to employability: Lessons for the UK's welfare-to-work agenda, *Policy & Politics*, 41, 2, 183–200

Mackie, JL, 1988, *The cement of the universe: A study in causation*, Oxford: Clarendon Press

Margetts, H, 6, P, Hood, CC (eds), *Paradoxes of modernisation: Unintended consequences of public policy reform*, Oxford: Oxford University Press

Maruyama, M, 1963, The second cybernetics: Deviation-amplifying mutual causal processes, *American Scientist*, 51, 2, 164–79

Maruyama, M, 1982, Mindscapes, management, business policy, and public policy, *Academy of Management Review*, 7, 4, 612–19

McMillan, E, 2004, *Complexity, organisations and change*, London: Routledge

Merali, Y, Allen, P, 2011, Complexity and systems thinking, in Allen, P, Maguire, S, McKelvey, B (eds), *The Sage handbook of complexity and management*, London: Sage, 31–52

Merton, RK, 1936, The unanticipated consequences of purposive social action, *American Sociological Review*, 1, 6, 894–904

Mintzberg, M, 1978, Patterns in strategy formation, *Management Science*, 24, 9, 934–48

Monagan, M, 2008, The evidence base in UK drug policy: The new rules of engagement, *Policy & Politics*, 36, 1, 145–50

Pawson, R, 2006, *Evidence based policy: a realist perspective*, London: Sage

Perrow, C, 1984, *Normal accidents*, New York: Basic Books

Pressman, JL, Wildavsky, A, 1984, *Implementation*, Berkeley, CA: University of California Press

Randers, J, 1980, *Elements of the system dynamics method*, Cambridge, MA: MIT Press

Rihoux, B, 2006, Qualitative comparative analysis (QCA) and related systematic comparative methods: Recent advances and remaining challenges for social science research, *International Sociology*, 21, 5, 679–706

Rhodes, RAW, 't Hart, P, Noordegraaf, M, 2007, Being there, in Rhodes, RAW, 't Hart, P, Noordegraaf, M (eds), *Observing government elites: Up close and personal*, Basingstoke: Palgrave Macmillan, 1–17

Richardson, GP, 1986, Problems with causal-loop diagrams, *System Dynamics Review*, 2, 2, 158–70

Richardson, GP, 1991, *Feedback thought in social science and systems theory*, Waltham, MA: Pegasus Communications

Richmond, B, 1993, Systems thinking: Critical thinking skills for the 1990s and beyond, *System Dynamics Review*, 9, 2, 113–33

Roberts, N, Andersen, NF, Garret, M, Deal, R, Shaffer, W, 1983, *Introduction to computer simulation: The system dynamics approach*, Reading, MA: Addison-Wesley

Roberts, EB, 1978, *Managerial applications of system dynamics*, Cambridge, MA: MIT Press

Saeed, K, 1994, *Development planning and policy design: A system dynamics approach*, Aldershot: Avebury

Senge, PM, 1990, *The fifth discipline: The art and practice of the learning organisation*, London: Century Business

Sieber, SD, 1981, *Fatal remedies: The ironies of social intervention*, New York: Plenum

Sigsworth, EM, Wilkinson, RK, 1972, Constraints in the uptake of improvement grants, *Policy & Politics*, 1, 2, 131–41, 11

Simon, HA, 1957, *Models of man*, New York: Wiley

Tilley, N, 2010, Realistic evaluation and disciplinary knowledge: Applications from the field of criminology, in Vaessen, J, Leeuw, F (eds), *Mind the gap: evaluation and the disciplines*, New Brunswick, NJ: Transaction Publishers, 203–35

Toole, TM, 2005, *A project management causal loop diagram*, paper presented at the Association of Researchers in Construction Management Conference, London

Van Twist, M, Van der Steen, M, Kleiboer, M, Scherpenisse, J, 2011, *Coping with very weak primary schools: Towards smart intervention in Dutch education policy*, paper presented at the First 'Governing Complex Education Systems project' Thematic Conference, The Hague, Netherlands, 21–22 November, 1–41

Weiss, RS, 1994, *Learning from strangers: The art and method of qualitative interview studies*, New York: Free Press

Wildavsky, A, 1988, *Searching for safety*, Oxford: Oxford University Press

Yanow, D, 1996, *How does a policy mean?*, Washington, DC: Georgetown University Press

Yanow, D, 2004, Translating local knowledge at organisational peripheries, *British Journal of Management*, 15, 1, 9–25

CHAPTER SEVEN

Toward policy coordination: alternatives to hierarchy

B. Guy Peters

Introduction

Coordination and coherence have been a challenge to government since the inception of government. The development of the public sector has been primarily through continuing specialisation and the creation of organisations that perform a limited number of functions (see Bouckaert, Peters and Verhoest, 2010). That pattern of development has tended to improve performance of the individual programmes, but that improvement has been bought with conflicting programmes, gaps in service, duplication, and a host of other ills that can arise from inadequate coordination in the public sector. As Aaron Wildavsky once argued, coordination has been the 'philosophers' stone' for government that presumably could produce better policy and administration were it to be achieved.

Coordination can mean a variety of different things, and there are also numerous similar concepts such as coherence and policy integration. More recently the term collaboration (Chen, 2010) has been used extensively to describe patterns of organisations working together. In addition, coordination is discussed as both a process and as an outcome of that process, sometimes creating confusion. In this chapter, I will be focusing on the outcomes of processes, and will think of coordination in terms of the rather old but still useful definition supplied by Charles Lindblom. For Lindblom (1965, 15):

> A set of decisions is coordinated if adjustments have been made in it such that the adverse consequences of any one decision for other decisions in the set are to a degree and in some frequency avoided, reduced, counterbalanced, or outweighed.

Although coordination has been a problem for the public sector since the creation of government, there has been an increasing emphasis on improving coordination over the past several decades. This enhanced need for coordination was at least in part in response to the impact of the New Public Management and the attendant tendency to fragment the public sector and increase the autonomy of public agencies (Verhoest et al, 2010). Governments have responded with a number of programmes, such as 'joined up government' in the United Kingdom (see Pollitt, 2003), with most of these programmes tending to rely upon restoring some aspects of hierarchical control over the organisations to create greater coherence. Politically the need for coordination has also been enhanced through the mobilization of client groups – children, women, the elderly – who require services from a range of traditional government departments.

Despite the importance of coordination for policy and governance, there has been relatively little systematic analysis of the politics of coordination (but see Challis et al, 1988; Jennings and Crane, 1994). There have been a number of studies of the barriers to coordination that have emphasised, among other factors, differences in professional understandings of policy, turf battles among public sector organisations (see Bardach, 1998), information hoarding, and a host of other familiar bureaucratic and political ills. Some of these problems of coordination result from the self-interest of the individuals and organisations involved, but many result simply from ignorance and from poor institutional design.

In this chapter I will analyse coordination from two perspectives. The major part of the analysis will be attempting to understand coordination as a collective action problem. Coordination involves multiple actors whose self-interest, or ignorance of the possibilities for improving public services, may prevent them from cooperating in ways that would improve overall performance. Thus, coordinating public policy involves many of the same issues as forming governing coalitions, and I will develop an argument about how to address the issue analytically, if not necessarily practically.

The other, and to some extent competing, perspective about policy coordination is identifying some means for promoting cooperation and collaboration among the actors (see Bardach, 1999). This approach to coordination is not based so much upon rational calculation and bargaining but more on perceived needs to work together, and also on ideational approaches. That is, the assumption of these collaborative approaches is that most people working within the public sector tend to want to produce better outcomes for their clients. Therefore, when those opportunities can be identified the actors involved will indeed cooperate. Even then, however, good ideas may not be enough and cooperation may not emerge autonomously and some agency will be required (see Williams, 2012).

Although having numerous different assumptions, both of these approaches to coordination depend more on agency, while the conventional approach of utilising hierarchy to promote coordination has relied more on structure. Even within these approaches depending on agency, however, there is a tendency to maintain some structural assumptions, for example that network structures are sufficient to generate coordination. There is also a tendency to revert to hierarchical solutions when there are difficulties with the more agency-based models. Therefore, one question which will arise in this chapter is whether coordination can be achieved without the use of hierarchical authority.

Collective action and coordination

One approach to coordination would be that policy and administrative coordination represent yet another example of the collective action problems that arise in political life (Ostrom, 1990; Baldassari, 2011). In the case of coordination there are two or more organisations that have some potential for gains from cooperating, or have the possibilities of creating better outcomes for their clients (and perhaps especially for the public in general) if they work together. While the organisations can potentially provide improved services through cooperation, they also have competing interests. If nothing else they depend upon the same common pool of resources – the public budget – and may therefore not want to risk losing resources through moving away form their status quo.

This combination of inherent competition and possible gains from cooperation is the foundation of much of the familiar problem of coordination. The locus of the benefits and costs, and their timing, may make coordination difficult to achieve even if there were to be some possibility of improvements. In part, the possible budgetary losses are very visible and are central to the existence of the organisation, while the gains from cooperation are more uncertain and remote.

Further, the gains arising from cooperation may accrue to someone else, notably clients or even the public treasury, while the possible losses of budget and power are felt directly by the individual organisation (Schlager, 1995).

Hierarchy has been the conventional means of addressing the problem of coordination in the public sector (but see Chisholm, 1989; Webb, 1991). Political leaders and central agencies in government have developed numerous structures and methods to impose their wills over the organisations within the public sector. The assumption generally is that the central actors have the capacity to produce the behaviours that they demand from other actors (in this case organisations), and can monitor compliance with their preferences. Even with those powers lodged in central agencies, however, coordination is often difficult to achieve as the numerous well-known failures will confirm.

The methods for imposing hierarchical control may be effective in many instances, although organisations often find ways to avoid the imposition of control. But these hierarchical methods for producing coordination may also be expensive for governments. The political actors must expend political capital to ensure that the organisations that are the targets of their coordination activities comply with their demands. Further, they may have to expend other valuable resources, notably information, in order to overcome the resistance of organisations to complying with the desires of the centre of government. Thus, even when hierarchical controls are being imposed, there will still be resistance from the actors that will impose costs on themselves and on government in general.

Options beyond hierarchy

If we assume that hierarchical coordination is the default option for coordination, then the interesting theoretical question is how to understand the possibilities for overcoming the inherent collective action problems without invoking hierarchy.[1] This does not mean, of course, that hierarchy will necessarily be effective in all cases, but only that if less intrusive mechanisms fail then governments will tend to revert to the familiar hierarchical solution to the problem. The fundamental question, again associated with Elinor Ostrom, is whether there is a capacity for self organisation to overcome collective action problems, with coordination being a particular example.

Some of Ostrom's work dealt with collaboration in solving common pool problems and other collective action problems. Other models, however, have been more explicit in addressing coordination among multiple actors who have both competitive and collective goals. One such model, developed by Thomson, Stokman and Torenvlied (2003; see also Stokman and van Oosten, 1994) assumes that the process proceeds through four stages – information sharing, proposing solutions, bargaining over the proposition, and terminating bargaining. Although this model for addressing collective action problems was designed to some extent to understand processes of coalition formation among political parties in a multi-party setting, the same logic may be relevant for policy coordination. There are important differences between these alternative political processes that will be discussed below, but the model may be sufficiently generic to permit to be used for this problem.

Information sharing

The first stage of the process of overcoming collective action problems is sharing information among the involved parties. In the case of government coalition-building this sharing of information means each party providing the other potential coalition partners with information about their preferred positions on policy issues, thus establishing the foundation for finding partners who have sufficient agreement on policy to make a viable partnership in governing. In this case the parties have an incentive to be truthful because they do not want to become part of a coalition with numerous misconceptions about each other's preferences.

Information sharing for public sector organisations may be more problematic than in coalition formation. First, there is the simple problem of with whom does one share the information. In the case of the political parties the potential coalition partners are relatively clear after an election. For policy coordination the relevant actors are less clear, and to some extent all public programmes have some relevance for all others. The important administrative and policy question is where, and how, to draw the demarcating line of relevance so that efforts can be concentrated on the most important coordination issues.

The relevance of different potential partners for sharing information may, in part, be defined by the particular policy problem being addressed. Ministries of Sports and Recreation may not be natural partners for Ministries of Agriculture, but they may both be relevant for addressing problems of health promotion. Further, it may be that organisations will be more willing to share information with organisations that are perceived as more different from themselves, given that they will not be perceived as competitors within the same policy space.

The other problem confronting would-be coordinators at this point is that many if not most public organisations do not want to share information. As has been noted any number of times, information is power in the public sector (see Stinchcombe, 1990) and organisations will tend to hold on to information. Even components of a single organisation may be unwilling to share information, wanting to preserve their own power and autonomy.[2] And if these organisations do engage in some exchanges of information they have incentives to be less than completely forthright about their programmes and their preferences.

The paradox is that in the case of many public sector coordination efforts, hierarchy may have to be invoked before the information exchange can be implemented. Although information sharing may, in itself, be insufficient to produce effective coordination, it often cannot even occur without the intervention of some external actor. In part, unlike formation of new coalitions within government, coordination among public sector organisations may not have a triggering event that virtually forces them to confer with each other. This absence of a trigger is especially true given that the organisations may be located in different cabinet departments, or may be independent organisations – executive agencies – which believe that they are meant to be independent (Verhoest et al, 2010).

The diffusion of information is assumed to play a positive role in promoting coordination, and in the case of forming political coalitions that may be true. In the case of policy coordination information, or at least knowledge, may also be an impediment. That is, one of the barriers to effective coordination is that public sector organisations are also the embodiments of particular epistemic communities (see Zito, 2001). The professional training and the expertise of individual organisations provide them with lenses through which they interpret the policy world. Even if confronted with a common problem, different organisations with different epistemic foundations may perceive the problems differently and therefore confront them differently, and therefore have a limited foundation for cooperation with other organisations.

In some instances coordination activity may simply cease after this information-sharing stage of the process has been completed. One version of the concept of negative coordination (see Scharpf, 1997) would be that if two actors are aware of each other's positions, and attempt to avoid conflicts and negative interactions, then some coordination has been achieved. This negative version is obviously a minimalist conception of coordination but may in some instances be all that is possible to achieve given the distribution of preferences of the parties involved. And negative coordination may function as a necessary first step toward achieving higher levels of coordination in subsequent interactions.

Bargaining: making proposals and bargaining over them

Leaving aside the potential problems, and possibilities, of information as a source of coordination, if we assume that the first stage of the process is fulfilled at least at some minimal level, and organisations do have some information about each other's goals and priorities, then the next two stages of the process involve bargaining toward some consensus. In the case of political parties forming coalitions, this bargaining is argued to proceed through two stages. The first stage is that one political party – typically the largest that will be at the centre of the coalition and provide the prime minister – makes a proposition to other parties for the coalition. The second stage then involves the reactions of the other party or parties to the proposal.

As in the first stage, the analogy to coordinating policy issues is not perfect, but there is sufficient similarity to utilise the model to employ the model in thinking about coordination. The first important difference is that there is not necessarily a natural initiator of the process. As Bates

(1988) and many others have noted, attempts at self-organisation may falter because of the absence of anyone willing to bear the organisational costs. The process is called 'self-organisation' but it does not occur as spontaneously as we all might like, and without overcoming the inertia of the status quo there will be no organisation.

As noted above, the typical model for initiating coordination is that the impetus will come from external actors such as central agencies or political leaders. However, when we attempt to consider more autonomous processes of change, there is often a lead agency that will have the responsibility of beginning the process (see Alexander, 1993; 1995).[3] In most cases this lead agency is identified by the relevant political leadership, while in others it may be quite apparent that one organisation is more central to the policy area than are others. The centre of government may thus be able to delegate and require someone else to bear the costs, or there may be truly autonomous action.

Again, there is the question of whether imposition from some hierarchical actor is necessary to produce the bargaining, or whether the actors themselves are interested in producing higher quality results. There is a large amount of anecdotal evidence pointing to the reluctance of organisations and institutions to move away from their well-established paths in order to coordinate with others, or indeed for any other reason (but see Streeck and Thelen, 2005; Mahoney and Thelen, 2010). This may be simple inertia on their part, or it may be that these organisations are receiving substantial positive returns (Pierson, 2000) from their current position and perceive little reason to endanger those returns by moving toward some uncertain possibility of an improved position.[4]

If we take the role of the lead agency to be the analogue of the initiator of bargaining involved in forming a coalition, then the bargaining will be initiated through this agency. Another way to consider this process of bargaining is to assume that the status quo position for the lead agency represents the initial proposal to form the coalition around the policy. This policy stance already exists and to some extent dominates the policy area, so therefore any bargaining must be about ways in which to modify that position, or perhaps simply to bring other actors more in line with that position.

Paul Sabatier's familiar arguments concerning the advocacy-coalition framework (ACF) (1988; Sabatier and Jenkins-Smith, 1999) provide one framework for approach to this policy bargaining. In this ACF there are two (or potentially more) organisations (or coalitions) seeking to preserve and/or to change policies. Each of these organisations has a policy core that they wish to defend, but they also have more peripheral elements in their policy activities and of their conceptions of public policy that they may be willing to bargain away in order to preserve their core. In the bargaining process that ensues between the actors if there is some common ground then the parties may be able to agree on a move toward that point of agreement.

The Sabatier framework is primarily about bargaining and policymaking within a particular policy subsystem, but the definition of that subsystem is itself an important consideration for issues of coordination. Where, for example, do we draw the boundaries of the health subsystem? Does it include nutrition (agriculture), income maintenance, recreation, housing, or what? Part of the politics of coordination, therefore, may arise in expanding the perceived boundaries of the subsystem and considering how the bargaining then can be conceptualised, or perhaps more appropriately considering policymaking as occurring within a range of overlapping subsystems with relatively permeable boundaries.

Several important points arise from considering coordination from the perspective of the ACF. The first and most basic point is that this bargaining is about public policy, although for many organisations the conflicts arising from coordination and coherence debates are more about power and 'turf.' This displacement of goals is a familiar and often accurate critique of organisations (see Thompson, 2000), both public and private, and certainly emerges clearly when considering bargaining to produce effective policy coordination. The apparent displacement of goals also has a political component, given that most public organisations will be protecting, and responding to, the interests of their clientele groups, so that they are playing a two-level game over policy.

Associated with the above point concerning the centrality of policy in this model is the point that the bargaining about coordination will tend to be about ideas. In many cases the self-interest of the organisation will be rationalised through a set of ideas, but much of the bargaining will be in terms of ideas about policy and mechanisms for delivering policy (Campbell, 2002). Thus, actors seen from the outside as obstructionist or merely self-interested may in their own terms be protecting the underlying concepts about policy that have informed their organisation.

As noted above, this reliance on ideas and bases of knowledge may present more difficulties than would bargaining over money and power. In the case of the latter factors there is a common understanding and a common metric, but when the discussion of coordination is in policy terms and ideas there may be some lack of mutual comprehension among the actors. The different epistemic foundations for understanding policies, and different understandings of the goals of policy, may make cooperation among the actors involved difficult. For example, in the best of all worlds labour market policies and social policies would be closely linked.[5] Even if the actors are closely linked, individuals coming from the labour market side will have as their primary concern jobs and skilling the clients, while those from social services will be more interested in income maintenance and social protection.

The ACF for policy change also appears to assume that there is a single dimension of policy within the subsystem about which the contending organisations have differing ideas. In many policy areas in which coordination is perceived to be important there may be multiple dimensions of policy in play, and some of the conflicts are over how to include and weight those different dimensions. Forming political coalitions also tends to involve multiple dimensions of policy so that the actors involved have to make calculations about how much they may be willing to trade on one dimension in order to gain on other dimensions. The expectation would be that each actor would have one central dimension on which trades may be more difficult, while agreement on peripheral issues may be more possible. This may again lead to coordination outcomes in which second or third best alternatives result from unwillingness to make exchanges on more salient dimensions, especially for the principal actors.

Although the policy bargaining may be reconcilable along the single dimension, or along a limited number of dimensions, there may be ploys available in administrative bargaining that are not available in coalition formation. As implied above, one of the more important means of trying to create coordination is to shift the dimensions of discussion. In this case, as opposed to forming political coalitions, shifting from policy questions to implementation may be a means of finding some common ground. For example, the Australian government has been successful in coordinating the implementation of a number of social policies through implementation, and cross-training the employees (Halligan and Wills, 2008).

An analogous strategy is to shift the discussion away from the points of conflict to policies on which there may be agreement. Similarly there are opportunities for log-rolling in which participants are willing to trade votes on issues for which they have less intense preferences for votes from other participants on issues they find less central to their values or their political goals (see Patty, 2008). By trading votes on those issues the total welfare may be enhanced, although underlying differences may not be resolved.

The final point, implicit throughout this discussion, is that producing coordination and coherence in government may be about conflict as much or more than about cooperation. The institutionalist logic of path dependence is again a useful point of departure for thinking about coordination. We have argued that little change is likely to occur in an ongoing path unless there is some conflict (Peters, Pierre and King, 2005), and the path dependence of uncoordinated programmes and policies is likely also to require some overt discussion. And again this may well be expressed in terms of ideas, with paths likely to persist until there is a good policy concept to replace them.

The conflicting preferences inherent to negotiations in coordination may not be resolvable. The ACF appears to have some rather felicitous assumptions about the willingness of the actors involved to find some common ground, albeit under particular circumstances. The important element in the model, however, appears to be social learning. The ACF assumes that the learning is about the other participant in the bargaining and its approach to policy, but the learning may also be about the possible gains from cooperation. As in the literature on iterative game theory (Axelrod, 1997), continued interaction of actors makes reaching some form of coordinated outcome more probable (see Schlager, 1995).

Termination of bargaining

The final stage in resolving collective action problems is achieving some termination of the bargaining process. Assuming that the initial proposal from the lead agency is not accepted, then the bargaining will continue with counter offers until some agreement is reached. The ACF model described above tends to assume that there will be some splitting of the difference between the parties involved in bargaining and that this will produce an acceptable compromise. This compromise is not, however, the only possible outcome, and that tends to assume that there will be more or less economic contracting along the locus formed by the intersection of the preferences of the actors involved.

Another possible outcome might be that the position of the lead agency dominates. This outcome would be most unlikely in the case of forming a coalition, given that the largest political party would need the involvement of smaller parties, and therefore would have to give away something to form the coalition. For policy bargaining, however, organisations that are more central to the area, and which have more political resources, may be more capable of imposing their own solutions. These influential organisations may also be able to appeal to central agencies and other political actors to impose their policy desires.

Collaboration and cooperation

The above provides one solution to the collective action problem produced through bargaining. There are also models of cooperation based on ideas that can lead to positive coordination outcomes. The assumption of the bargaining is that the solution will almost certainly be somewhere between the preferences of the actors involved. Thus, the general response would be an outcome that is suboptimal from the perspective of all concerned. Using ideas as a means overcoming the inherent conflict among organisations, however, may be able to produce more positive results.

Framing

Ideas may be more important than are other resources or even power (Beland and Cox, 2011). If would-be coordinators can develop ideas for policy that are acceptable to the parties involved, then the goal of common responses to problems across agencies can be achieved. The Sabatier framework mentioned above contains some of the same logic, albeit still assuming that organisational interests, and protection of the policy core of the organisation, are paramount concerns. The ideational approach assumes that those interests can be overcome through the development of ideas and prospective policies that can appeal to them all.

The logic of coordination based on ideas can be seen in part in the 'frame reflection' arguments of Schon and Rein (1994). These two scholars were concerned about policy conflicts in which participants found their disagreements quite basic and could find no common ground. They argued that the basic conflict was over policy frames that were incompatible (on policy framing see Jones, 1994). So long as the participants had these differing fundamental conceptions about what the problem was, and therefore what the solutions might be, then there was little hope of a resolution without the imposition of hierarchy.

The solution to the intractable issue in this model was, therefore, reframing the contentious issues in a manner that was more agreeable to the participants. What is important here is that the assumption is no longer that dispute resolution will be some version of splitting the difference. The hope, and perhaps even expectation, becomes that through reframing the dispute can produce a resolution that is not only acceptable to the participants but also a superior policy solution. Assuming this positive outcome may be excessively optimistic, but it does point to the capacity of thinking about policy and developing new understandings, creating the possibility of producing superior solutions.

The major challenge in this (overly) optimistic perspective is identifying what social mechanisms are available to produce this movement of ideas. Ideas may have some power of their own in policy (see Braun and Busch, 1999; Surel, 2000) but generally will require some means of activation to make them influential, especially when there is another entrenched policy. One way to consider this question is from the perspective of analytic sociology, and consider very fundamental social instruments involved in the process (see Hedstrom 2005; Demeulenaere, 2011). Perhaps the best candidate for the fundamental instrument producing enhanced coordination would be power, and its associated concept of authority, operating through formal hierarchies. But there are also less intrusive instruments that could be utilised to encourage cooperation. Again, we should think about means for creating cooperation and coordination without having to invoke the usual remedy of hierarchy.

Networks

Several of the fundamental mechanisms available for producing the necessary collaboration operate through networks (see Torfing et al, 2011). The assumption here is that although organisations and individuals do have self-interest, most still participate in network structures. Networks surrounding policy areas are now ubiquitous, and form a locus for learning and for tacit if not explicit bargaining among the participants. The huge literature on governance through networks appears to impute almost magical properties to the existence of the networks, but generally fails to consider the mechanisms operating within them.

Thus, while the networks may be a location for producing coordination, they still require some process to produce the coordination. As noted above, diffusion and learning may be one of those processes. Policy diffusion is usually conceptualised as occurring within the same policy area but across government boundaries, whether cross-national or among local governments, or perhaps even across levels within a single system (see Shipan and Volden, 2008). We can, however, consider learning across policies within the same government structure, or within the same policy network that may include government and non-government actors.

Thinking of networks as a means of learning, and therefore of collaboration, makes the point that although we tend to consider coordination occurring through bargaining among organisational leaders, it may be produced more readily lower down in organisations. Public servants in the field charged with implementing programmes when faced with real clients with multiple needs may find better ways of addressing the issues than would senior public servants back in the national capital. Given the prevalence of 'implementation structures' – another form of network if not conceptualised in that manner – responsible for delivering services, the interactions within these can facilitate cooperation and coordination; Hupe, 2011).[6]

Eugene Bardach's (1999) analysis of how to encourage agencies to work together for improved policies also focuses on the lower echelons of organisations, and the seemingly greater capacity of those 'street level bureaucrats' to collaborate when compared to the possibilities in the same organisations at the upper levels. The argument in this case appears more analogous to that of Schon and Rein (1994), in that it depends on reframing the conflicts across policies and programmes in ways that are compatible to the participants. Again, this may be easier to do with lower echelon workers who may not perceive as much need to protect organisational interests. They may, however, perceive the need to defend personal interests, most importantly their jobs. Thus, collaboration may be acceptable so long as it does not result in reducing the number of positions in the organisations involved in the negotiations.

The above discussion of the necessity for agency within policy networks leads to the second possible instrument for generating collaboration – policy entrepreneurship. Or this could simply be characterised as leadership. John Kingdon (1984) is usually associated with the term policy entrepreneur, but scholars before and since and others have discussed the importance of entrepreneurship in making public policy (see especially Roberts and King, 1991). This mechanism for producing cooperation is clearly based on agency, and may be a function of particular leadership abilities, or may arise simply because of the confluence of streams of ideas and opportunities.

Boundary spanners

In the context of producing coordination, one approach to conceptualising leadership is the role of the 'boundary spanner' (Radin, 1996; Williams, 2012) in organisations. Some individuals in organisations, whether because of their structural position (perhaps having more contact with the external environment and other organisations than is common among all members) or because of their personal attributes, play a role that connects two or more organisations. The lower echelons of organisations, and perhaps the very top of public organisations operating in a political environment, may be especially suited for playing this role. But paradoxically these positions may not be as powerful as others within the organisation, and hence may have some difficulty in fostering collaboration.

The potential importance of boundary spanners in producing coordination also raises interesting questions about levels of institutionalisation within the organisation (Martin, 1992). Having a strong and pervasive organisational culture is often cited in the management literature as important for a successful organisation. However, creating that strong internal culture may be a barrier to boundary spanning, given that individuals within any one organisation will be strongly committed to their ideas and goals. To some extent the idea of 'orthogonal cultures' within one organisation, representing the incomplete institutionalisation of the dominant culture, may therefore facilitate boundary spanning (Martin and Siehl, 1990). Boundary spanners encounter the risk of being considered traitors within their own organisations if they become too cooperative with other organisations that may be conceptualised as being competitors (Webb, 1991, 237). This sense of betrayal may be more apparent for the upper echelons of the organisation who are expected to 'fight their corner' and defend the organisation in budgetary and policy debates.

In summary of this section, in addition to the bargaining model of coordination based on the interests of the participants, a somewhat more optimistic approach to coordination is based on the capacity of ideas to create agreement and collaboration among the parties. But ideas, as important as they may be (Schmidt, 2010), can not necessarily move people away from their established positions on their own. Therefore, some means of agency must be introduced in order to make the approach to coordination function. This need for agency is evident whether the emphasis in the argument is on the role of networks in collaboration, or the emphasis is on collaboration through reframing and boundary spanning.

Conclusion: explaining coordination choices

While hierarchy is the default option in situations demanding policy coordination, there are other options. Although hierarchy may appear to be the simplest option, it also involves costs for the actors involved in imposing controls over the other organisations. Not only does hierarchy involve the use of political capital, it also involves significant transaction costs among the actors. Even then, most governments have been developing their central capacities for coordination (Dahlström, Peters and Pierre, 2011), but if there are means of generating coordination without using that authority then the political capital does not have to be expended.

To hierarchy we can add at least the two approaches to coordination developed above. If we continue to assume that hierarchy is the default option for coordination, then the analytic question is when is one alternative approach likely to be successful, or even when is it likely to be invoked by the participants. The first necessary condition for either alternative approach to be used, however, may be that political and administrative leaders at the centre of government do not perceive a necessity for their own intervention. In other words, the issues involved must be considered either sufficiently unimportant, or sufficiently intractable, that there is little advantage for the centre to become involved. If, indeed, a good deal of politics is about avoiding blame for failures (Hood, 2011), then eschewing any involvement in intractable issues will potentially be good politics.

One characteristic issue that would help shape the possibilities of utilising either of these self-organising approaches is just how much an issue can be disaggregated. Bargaining to some extent assumes that there is a common metric for bargaining – usually money – and that a contract of some sort can be reached along that dimension. The monetary metric is useful for both the budgets of organisations and for the distributional consequences of public programmes. Other public programmes, such as those concerned with basic rights, are difficult to disaggregate and bargain about – they are created or they are not. Further, other programmes may be 'large-scale' so that they have to be provided in their entirety or not at all (see Schulman, 1985; see also Steinacker, 2010).

Following from the above is the question of to whom any benefits and costs of coordination accrue. To the extent that an organisation can capture the benefits of cooperating with others then they will be more willing to cooperate. Coordination also inherently involves some transaction costs, so to the extent that these costs can be displaced on another organisation, for example the lead organisation or the hierarchical coordinator, then cooperation is more feasible. While these costs and benefits are to some extent real budgetary consequences of changes in governance arrangements, they may also be politically constructed and may include political and reputational costs and benefits.

Another dimension affecting the selection of approaches to coordination would be the rigidity of the frames being employed by the organisations involved. For example, policy frames that are linked to strong epistemic communities and associated professional communities would be more difficult to alter than would those merely tied to an organisation's path dependence. This is not to denigrate the significance of path dependence in explaining the behaviour of organisations, but when that inertia is reinforced by professional commitments then reframing becomes all the more difficult. In those cases some bargaining and logrolling may be possible, but moving the policy toward a fundament shift of any sort is unlikely.

Structurally, the absence of a lead agency or other formal initiator of cooperation (or the unwillingness of participants to accept the attempted leadership of the lead agency) may make overcoming collective action problems through some the mechanisms of self-organisation difficult. Similarly, the absence of an effective policy entrepreneur or other policy leadership may make the reframing approach less viable. In both these cases the absence of those key role players for self-organisation in the process of coordination may require some hierarchical intervention.

In the end none of these methods for achieving coordination, including the use of formal, hierarchical means, is guaranteed success. The history of government has been that organisations and individuals often feel compelled not to cooperate. This may be because of self-interest, or because of inertia, but the outcomes of attempts at coordination are often disappointing. That is not, however, a reason not to continue trying. And perhaps especially it is not a reason to continue attempting to understand the underlying processes involved in coordination and collaboration within the public sector.

Notes

[1] This question then is analogous to the question posed by Arrow concerning the capacity to overcome collective action problems without imposing hierarchy. The nature of organisational behaviour in the public sector is, if anything, more complex than the questions of individuals operating in voting situations.

[2] One recent example is that the Boston and New York offices of the Securities and Exchange Commission each had some relevant information concerning the Bernie Madoff 'Ponzi Scheme', but did not want to share. Their hope to resolve the problems themselves led the two organisations not to cooperate or share information, and allowed the scheme to persist for another year at least (SEC, 2009).

[3] Alexander (1995) refers to these lead organisations as the 'meso' level of coordination, in contrast to the formal structures at the centre and the actions of individuals at the micro-level.

[4] This was the argument in the original economic approaches to path dependency (see Liebowitz and Margolis, 1995). Although the status quo was suboptimal there was no logic in deserting that suboptimal point and to bear the transaction costs of reaching a presumably superior position.

[5] Some governments, such as Canada, have moved these policies into a single large cabinet department: HRSDC (Human Resources and Skills Development Canada).

[6] Organisations at the centre of government can function as impediments to this potential coordination at the bottom, by imposing rigid rules on the formats for implementation, or through seemingly simple matters such as information systems that are incompatible with each other.

References

Alexander, ER, 1993, Interorganisational theory and practice, *Journal of Planning Literature*, 7, 3, 328–43

Alexander, ER, 1995, *How organizations act together: Interorganisational coordination in theory and practice*, Amsterdam: Gordon and Breach

Axelrod, R, 1997, *The complexity of cooperation: Agent-based models of competition and collaboration*, Princeton, NJ: Princeton University Press

Baldassari, D, 2011, Collective action, in Hedström, P, Bearman, P (eds), *Oxford handbook of analytic sociology*, Oxford: Oxford University Press

Bardach, E, 1998, Turf barriers to interagency collaboration, in Kettl, DF, Milward, HB (eds), *The state of public management*, Baltimore, MD: Johns Hopkins University Press

Bardach, E, 1999, *Getting agencies to work together*, Washington, DC: Brookings Institution

Bates, RH, 1988, Contra-contractarianism: Some reflections on the new institutionalism, *Politics & Society*, 6, 3, 387–401

Beland, D, Cox, RH, 2011, *Ideas and politics in social science research*, Oxford: Oxford University Press

Bouckaert, G, Peters, BG, Verhoest, K, 2010, *Coordination of public sector organizations: Shifting patterns of public management*, Basingstoke: Palgrave

Braun, D, Busch, A, 1999, *Public policy and political ideas*, Cheltenham: Edward Elgar

Campbell, JL, 2002, Ideas, politics and public policy, *Annual Review of Sociology*, 28, 1, 21–38

Challis, L, Fuller, S, Henwood, M, Klein, R, Plowden, W, Webb, A, Whittingham, P, Wistow, G, 1988, *Joint approaches to social policy: Rationality and practice* Cambridge: Cambridge University Press

Chen, B, 2010, Antecedents or processes? Determinants of perceived effectiveness of interorganisational collaborations for public service delivery, *International Public Management Journal*, 13, 3, 381–407

Chisholm, DW, 1989, *Coordination without hierarchy: Informal structures in interorganisational systems*, Berkeley, CA: University of California Press

Dahlström, C, Peters, BG, Pierre, J, 2011, *Governing from the centre*, Toronto: University of Toronto Press

Demeulenaere, P, 2011, *Analytical sociology and social mechanisms*, Cambridge: Cambridge University Press

Halligan, JA, Wills, J, 2008, *The Centrelink experiment: Innovation in service delivery*, Canberra: Australian National University Press

Hedström P, 2005, *Dissecting the social on the principles of analytical sociology*, Cambridge: Cambridge University Press

Hood, C, 2011, *Blame game: Spin, bureaucracy and self-preservation in government* Princeton, NJ: Princeton University Press

Hupe, P, 2011, The thesis of incongruent implementation: Revisiting Pressman and Wildavsky, *Public Policy and Administration*, 28, 1, 63–80

Jennings, ET, Krane, D, 1994, Coordination and welfare reform: The quest for the philosophers' stone, *Public Administration Review*, 54, 2, 341–8

Jones, BD, 1994, *Reconceiving decision-making in democratic politics: Attention, choice and public policy*, Chicago: University of Chicago Press

Kingdon, JW, 1984, *Agendas, alternatives and public policies*, Boston: Little, Brown

Liebowitz, SJ, Margolis, SE, 1995, Path dependence, lock-in and history, *Journal of Law, Economics and Organisation*, 11, 2, 205–26

Lindblom, E, C, 1965, *The intelligence of democracy. Decision making through mutual adjustment*, New York: Free Press

Mahoney, J, Thelen, K, 2010, *Explaining institutional change: Ambiguity, agency and power*, Cambridge: Cambridge University Press

Martin, J, 1992, *Culture in organizations: Three perspectives*, Oxford: Oxford University Press

Martin, J, Siehl, C, 1990, Organisational culture and counterculture: An uneasy synthesis, in Sypher, BD (ed), *Cases in organisational communication I*, New York: Guilford Press

Ostrom, E, 1990, *Governing the commons: The evolution of institutions for collective action*, Cambridge: Cambridge University Press

Patty, JW, 2008, Arguments-based collective choice, *Journal of Theoretical Politics*, 20, 3, 379–404

Peters, BG, Pierre, J, King, DS, 2005, The politics of path dependence: Political conflict in historical institutionalism, *Journal of Politics*, 67, 4, 1275–1300

Pierson, P, 2000, Increasing returns, path dependence and the study of politics, *American Political Science Review*, 94, 1, 251–67

Pollitt, C, 2003, Joined-up government: A survey, *Political Studies Review*, 1, 1, 34–49

Radin, BA, 1996, Managing across boundaries, in Kettl, DF, Milward, HB (eds), *The state of public management*, Baltimore, MD: Johns Hopkins University Press

Roberts, NC, King, PJ, 1991, Policy entrepreneurs: Their activity structure and role in the policy process, *Journal of Public Administration Research and Theory*, 1, 1, 147–75

Sabatier, PA, 1988, An advocacy coalition framework for policy change and the role of policy learning therein, *Policy Sciences*, 21, 2, 129–68

Sabatier, PA, Jenkins-Smith, H, 1999, The advocacy-coalition framework: An assessment, in Sabatier, PA (ed), *Theories of the policy process*, Boulder, CO: Westview

Scharpf, FW, 1997, *Games real actors could play: Actor centred institutionalism*, Boulder, CO: Westview

Schlager, E, 1995, Policy-making and collective action: Defining coalitions within the advocacy-coalition framework, *Policy Sciences*, 28, 2, 242–70

Schmidt, VA, 2010, Taking ideas and discourse seriously: Explaining change through discursive institutionalism and the fourth new institutionalism, *European Political Science Review*, 2, 1, 1–25

Schon, DA, Rein, M, 1994, *Frame reflection: Toward the resolution of intractable policy disputes*, New York: Basic Books

Schulman, P, 1985, *Large-scale policymaking*, New York: Elsevier-North Holland

SEC (Securities and Exchange Commission), 2009, *Investigation of the failure of the SEC to uncover the Bernard Madoff Ponzi scheme – public version*, Washington, DC: SEC, Office of Investigation, OIG 509, August 31

Shipan, CR, Volden, C, 2008, The mechanisms of policy diffusion, *American Journal of Political Science*, 52, 3, 840–57

Steinacker, A, 2010, The institutional collective action perspective on self-organising mechanisms: Market failures and transaction cost problems, in Feiock, RC, Scholz, JT (eds), *Self-organising federalism*, Cambridge: Cambridge University Press

Stokman, F, van Oosten, R, 1994, The exchange of voting positions: An object-oriented model of policy networks, in Bueno de Mesquita, B, Stokman, F (eds), *European Community decision-making*, New Haven, CT: Yale University Press

Stinchcombe, A, 1990, *Information and organisations*, Berkeley, CA: University of California Press

Streeck, W, Thelen, K, 2005, *Beyond continuity: Institutional change in advanced political economies*, Oxford: Oxford University Press

Surel, Y, 2000, The role of cognitive and normative frames in European policymaking, *Journal of European Public Policy*, 7, 4, 495–512

Thompson, JD, 2000, *Organisations in action: Social sciences basis of administrative theory*, New Brunswick, NJ: Transaction Press

Thomson, R, Stokman, F, Torenvlied, R, 2003, Models of collective decision-making: Introduction, *Rationality and Society*, 15, 1, 5–14

Torfing, J, Peters, BG, Pierre, J, Sørensen, E, 2011, *Interactive governance: Advancing the paradigm*, Oxford: Oxford University Press

Verhoest, K, Roness, P, Verschuere, B, Rubecksen, K, MacCarthaigh, M, 2010, *Autonomy and control of state agencies*, Basingstoke: Macmillan

Webb, A, 1991, Co-ordination: A problem in public sector management, *Policy & Politics*, 19, 2, 229–41

Williams, P, 2012, *Collaboration in public policy and practice*, Bristol: Policy Press

Zito, AR, 2001, Epistemic communities, collective entrepreneurship and European integration, *Journal of European Public Policy*, 10, 4, 585–603

Governing local partnerships: does external steering help local agencies address wicked problems?

Steve Martin and Valeria Guarneros-Meza

Introduction

The increasing importance of partnership working has been one of the most notable developments in public policy over the last 40 years (Stoker, 2004; 2011). Collaboration has, it is claimed, become a hegemonic discourse (Skelcher and Sullivan, 2002; 2008), and partnerships have emerged as the instrument of choice when it comes to implementing most public programmes (Turrini et al, 2010). This trend has been reflected in contributions to *Policy & Politics*. Over the last decade, the journal has featured more than 30 papers – spanning health, social care, community policing, child care, community cohesion, the knowledge economy and regeneration – which have referred to partnership in their title, keywords and/or abstract. One of the recurring themes in these papers has been the interplay between hierarchy and networks, and the role of external steering of partnerships (see for example Glendenning, 2002; Hudson and Henwood, 2002; Kuhlman and Allsop, 2008; Fenwick et al, 2012). There are scholars who believe networks are inherently self-organising and self-sustaining – for example Rhodes emphasises the role of '*self-organising, interorganisational networks*' that enjoy a significant degree of autonomy from the state (1997a, 15, italics in the original). Seen from this perspective, external intervention can appear to be an impediment to effective partnership working. However, others have argued that networks continue to operate in the shadow of hierarchy and may in fact benefit from external steering by governments (Scharpf, 1997; Klijn and Koppenjan, 2000).

This chapter contributes to the understanding of the impact of external steering through an analysis of the activities of three multi-sectoral public service partnerships and their ability to deal with complex public policy issues. It addresses three research questions. How have the partners in these networks collaborated in order to address 'wicked problems'? What forms of self-steering do these partnerships exhibit? Has external steering by government helped or hindered them? We conclude that, contrary to some theories of network effectiveness, external steering has been beneficial. However, it is important to differentiate between 'hard steering', by which we mean attempts by government to dictate how partnerships operate through the imposition of top down targets and performance regimes, and 'soft steering', which we define as the provision by governments of funding, information and expertise. We find that soft steering played an important role in helping to establish and mobilise the local partnerships. They also needed self-steering capacity but its nature and extent varied according to context and kinds of issues which they sought to tackle.

The next section of the chapter develops a framework for analysing the kinds of collaborative activities that public service partnerships engage in, the types of self-steering capacity they may exhibit, and the sorts of external steering to which they may be subject. The chapter then describes the policy context in which the three local partnerships that we studied operate. Next, we outline our data sources and research methods. The chapter then provides an empirical analysis of the collaborative activities that the case study partnerships engaged in, their achievements, and the factors which influenced their ability to address 'wicked problems'. The concluding section draws together the main findings, discusses the contribution of our study to understanding of steering of public service networks, and suggests avenues for future research.

Local public service partnerships

Networks are characterised by lateral linkages between autonomous actors displaying a degree of stability and formality (Kickert et al, 1997; Keast et al, 2004). Blanco et al, (2011) draw an important distinction between policy networks (Marsh and Rhodes, 1992), which are dominated by state actors, and network governance (Sorensen and Torfing, 2007), which is a more pluralist concept that decentres public sector bodies. The public service partnerships with which this chapter is concerned are an expression of the former, and their proliferation in recent years reflects a broader, transnational shift away from vertically integrated hierarchical bureaucracies in favour of networked organisational forms (Kickert et al, 1997, Bovaird et al, 2002; Goldsmith and Eggers, 2004). In the private sector networks have been recognised as a source of 'collaborative advantage', particularly in markets that are characterised by rapid innovation and short product cycles (Miles et al, 2005; Bøllingtoft et al, 2009). In the public sector they have been theorised as a response to problems of ungovernability (Mayntz, 1993); a means whereby governments can secure the cooperation of non-state actors (Kooiman, 2003; Van Bueren et al, 2003). In particular they are seen as offering a way of (re)integrating the 'hollowed out' state (Rhodes,

1997b; Fenwick et al, 2012) and as especially suited to addressing 'wicked problems', that is, long-standing public policy issues such as crime and disorder, social exclusion, public health and climate change, for which there are no obvious or straightforward solutions (Ferlie et al, 2011).

Because wicked problems cut across sectors and transcend organisational boundaries (Clarke and Stewart, 1997), they cannot be addressed by agencies working in isolation (Alter and Hage, 1993; Rhodes, 2000; Agranoff, 2007) and are an obvious focus for collaborative efforts. However, the literature demonstrates that partnership working is itself frequently fraught with difficulty. In practice, 'making collaboration work effectively is highly resource consuming and often painful' (Huxham 2003, 420). Managers are concerned primarily with services for which they and their organisations are directly responsible (Martin, 2010). Professional groups hoard information, thus impeding inter-organisational learning (Rashman and Hartley, 2002; Currie et al, 2008), and the fragmentation of career paths and absence of formal record keeping in post-bureaucratic organisational forms, like public service partnerships, renders them particularly susceptible to 'memory loss' (Pollitt, 2009). Some scholars suggest that attempts by central government to steer local partnerships make the task of collaborating even more difficult. In the UK, for example, the Blair government's top down 'modernisation agenda' was at odds with its rhetoric of network governance and emphasis on partnership working (Newman, 2001). Targets and inspection regimes imposed by activist government departments corrupted local networks, preventing knowledge transfer within the health service (Currie and Suhomlinova, 2006; Addicott et al, 2007; Currie et al, 2007) and distorted local authorities' priorities (Wilson, 2003; Davies, 2008). Some scholars argue that local partnerships must therefore be free from government intervention so they can be 'equal, spontaneous, naturalistic and improvisatory, and less routine, hierarchical, structured and orchestrated... more self-managing and self-organising' (Bate and Robert, 2002, 600).

However, there are studies which suggest that external steering can, in fact, be beneficial. Turrini et al (2010) cite evidence that the exercise of fiscal control by a higher tier of government enhances performance. Ferlie et al (2011) found that managers of local networks used the threat of central government intervention to force local actors to work together. Kooiman (2003, 115) argues that the bureaucratic state remains 'a major governing actor' by virtue of its ability to frame the conditions in which networks operate. In this way, hierarchical control is reintroduced into governance of networks, albeit in a somewhat oblique and opaque form (Jessop, 1998), and it follows that central government's influence need not be pernicious if it uses its power to create conditions in which local actors are better able to collaborate (Scharpf, 1997; Klijn and Koppenjan, 2000). These conflicting accounts of the impact of external steering on networks is relevant to wider debates about 'meta-governance', a relatively new term encompassing the governance of external and self-steering of networks (Sorensen and Torfing, 2007), by which we mean the ways in which governments (and other organisations) may seek to initiate, facilitate or constrain network processes (Klijn and Koppenjan, 2012). The impact of external steering is, therefore, central to understanding the role of government in processes of governance.

This chapter seeks to contribute to understanding of the impact of self-steering and external steering through an empirical analysis of the activities and achievements of three Local Service Boards (LSBs), a form of local public service partnership introduced in the UK in 2008. By activities we mean the ways in which agencies worked together to address wicked problems. We analyse these using a framework developed by Keast et al (2007) who identify three types of integration: cooperation, coordination and collaboration. These different forms of partnership working can be seen as situated on a spectrum from low to high levels of integration, that are differentiated by variations in the 'intensity of linkages between organisations, the degree of formalisation involved... the amount of resources and primary actors involved, and the relative threat to autonomy and risk' (2007, 25). According to Keast et al, cooperation describes situations in which agencies maintain a high degree of independence and retain their own budgets, staff, plans and protocols, but are aware of and take into account each other's goals and activities. Coordination describes joint working where agencies align their resources, strategies and activities with each other in order to achieve shared goals. Collaboration involves 'much closer relationships, connections and resources and even a blurring of the boundaries between agencies' (2007,19). In this case, organisations sacrifice autonomy by pooling finances and other resources such as staff and knowledge. There is a significant redistribution of power and major changes in operations, employment conditions and organisational cultures.

We define the partnerships' achievements as the progress they made in addressing wicked problems, including the development of new approaches to service delivery and the securing of improved outcomes for service users and citizens. We analysed self-steering by assessing the extent to which LSBs possessed internal collaborative capacity, which the literature associates with effective partnership working, including a degree of reciprocity, a sense of common purpose, effective communication and joint problem solving by local actors (Huxham and Vangen, 1996; Shortell et al, 2002; Entwistle, 2009); the degree of formalisation of partnership processes (Turrini et al, 2010); the level of network stability (Ferlie and Pettgrew, 1996); and the extent of member activation, by which we mean whether local actors are well connected (Klijn et al, 2010). To examine external steering we analysed the extent to which government promoted, shaped and/or constrained local partnerships through its ability to enact legislation, issue guidance, confer legitimacy, provide funding, impose standards, monitor performance, and share information and expertise (Bache, 2000; Jas and Skelcher, 2005).

Local service boards

Over the last two decades, and particularly under 'New Labour', partnership became the 'new paradigm' for both policy making and public service delivery in the UK (Newman 2001, 104). Local partnerships took centre stage in policy arenas as diverse as regeneration, community safety, employment, education, environmental sustainability and health care (Lowndes and Sullivan, 2004; Perkins et al, 2010). The Welsh Government (hereafter referred to as 'the government') has overall responsibility for the delivery of most local public services in Wales, with the exception of policing, and has placed particular emphasis on the need for collaboration (Martin and Webb, 2009; Simpson, 2011; Sullivan et al, 2012; Welsh Government, 2012). It actively encouraged the formation of LSBs to bring together councils, health authorities, the police and other local organisations to tackle what policy documents described as 'wicked problems' (Welsh Assembly Government, 2008). According to the government's own guidance, these new partnerships were to act as 'local leadership teams pulling together all the partners to agree joint action to achieve better outcomes for citizens' (Welsh Assembly Government, 2007). The intention was not to replace or replicate existing statutory partnerships. Instead, LSBs were encouraged to focus on issues that local agencies believed were not being addressed adequately by existing ways of working.

The government did not insist that every area create a LSB, nor did it prescribe in detail what form they should take. Local agencies were free to choose which wicked problem(s) they addressed, and there was no formal monitoring of their performance. Because of this there was considerable variation in the composition of the partnerships and the activities they engaged in. All LSBs included senior representatives of the police, health service, local authority and third sector, but they varied considerably in size from just five members in some partnerships to more than twenty in others. The issues they chose to focus on spanned a panoply of contemporary policy dilemmas including carbon reduction, regeneration, training for unemployed youth, care for the elderly, criminal and antisocial behaviour, alcohol abuse and rural transport needs.

The government did not, however, leave the partnerships entirely to their own devices. It provided funding and a variety of other forms of support. Each LSB received a core grant of £50,000 per annum and was invited to apply for additional funding to support specific initiatives to address the wicked problem(s) they had chosen to focus on. The government also provided expertise in the form of senior civil servants who were assigned to work with LSBs to give them advice and act as a direct channel of communication with government departments.

Methods

Our fieldwork was carried out in 2010 and focused on three LSBs. These were selected through a three-stage process. First, we analysed published and unpublished documents, including independent baseline evaluations of the pilot programme (CQ Consultancy and CARPP, 2008), policy papers produced by the government and quarterly reports prepared by each of the 22 partnerships which described their achievements. Next, we interviewed senior civil servants who had been responsible for overseeing the implementation of LSB policy and asked them to identify the partnerships which they judged to have made the most progress in addressing wicked problems. By triangulating their views and the documentary evidence we arrived at a shortlist of six LSBs that were seen as the most effective. We then conducted semi-structured interviews with the coordinators of each of these LSBs and the senior civil servants designated to work with them, to learn more about the way in which agencies had worked together and the results they had achieved. We paid particular attention to verified evidence of achievements, such as audited performance indicators and inspection reports. From the six shortlisted LSBs, we selected three that were very different in terms of the communities they served, their size, the wicked problems they had sought to address, and the levels of funding they had received (Table 8.1). Our methodology was therefore a multiple-case, replication design (Yin, 2009). If self-steering and government steering had similar effects in all three cases, there would be reasonable grounds for believing that our findings may be applicable more widely. If however there were variations in the impacts which steering had, we would be less confident about drawing general conclusions from our cases.

Data were collected from the three case studies in two phases. First, we undertook an in-depth analysis of their internal (usually unpublished) papers including project reports and presentations and the minutes of partnership meetings. This supplemented the evidence we had already collected in the process of selecting cases. Second, we conducted semi-structured interviews with the leaders of the main agencies involved in each

Table 8.1: Partnership characteristics and contexts

Network	Socio-economic context	Created	Network members	Wicked issue	Key actors	Funding
Partnership A	Population: 233,000 Former mining communities with high levels of long term unemployment and deprivation including low educational attainment; inadequate housing; and ill health.	2008	Leader of local authority; police chief superintendent; chief executives of local authority, health trust, and local NGO; senior civil servant.	Domestic abuse	Police, local authority (community safety and housing departments), health service, voluntary sector, courts, probation and prison services	£50,000 (from Welsh Government 'Making the Connections' Fund)
Partnership B	Population: 340,000 Capital city of Wales. Ethnically diverse population and prosperous economy (based on finance, service, retail and leisure industries) but with large disparities in quality of life between different parts of the city.	2007	Chief executives of city council; health trust and third sector umbrella organisation; police chief superintendent; chief of fire and rescue service; senior civil servant.	Crime and antisocial behaviour	Police and city council (housing, community safety, waste and parks departments) and then later health service and voluntary sector	£400,000 (initial budget pooled from police and council)
Partnership C	Population: 180,000 Large, rural county with geographically dispersed and relatively elderly population. Economy dependent on agriculture.	2007	Council leader; chief executives of county council, local health board, environmental agency and third sector umbrella organisation; police superintendent; directors of local health board; university and college of further education.	Integration of health and social care	Health board (hospitals, local surgeries), county council (social services department)	£2.5 million (Welsh Government Continuing Health Care Fund)

of the partnerships (including the chief executives of local councils and health authorities and chief police officers), and managers working in their organisations who had been responsible for the day-to-day implementation of the projects initiated by the partnership. A total of seventeen interviews were conducted, and data from these were combined with the evidence from our earlier interviews with partnership coordinators and senior civil servants. Interviews were recorded and transcribed. They followed a topic guide which covered a core set of questions (about the membership and management of the LSB, its activities, achievements and the impacts of self-steering and government steering on its ability to address wicked problems) whilst also allowing scope for interviewees to raise additional issues that they believed to be important.

Following completion of the interviews we coded the activities in which each partnership had engaged in terms of the three forms of integration – cooperation, coordination and collaboration – identified by Keast et al. We analysed the achievements of each of the partnerships using verifiable data including statutory performance indicators and audit and inspection reports, together with evidence provided by interviewees and analysis of reports produced by LSBs. The determinants of the effectiveness of the partnerships were identified from open-ended questions, which enabled interviewees to report those factors that had helped partnerships to address wicked problems. Based on the responses of all interviewees from a LSB we reached an overall judgement of the salience of each form of steering which they had mentioned and coded them as 'low', 'medium' or 'high'.

Findings

Partnership A – Rhondda Cynon Taf

Network A served Rhondda Cynon Taff (RCT), a former mining area now suffering from chronic multiple deprivation including poor health, high levels of unemployment and housing need, and low levels of educational attainment. In 2008 the area also had one of the highest rates of recorded domestic abuse in the UK, and this was the wicked problem that the LSB chose to focus on. Domestic abuse accounted for 16% of all recorded crime and a quarter of violent crime in the area. The majority of victims were young women who were attacked by their partners. Many of the perpetrators were unemployed and incidents were often linked to excess alcohol consumption. Local agencies knew of more than 3,000 victims, but believed that the full extent of the problem was far worse with many incidents in the home going unreported.

A senior civil servant who was working with the LSB recommended adopting an action learning method which analysed the problem from the viewpoint of victims (Turbitt et al, 2010). Consultants were employed to interview a sample of victims and identify a typical case for managers to learn from. The woman who was selected (known by the pseudonym 'Emma') was invited to participate in a day-long event with 60 public managers, at which she spoke in detail about her experiences. The meeting proved a powerful means of demonstrating to public service leaders how existing policies failed victims. It became clear that doctors had not assessed Emma for signs of domestic violence or referred her to other services; the prison service had failed to prevent her assailant from harassing her whilst he was in jail; the local authority had refused to re-house her; and social services had not given her children adequate support. The activities that they agreed in response were indicative of what Keast et al define as 'cooperation'. Most agencies revised their own internal procedures. They also agreed to improve data sharing, provide better information to victims, and put in place stronger safeguards for their children (Table 8.2). But they refrained from deeper forms of integration, such as pooling staff and funding or integrating their information systems. In part this was because data protection requirements restricted their ability to share case notes or identify victims to each other, but it also reflected a lack of incentives for closer joint working. As one of the project managers who worked with victims explained:

> the agencies which would need to hand over funding are not necessarily those who benefit from cross-cutting working.

In spite of these obstacles, interviewees were very confident that agencies had made significant improvements to services for victims of domestic abuse in a short space of time, and that this was already having a discernible impact on the level of domestic violence in RCT. The most recent data available at the time of our research, showed that by 2009/10 the number of recorded minor assaults had fallen by 12%, the number of victims who were harassed by their attackers from prison had gone down, and referrals by other agencies to the police safety unit had increased (an indication of more effective joint working between organisations) (WLGA, 2012). The problems Emma described were well known to specialists in the field, but not to public service leaders. The chief executive of a key local organisation told us that Emma's was 'a harrowing story', and the event at which she had spoken was:

one of the most uncomfortable days of my 38 years in local government.

The project manager explained that the LSB had been able to:

> achieve more in a short time than I could've done plodding on my own trying to influence people from my middle management level…. Having the people at the top saying what they wanted to happen was essential.

There was a strong sense of reciprocity among the leaders of the key agencies in the partnership. None of them wanted to be seen as letting the other members of the LSB down, and they communicated this sense of peer pressure to their subordinates. One chief executive explained:

> you don't actually have power, but you do have influence… the influence you had as leaders within your various fields to go back to your organisation and to make sure [they are]… holding up their part of the bargain.

The partnership had experienced a high level of turnover of public service leaders – only one of the original members of the LSB was still in post at the time of our research. However, it had coped with this instability because their successors were committed to seeing through the service changes that had been agreed.

External steering had been an important factor. Interviewees were unanimous that the LSB would not have been created had it not been encouraged by the government. The partnership's decision to focus on domestic abuse was prompted by government performance indicators that had highlighted the extent of the problem. Initially, the senior civil servant assigned to the LSB was viewed with suspicion by some local agencies who regarded him as 'a spy' sent to check on them. However, he rapidly became 'part of the team':

> [Name of civil servant] has been excellent because, you know, he did embrace the role immediately in that there was the conduit back to WAG [an abbreviation for the Welsh Government].

As well as suggesting that they assess the problem from the victim's perspective, he was also instrumental in securing funding for the project and persuading a government minister to attend key meetings. Network members reported that this helped to secure the participation of the courts, probation and prison services over which the LSB had no formal influence.

Partnership B – Cardiff

Partnership B served Cardiff, a major metropolitan area with an ethnically diverse population and relatively buoyant economy. It had focused on measures to reduce crime and antisocial behaviour in deprived neighbourhoods in the south and south-east of the city. In 2008 Cardiff was languishing at the bottom of the 'Priority 44' league table used by the UK government to measure community safety. The police knew they could not improve matters on their own and welcomed the LSB as a means of establishing stronger links with other agencies. The activities they engaged in involved a combination of cooperation and coordination as defined by Keast et al (Table 8.2). In line with national policy (Home Office, 2010), the police had adopted a neighbourhood-based approach which divided the

Table 8.2: Partnership activities and results

Partnership	Activities	Results
Partnership A	Cooperation Partner organisations taking others' goals into account to reduce barriers encountered by Emma Better data sharing Strengthening of police safety unit New protocols in housing, social care, health, police, prisons, criminal courts, and women's rights services	12% reduction in recorded minor assaults and harassment of victims within a year of implementation
Partnership B	Cooperation and coordination Joint working to reduce crime rates in an efficient and effective way Reconfiguration of service delivery into six neighbourhoods Creation of six virtual teams Information sharing Pooled financial resources Slow inclusion of health and voluntary sectors	Between 2008–10 reduction in: 10% overall crime 19% domestic burglaries 25% antisocial behaviour 27% auto crime
Partnership C	Coordination and collaboration Joint working to reduce delayed transfers of care and deliver a comprehensive health care assessment. Information sharing Pooled assets – buildings, IT, payroll systems Shared staff Legally binding through Section 33 Agreement	Between 2008–10 reduction in delayed transfers of care: from 10,000 to 7 hospital beds In 2010 CRT pilots were delivering home treatment

city into six operational areas. To facilitate joint working, the city council reconfigured its services along the same lines, and the two organisations created six 'virtual' teams comprising staff from both (Carr and Lawson, 2009). They also pooled funding and data. They created a substantial shared budget (£400,000 in 2008/09 and £722,000 in 2009/10) to support community based projects developed by the neighbourhood teams, and employed an analyst to compile regular reports identifying crime 'hotspots' and neighbourhood-level data on public confidence, public satisfaction and community cohesion. In 2010, consortia of General Practitioners (family doctors) were linked to the neighbourhood teams, and new health 'locality teams' (comprising a locality manger, an assistant manager and a locality nurse) were created. The city's third sector umbrella organisation also restructured its operations to create six new neighbourhood officers to work closely with the neighbourhood teams.

Interviewees believed that the partnership had made significant progress in reducing crime and antisocial behaviour. National performance data show that the overall level of reported crime in Cardiff fell by 10% between 2008 (when the LSB was created) and 2010. Domestic burglaries declined by 19%; calls to the police about antisocial behaviour decreased by 25%, and auto crime fell by 27%. Victim satisfaction rose by 7% (the largest improvement in England and Wales), and the city moved in to the top quartile of the 'Priority 44' league table (Cardiff City Council, 2010).

As in Partnership A, interviewees believed that a strong sense of reciprocity among public service leaders had been important. The police chief superintendent and chairs of neighbourhood teams had considerable 'clout', and their staff felt mandated 'from the top' to work in ways that would not previously have been possible. One service manager explained:

> we needed that very, very senior level buy-in from the LSB executive and the chiefs of all the organisations,

and a service director told us that this had:

> brought an unprecedented sense of urgency. For the first time we were in the spotlight.

It was also important that public service leaders understood each other's priorities. A civil servant who had worked closely with the partnership told us that it had been important to:

> get to know each other at a personal level and develop an appreciation of each others' realities.

According to a key member of the LSB, this created a sense of:

> give and take… a willingness to share the credit for successes.

Agencies learnt to support each other publicly and challenge each other in private:

> We put in a lot of time and energy because everyone's reputation is at risk. We hold each other accountable for the whole of our organisations.

A high level of turnover of public service leaders was seen as a potential threat to the LSB's effectiveness. Three of the six founding members had moved on by 2010 and another was due to retire shortly. The senior police officer told us that it would be important that whoever took over from him was committed to the 'ethos of partnering'.

Interviewees believed that external steering had been important. Like their counterparts in Network A, they said that they would not have formed the partnership without encouragement from the government. One service manager explained that his organisation:

> wasn't really keen on the concept, but equally they didn't want to be told two years down the line by the Government, this is what an LSB is and you to have one like this. So they decided that the best approach was probably to be one of the pilots and actually pilot something that suited Cardiff.

UK government policies were also important. They promoted the adoption of a neighbourhood approach to policing, and national league tables highlighted the relatively high level of crime in Cardiff. The UK government backed 'pathfinder projects' in other parts of the country that Cardiff police visited and learned from. Crucially, the Welsh and UK Governments provided much of the funding for the projects developed by neighbourhood teams. This meant that interviewees saw cuts in public spending as a serious threat to future effectiveness. A service manager feared that they would cause organisations to shy away from wicked problems and:

> retreat into their day jobs. If your budgets are under threat the last thing you want to be doing is working in partnership.

Partnership C – Carmarthenshire

Partnership C served Carmarthenshire, a relatively remote rural area with a longstanding problem of lengthy delays in finding suitable care for frail older people who were medically fit to be discharged from hospital, but could not support themselves at home. As a result, hospital beds were 'blocked', forcing others to wait for operations. This is a problem in many parts of the UK. It stems from a lack of coordination between the health service (which is responsible for acute care) and local government (which has a statutory duty to provide community-based care) (Glendinning et al, 2005), and reflects deeply entrenched differences in the organisational structures, professional backgrounds, funding regimes and performance monitoring frameworks in the two sectors (Ferlie et al, 2005).

The relationship between senior health service and local authority managers in Carmarthenshire had broken down amid disputes about who was to blame for the delays and accusations of 'cost shunting'. A service manager explained:

> When I was first appointed it was a horrendous time. The local health board and health trust were at each other's throats... there was no cooperation between directors within the council and no contact with health.

A series of critical inspection reports in 2003 led to the introduction of multi-agency case reviews and improved monitoring systems. This reduced the number of incidents, but the average length of the remaining delays increased, so that by 2007 Carmarthenshire had one of the highest rates of lost bed-days in Wales (Wales Audit Office, 2007). LSB members identified this as an issue requiring their immediate attention, and demanded that the health service and local authority devise a joint strategy to create capacity to treat patients in their own homes, thus freeing up hospital beds. The result was an ambitious plan to create a new category of staff (known as 'generic workers') who were able to provide health and social care in the home, and new multidisciplinary teams (known as Community Resources Teams, CRTs), which brought together a wide range of professions (including social work, enablement, domiciliary care support, chronic disease management, occupational therapy, physiotherapy, and disability resources) under a unified management structure (Table 8.2). Health care professionals and social workers whose roles were being merged viewed the plan with suspicion. Staff came from different professional backgrounds and had different working patterns and pay scales. Trades unions objected to changes in terms and conditions. There were practical problems in sharing patient records because the two agencies' IT systems were incompatible. However, interviewees reported that progress had been made. CRTs were only operating in part of the county by 2010, but the new working practices were enabling procedures such as blood transfusions and the intravenous administration of antibiotics to be performed in patients' homes, and the number of delayed transfers of care had been reduced from 140 in 2008 to just six.

Interviewees reported that the LSB was the driving force behind these changes. A senior officer explained:

> From within our organisations we saw the operational challenges to integration, but the LSB was above that. They ignored operational challenges. They just said 'we want that to happen by such and such a date, do it'. In a bizarre way it was quite refreshing because you did not sit there defending yourself, explaining what you couldn't do, you just knew you had to find a way around it.

Joint working in the Carmarthenshire LSB was much more formalised than in the other two case study partnerships. The history of difficult working relationships meant that the health authority and local council decided to 'lock in' joint working by entering into a legally binding contract (known as a 'Section 33 Agreement') which specified accountability arrangements, complaint and grievance procedures, staff pay and conditions, and responsibilities for overspends. A senior officer explained that:

> by going through that process you'll have got something that won't all unravel,

and a service manager told us:

> It is so interlocked now with the joint posts… and more pooling of budgets… When you interlock all that then it is more sustainable.

As in the other two partnerships, interviewees reported that external steering had been important. Ministers wanted to encourage community-based provision throughout Wales (Welsh Assembly Government, 2010), and saw Carmarthenshire as a 'test case'. So the senior civil servant who was responsible for Health and Social Care asked to be assigned to the LSB. She was credited by interviewees with having helped agencies to resolve their differences. Because of her senior position in the government, health service managers felt compelled to attend LSB meetings and embrace joint working. She was also able to help the partnership access substantial government funding to pilot the generic worker model. Interestingly, interviewees also identified as important a decision by ministers not to accede to a request from trade unions to intervene in disputes about changes to pay and conditions resulting from the formation of CRTs.

Discussion

As explained in the opening section of this chapter, previous studies have reached contrasting conclusions about external steering of networks. Some see it as a hindrance; others believe it is helpful, perhaps even essential, to effective partnership working. Our research contributes to this debate by examining the kinds of steering which enabled LSBs to address wicked problems.

The three partnerships we studied served different types of area, focused on different problems and adopted different integration strategies. The agencies in Partnership A developed a shared analysis of the problem but pursued their own individual solutions. In Keast et al's terms, they cooperated but did not coordinate or collaborate. Partnership B was characterised by cooperation and coordination. Organisations shared information, agreed joint strategies and shared objectives, created cross-agency teams and pooled budgets. In Partnership C the health service and local authority agreed a fundamental and irreversible reconfiguration of staff and services, which has many of the features of collaboration as defined by Keast et al.

Interviewees in all three partnerships believed they had made significant progress in addressing wicked problems, and were able to provide independent evidence to corroborate these claims. Their accounts of what had enabled them to do this, together with the evidence from documentary sources, point to seven important factors. Four relate to capacity for self-steering: a sense of reciprocity, member activation; formalisation of partnership processes; and stability of membership. Three involve external steering by government: ministerial encouragement for the creation of LSBs, the provision of additional finance to the partnerships, and expertise provided by the senior civil servants who were assigned to work with the partnerships. Table 8.3 shows the significance of these seven factors in each of the three partnerships.

These findings lead us to two main conclusions. First, it is clear that LSBs benefitted from government steering, but it is important to note that this was a particular kind of intervention. The government eschewed top down targets and delivery agreements, opting instead for soft steering. Its approach was all 'carrot' and no 'stick'. Moreover, it is striking that

Table 8.3: Factors influencing partnerships' capacity to address wicked problems

	Partnership A	Partnership B	Partnership C
Self-steering			
Reciprocity	High	Medium	Medium
Member activation	High	Medium	Low
Formalisation	Low	Medium	High
Membership stability	Low	Low	High
Government steering			
Legitimacy	High	High	High
Funding	Medium	High	High
Personnel	High	High	High

interviewees from all three LSBs repeatedly identified the same three forms of external steering as having been helpful to them. Ministers gave the partnerships legitimacy and national performance data helped them to define the wicked problems which they chose to address. In all three cases, the civil servant assigned to work with them had provided valuable advice and secured the participation of reluctant partners. They also enabled LSBs to access government funding which Partnerships B and C needed to create new models of service delivery.

Our second conclusion is that while soft steering by government was important it was not the whole story. We purposefully studied partnerships which had made progress in addressing wicked problems. Other LSBs received similar government support but achieved far less. So it seems that external steering is not sufficient on its own to enable partnerships to address wicked problems, success also depends on the capacity of local actors. Our case studies also show that the type of self-steering which is needed varies according to the contexts in which partnerships operate and the types of activities they engage in. Cooperation among the key agencies in Partnership A was facilitated by a strong sense of reciprocity, and the level of activation of public service leaders was much higher than in the other two partnerships. The fact that this partnership was able to rely on loose, informal arrangements, rather than formalised partnership processes, reflected the good personal relations which existed between leaders, and the fact that they were attempting only a limited degree of integration involving low cost actions. Interviewees in Partnership B reported a high level of reciprocity between the police and local council, but only limited involvement of other agencies. There was a moderate level of formalisation of partnership processes: the police and city council agreed a common template for the structure, roles and leadership of neighbourhood teams, but stopped short of legally binding commitments. The history of conflict between the health service and local authority in Partnership C meant that it could not rely on informal agreements. Because of this and the fact that they were attempting to achieve a very high level of integration, the health service and local authority decided to formalise their collaboration in a legally binding contract. Unlike Partnerships A and B, the membership had been stable and interviewees believed that without this it would have been difficult to see through the changes.

It is also important to note that our case studies were multi-sectoral networks seeking to address wicked problems. Local agencies were therefore operating outside of their core competencies and statutory roles. It may be that because of this they were particularly receptive to government support and advice. It is also possible that local public services in the UK are particularly prone to looking to the government for legitimacy and funding because of its history of centralisation. Perhaps their counterparts in other countries are more self reliant. Finally, we studied LSBs at an early stage in their development. It may be that the interplay between external and self-steering will change as partnerships mature.

Notwithstanding these caveats, our findings have some significant implications for theory. They suggest that studies of local partnership working need to pay more attention to the positive impacts which the right kinds of government support can have. Scholars should in future differentiate between soft and hard steering. They also need to consider the interplay between external steering and local capacity. Local partnerships are unlikely to be self-generating or self-sufficient when it comes to addressing complex 'wicked problems'. They require the legitimacy, finance and external expertise that governments can bestow. However, our research suggests that the best outcomes are likely to be achieved where local partnerships are allowed to determine what issues they address and how they operate.

Our conclusions suggest some interesting avenues for further research. Future studies might usefully test whether our findings are replicated in other partnership settings and other countries. There could be value in longitudinal research that charts the interplay between and impact of soft steering and self-steering as partnerships mature. It would also be interesting to analyse the impact of austerity on the ability of governments to provide the kind of soft steering which our case studies benefitted from. Previous research has shown that instability in external environments detracts from network effectiveness and network performance is positively associated with resource munificence (Conrad et al, 2003; Turrini et al, 2010). This suggests that our interviewees were right to see spending cuts as a threat to their ability to address wicked problems, and highlights the need for research to investigate whether local partnerships are able to address wicked problems at a time when governments are no longer willing or able to provide the kinds of support that our case studies received.

Acknowledgement

We thank two anonymous reviewers and the editor for their very helpful comments on an earlier draft of this chapter.

References

Addicott, R, McGivern, G, Ferlie, E, 2007, The distortion of a managerial technique? the case of clinical networks in the UK health care, *British Journal of Management*, 18, 93–105

Agranoff, R, 2007, *Managing within networks: Adding value to public organisations*, Washington, DC: Georgetown University Press

Alter, C, Hage, J, 1993, *Organizations working together*, Newbury Park, CA: Sage

Bache, I, 2000, Government within governance: Network steering in Yorkshire and the Humber, *Public Administration*, 78, 3, 575–92

Bate, SP, Robert, G, 2002, Knowledge management and the communities of practice in the private sector: Lessons for modernising the National Health Service in England and Wales, *Public Administration*, 80, 4, 643–63

Blanco, I, Lowndes, V, Pratchett, L, 2011, Policy networks and governance networks: Towards greater conceptual clarity, *Policy Studies Review*, 9, 297–308

Bøllingtoft, A, Håkonsson, DD, Nielsen, JF, Snow, CC, Ulhøi, JP, 2009, *New approaches to organisation design: Theory and practice of adaptive enterprises*, New York: Springer

Bovaird, T, Loffler, E, Parrado-Diez, S, 2002, *Developing local governance networks in Europe*, Baden Baden: Nomos Verlag

Cardiff City Council, 2010, Options for area based working in Cardiff: Report of the City and County Solicitor, Cardiff: City Council Agenda Item 6, www.cardiff.gov.uk/objview.asp?object_id=16697

Carr, S, Lawson, S, 2009, Cardiff: Transforming neighbourhoods in the Welsh capital, Cardiff: Safer Capital Partnership

Clarke, M, Stewart, S, 1997, Handling the wicked issues: A challenge for government, School of Public Policy discussion chapter, University of Birmingham

Conrad, DA, Cave, SH, Lucas, M, Harveille, J, Shortell, SM, Bazzoli, GJ, Hasnain-Wynia, R, Sofaer S, Alexander, JA, Casey E, and Margolin, F, 2003, Community care networks: Linking vision to outcomes for community health improvements, *Medical Care Research*, 60, 4, 95–129

CQ Consultancy and CARPP (Centre for Action Research for Professional Practice, University of Bath), 2008, *Local service boards: A baseline for evaluation*, Cardiff: Welsh Assembly Government

Currie, G, Suhomlinova, O, 2006, The impact of institutional forces upon knowledge sharing in the UK NHS: The triumph of professional power and the inconsistency of policy, *Public Administration*, 84, 1, 1–30

Currie, G, Finn, R, Martin, G, 2007, Spanning boundaries in pursuit of effective knowledge sharing within networks in the NHS, *Journal of Health Organisation and Management*, 21, 4/5, 406–17

Currie, G, Waring, J, Finn, R, 2008, The limits of knowledge management for UK public services modernisation: The case of patient safety and service quality, *Public Administration*, 86, 2, 363–85

Davies, JS, 2008, Double devolution or double-dealing? The local government white paper and the Lyons review, *Local Government Studies*, 34, 1, 3–22

Entwistle, T, 2009, Partnerships, networks and alliances in collaborative public service delivery, in Ashworth, R, Boyne, GA, Entwistle, T, (eds), *Theories of public service improvement*, Oxford: Oxford University Press

Fenwick, J, Johnston Miller, K, McTavish, D, 2012, Co-governance or meta-bureaucracy? Perspectives of local governance partnership in England and Scotland, *Policy & Politics*, 40, 3, 405–22

Ferlie, E, Fitzgerald, L, Wood, M, Hawkins, C, 2005, The nonspread of innovations: The mediating role of professionals, *Academy of Management Journal*, 4, 1, 117–34

Ferlie, E, Fitzgerald, L, McGivern, G, Dopson, S, Bennett, C, 2011, Public policy networks and wicked problems: A nascent solution?, *Public Administration*, 89, 2, 307–24

Ferlie, E, Pettigrew A, 1996, Managing through networks: Some issues and implications for the NHS, *British Journal of Management*, 7, S81–S99

Glendinning, C, 2002, Partnership between health and social services: Developing a framework for evaluation, *Policy & Politics*, 30, 1, 115–27

Glendinning, C, Hudson, B, Means, R, 2005, Under strain? Exploring the troubled relationship between health and social care, *Public Money and Management*, 24, 4, 245–51

Goldsmith, S, Eggers, W, 2004, *Governing by network: The new shape of the public sector*, Washington, DC: Brookings Institute

Home Office, 2010, Safe and confident neighbourhoods strategy: Next steps in neighbourhood policing, London: Home Office

Hudson, B, Henwood, M, 2002, The NHS and social care: The final countdown?, *Policy & Politics*, 30, 2, 153–66

Huxham, C, 2003, Theorising collaboration practice, *Public Management Review*, 5, 3, 401–23

Huxham, C, Vangen, S, 1996, Working together: Key themes in the management of relationships between public and non-profit organisations, *International Journal of Public Sector Management,* 9, 7, 5–17

Jas, P, Skelcher, C, 2005, Performance decline and turnaround in public sector organisations: A theoretical and empirical analysis, *British Journal of Management,* 16, 195–210

Jessop, B, 1998, The rise of governance and the risks of failure: The case of economic development, *International Social Science Journal,* 50, 155, 29–45

Keast, R, Mandell, M, Brown, K, Wooodcock, G, 2004, Network structures: Working differently and changing expectations, *Public Administration Review,* 64, 3, 363–71

Keast, R, Brown, K, Mandell, M, 2007, Getting the right mix: Unpacking integration meanings and strategies, *International Public Management Journal,* 10, 1, 9–33

Kickert, W, Klijn, E, Koppenjan, J, 1997, *Managing complex networks,* London: Sage

Klijn, E, Koppenjan, JFM, 2000, Public management and policy networks: Foundations of a network approach to governance, *Public Management Review,* 2, 135–58

Klijn, E, Koppenjan, JFM, 2012, Governance network theory: Past, present and future, *Policy & Politics* 40, 4, 587–606

Klijn, EH, Steijn, B, Edelenbos, J, 2010, The impact of network management on outcomes in governance networks, *Public Administration,* 88, 4, 1063–82

Kooiman, J, 2003, *Governing as governance,* London: Sage

Kuhlmann, EC, Allsop, J, 2008, Professional self-regulation in a changing architecture of governance: Comparing health policy in the UK and Germany, *Policy & Politics,* 36, 2, 173–89

Lowndes, V, Sullivan, H, 2004, Like a horse and carriage or a fish on a bicycle: How well do local partnerships and public participation go together?, *Local Government Studies,* 30, 1, 51–73

Marsh, D, Rhodes, RAW (eds), 1992, *Policy networks in British government,* Oxford: Oxford University Press

Martin, SJ, 2010, From new public management to networked community governance? Strategic local public service networks in England, in Osborne, SP (ed), *The new public governance: Emerging perspectives on the theory and practice of public governance,* London: Routledge, 337–48

Martin, SJ, Webb, A, 2009, Citizen-centred public services: Contestability without consumerism, *Public Money and Management* 29, 2, 123–30

Mayntz, R, 1993, Governing failure and the problem of governability: Some comments on a theoretical paradigm, in Kooiman, J (ed), *Modern governance: New government-society interactions,* London: Sage, 9–21

Miles, RE, Snow, G, Snow, CC, 2005, *Collaborative entrepreneurship: How communities of networked firms use continuous innovation to create economic wealth,* Palo Alto, CA: Stanford University Press

Newman, J, 2001, *Modernising governance: New Labour, policy, and society,* London: Sage

Perkins, N, Smith, K, Hunter, DJ, Bambra, C, Joyce, K, 2010, What counts is what works? New Labour and partnerships in public health, *Policy & Politics* 38, 1, 101–17

Pollitt, C, 2009, Bureaucracies remember, post bureaucratic organisations forget?, *Public Administration,* 87, 2, 198–218

Proven, KG, Milward, BH, 1995, A preliminary theory of interorganisational network effectiveness, *Administrative Science* Quarterly, 40, 1, 1–33

Rashman, L, Hartley, J, 2002, Leading and learning: Knowledge transfer in the beacon council scheme, *Public Administration* 80, 3, 523–42

Rhodes, RAW, 1997a, *Understanding governance: Policy networks, reflexivity and accountability,* Buckingham: Open University Press

Rhodes, RAW, 1997b, From marketisation to diplomacy: It's the mix that matters, *Public Policy and Administration,* 12, 2, 31–50

Rhodes, RAW, 2000, The governance narrrative: key findings and lessons from the ESRC's Whitehall Programme, *Public Administration* 78, 2, 345–63

Scharpf, FW, 1997, *Games real actors play: Actor-centred institutionalism in policy research,* Boulder, CO: Westview

Shortell, SM, Zukoski, AP, Alexander, JA, Bazzoli, GJ, Conrad, DA, Hasnain-Wynia, R, Sofaer, S, Chan, BY Casey, E, Margolin, FS, 2002, Evaluating partnership for community health improvement: Tracking the footprints, *Journal for Health Politics, Policy and Law,* 27, 1, 49–91

Simpson, J, 2011, Local, regional, national: What services are best delivered where? A report to Carl Sargeant, Assembly Member, Minister for Social Justice and Local Government, Cardiff: Welsh Government

Skelcher, C, Sullivan, H, 2002, *Working across boundaries: Collaboration in public services,* Basingstoke: Palgrave-Macmillian

Skelcher, C, Sullivan, H, 2008, Theory driven to analysing collaborative performance, *Public Management Review,* 10, 6, 751–71

Sorensen, E, Torfing, J, 2007, Governance network research: Towards a second generation, in Sorensen, E, Torfing, J (eds), *Theories of democratic network governance,* Basingstoke: Palgrave-Macmillan

Stoker, G, 2004, *Transforming local governance,* Basingstoke: Palgrave-Macmillan

Stoker, G, 2011, Was local governance such a good idea: A global comparative perspective?, *Public Administration,* 89, 1, 15–31

Sullivan, H, Williams, P, Jeffares, S, 2012, Leadership for collaboration: Situated agency in practice, *Public Management Review* 14, 1, 41–66

Turbitt, I, Mathias, M, de Jong, J, 2010, The Kafka Brigade: Public management theory in practice, Cardiff: The Kafka Brigade

Turrini, A, Cristofoli, D, Frosini, F, Nasi, G, 2010, Networking literature about determinants of network effectiveness, *Public Administration*, 88, 2, 528–50

Van Bueren, EM, Klijn, EH, Koppenjan, JFM, 2003, Dealing with wicked problems in networks: Analysing an environmental debate from a network perspective, *Journal of Public Administration Research and Theory*, 13, 2, 193–212

Wales Audit Office, 2007, *Follow up review of delayed transfers of care across the whole system – Carmarthenshire Health and Social Care Community*, Cardiff: Wales Audit Office

Welsh Assembly Government, 2007, *Local service boards in Wales – A prospectus for the first phase 2007–08*, Cardiff: Welsh Assembly Government

Welsh Assembly Government, 2008, *Local service boards in Wales – Realising the potential*, Cardiff: Welsh Assembly Government

Welsh Assembly Government, 2010, *Setting the direction: Primary and community strategy delivery programme*, Cardiff: Welsh Assembly Government

Welsh Government, 2012, *Shared purpose – shared delivery: Guidance on integrating partnerships and plans*, Cardiff: Welsh Government

WLGA (Welsh Local Government Association), 2012, *1000 Safer lives project: Final report*, www.1000livesplus.wales.nhs.uk/opendoc/179927

Wilson, DJ, 2003, Unravelling control freakery: Redefining central-local government relations, *The British Journal of Politics and International Relations*, 5, 3, 317–46

Yin, RK, 2009, *Case study research: Design and methods*, Thousand Oaks, CA: Sage

All tools are informational now: how information and persuasion define the tools of government

Peter John

Introduction

One of the most important advances in the study of public policy – occurring over the lifetime of the Policy & Politics journal – is the categorisation of the tools of government into a small number of discrete types.[1] Salamon and Lund (1989, 4) sum up what underlies the concept: 'the notion that the multitude of government programmes actually embody a limited array of mechanisms or arrangements that define how the programmes work'. Analysts should not be dazzled by the variety of different labels governments use, as they usually reduce to a much smaller set of categories based on distinct causal claims. Seminal is the work of Hood (1986; 2007), and of Hood and Margetts (2007), who developed the NATO classification system: Nodality, Authority, Treasure and Organisation. Hood's influential acronym has been complemented by Salamon's more complex and differentiated 14-point scheme (Salamon and Elliott, 2002; Salamon and Lund, 1989); Howlett's classification of continua (Howlett, 2005; Howlett, Ramesh and Perl, 2009; Howlett, 2011); and John's addition of institutions and networks into the mix (John, 2011). Then there is conceptual work on the different dimensions of tools, which seeks to understand the processes of instrumentation and maps out guiding principles behind the tools, what are called meta-tools (Peters and Nispen, 1998; Lascoumes and Le Galès, 2004; 2007; Kassim and Le Galès, 2010).

Nothing in this chapter should detract from the value of such schemes, as they assist an understanding of how the capacity of government may be enhanced or weakened by the resources at its disposal. But such accounts need a second step. As well as an elaboration of the tools of government, it is important to consider the communication between the instrument and those who are intended to receive such commands or encouragements once the tool has been applied. There is, for example, the publication of a law, and then the ways in which the targets of the law get information about the change; or there can be an adjustment in the level of taxation and then citizen or company compliance based on awareness of the new rate. Once this distinction is conceded, there may be less difference between instruments of government as each is mediated and processed by the means of communication, whether encouraging, manipulating, commanding, or conveying norms, which themselves can be customised and shaped by the very same institutions of the state that control the instruments. In this way, the tools of government are all informational to a certain degree.

The tools of government have always had an informational component, but they are more informational now because of a growing awareness among policy makers of the power of signals and norms. Those in government and other public agencies increasingly realise how their messages may be conveyed in ways that yield a far greater effect on outcomes than might be supposed from their lightness of touch. As governments seek to reshape the state in a period of fiscal austerity, they increasingly recognise the importance of carefully crafting the tools of government, refashioning them so they work much better, and do not default to their core characteristics, whether it is over-authoritarian laws that do not work or public finances that crowd out other forms of motivation. Such trends are likely to increase with the greater reliance by government on information technology and digital forms of service delivery (Hood and Margetts, 2007). In short, information provision can guard tools from themselves, and help craft interventions that are more appropriate and effective.

The aim of this chapter is to develop the argument that the tools of government are informational, and are increasingly so in today's environment. It does so through drawing on the literatures on the tools of government, public information campaigns, citizen mobilisation, behavioural economics and risk regulation. The review of the literature shows that the traditional approach to informational provision only yielded weak effects, even if these were valuable for policy makers. But new work in psychology can help policy makers recalibrate the state to get much more from the informational aspect of tools, in particular by using nudge techniques such as defaults and peer effects. With these ideas, policy makers may redesign the tools of government, not just improving the traditional means of conveying information, but in helping laws and financial instruments work more effectively.

The chapter is in six sections. It starts with a review of the use of information and persuasion by government as a discrete activity; secondly, recent debates in behavioural economics and about nudging citizens are introduced; thirdly, the argument is presented that nudge may be applied to a wide range of government activities, taking examples from the recent work of the UK Cabinet Office Behavioural Insights Team; fourthly, there are two brief case studies of research on taxation and of legal regulation; and, finally, in the conclusion there is a discussion of the implication for the literature on the tools of government, and on the capacity of the public sector more generally. The chapter contributes to the literature on the tools of government by stressing how the provision of information and feedback enhance the effectiveness of public policy.

Information as a tool of government

The use of information as a key resource of government has been recognised by writers on the tools of government, such as Hood and Margetts' discussion of nodality. The kinds of activities that are purely information or persuasion-based are public information campaigns, which may contain key messages backed up by evidence. There may be – in addition to or in place of – efforts at persuasion using symbols to try to influence behaviour, where the means are exhortation, encouragement and even negative warnings. The means of information and persuasion might be a leaflet, a magazine, a media campaign on the radio or on television, a door-to-door canvassing exercise, putting up posters, and an attempt to get someone to pledge to do something. Alternatively, it might be more indirect through carrying out interviews with the media, the dissemination of research findings, the briefing of journalists and the sponsoring of events. These campaigns are sometimes targeted to the general population, such as with health or car-driving campaigns, or towards specific groups, such as the elderly, those in ill health or young car drivers. Hood and Margetts discuss the way in which governments provide bespoke messages, which are directed to certain kinds of citizens, say in the form of a customised letter, or where citizens can access, say electronically, if they search for it. Alternatively, some interventions can be information rich. There may be an incentive, but the key to the intervention is the provision of information to change behaviour.

Information provision is not costless. It needs to be collected, designed and commissioned; but it is not at the high end of expenditure choices of governments. It is an attractive policy tool because it appeals to the higher human motivations, both in government as it uses evidence and considered actions, and to the citizens because it appeals to their goodwill, their willingness to listen and to decide for themselves what is the best thing to do. There are also situations where providing information is a no-brainer option. As Balch (1980, 30) writes:

> Often people fail to use a new product, service or behaviour because they are unaware of it or uncertain about its consequences... In such case, where information is the main gap between the potential and the new behaviour, information is what must be

provided. There are numerous examples of this kind of information provision, which we do not appreciate much normally, such as notices saying that the cliff edge is near or the water is deep. And people even ignore these pieces of information.

It is more likely information and persuasion is directed to people who might not necessarily act on it immediately or see it as in their interests to act. So the information needs to persuade as well. An effective message depends on its presentation and ensuring the message is adapted to whoever is likely to respond. There is a marketing industry, which governments have employed, to try to do this. Why should many activities of government, such as actions to promote the take-up of welfare benefits, be any different to the private sector? Effectively the state is persuading individuals to do something and to see the action as beneficial to themselves, with the difference – and advantage – that the state can appeal to wider motivations, such as the desire to do good.

The main weakness of information and persuasion is that there is no compulsion involved, so these messages can be avoided without immediate cost. By being information, the public authority might even be giving permission for them not to be obeyed. It is saying in effect that 'we can't force you not to eat high fats, and we will treat your heart disease that may result, but we would like you to stop because there is this evidence that shows it would be bad'. It is possible to imagine several kinds of response to public information of this kind. One may be immediate cessation of a diet of chips, burgers, sweets, cakes and soft drinks, and their replacement with muesli, steamed fish, vegetables and spring water based on the power of this new information. But it is not likely that one act of providing information will have this effect. It is more likely that people will ignore the message because they enjoy their foods of habit, which are provided cheaply and are easily available locally, and which do not require much effort and knowledge to cook and eat. People cannot observe the immediate consequences of their habits, so they may choose to ignore the message or think that it is really not so bad. They may even decide they enjoy their lifestyle so much they do not care what happens later or prefer to have shorter unhealthy life, positively valuing current pleasure and negatively valuing future costs. This is a well-known phenomenon, called hyperbolic discounting, and explains a range of apparently non-rational behaviours, such as why people do not save for retirement even though they know they should if they are to be comfortable in old age. The problem for information and persuasion is that the need to persuade arises from the future costs that people do not take into account, but changing the way people approach their choices is hard because it is so engrained. Information can make people aware of the costs and benefits, and might induce a short-term change in behaviour, such as towards healthy eating; but it is likely that people will return to their long-term pattern of behaviour once the short-term stimulus has been removed. The diet is kept to for a few weeks, but then they remember the old foods and how nice they were and encouragement by family and friends takes its course. This is the term preference reversal, where a commitment to a new lifestyle can be reversed by even a weak counter stimulus – so the dieter sees a box of chocolates in the office and then consumes them voraciously. Once the diet is broken, there is a downward slide and the person returns to what they were doing before.

There is the tendency for people to resist the message, as a kind of reaction, which is equivalent to taking the opposite point of view in an argument even if you agree with the position of the opponent. Halpern et al (2004, 25) refer to the psychological concept of reactance, where people see an act of persuasion as a threat to their freedom. Finally, too much information makes the information itself routine as it loses its effect – the recipient becomes bored with it. This is easily done in the information-rich western societies with many sources of information. Government announcements will be easily lost amid the many messages the public receives.

So it is no surprise to find a line of sceptical thinking about the power of information and persuasion, partly in reaction. Hyman and Sheatsley, in *Some reasons why information campaigns fail* (1947), argue that 'the very nature and degree of public exposure to the material is determined to a large extent by certain psychological characteristics of the people themselves' (1947, 413). The power of human beings to resist new information and to trust information from peers, family and friends is a powerful obstacle to the impact of new, potentially beneficial information. This does not mean messages are bound to fail. There have been significant changes in behaviour as a result of information. Thus research on the harmful effects of smoking has diffused over time, helped by government information campaigns and by other instruments, such as taxation. The question is how much and over what time period. In addition the academic consensus has switched around again. In a riposte to the earlier article about why information campaigns fail, in 1973 an article appeared in the same journal, called *Some reasons why information campaigns can succeed* (Mendelsohn, 1973). Mendelsohn draws attention to the design of studies, and where more targeted campaigns can have an effect, particularly if they give some thought to the context and viewpoints of the individuals being targeted as well as use evidence about what works. This line of thinking about media influence highlights the many practical things governments and other public actors can do to improve the quality of the information, such as improving the clarity of the message. It is possible to use some well-known techniques of persuasion that involve implying reciprocation, giving a commitment, the appearance of more people doing this, respect for authority (important in public policy) and liking the persuader (Cialdini, 1993; 2012). It is on these developments that the more radical behaviour change or nudge agenda has built.

The simplest example of a persuasive tool is the public information campaign. Here information is presented in an attractive noticeable way to seek to change behaviour. This kind of campaign has been subject to many studies and reviews, in particular meta-analyses and systematic reviews that allow some general inferences to be made about the impact. One area where research is common is health promotion, so it is not surprising to find a meta-analysis, such as Snyder et al (2004), who find an average effect size of 9%. As predicted, they find studies that show addictive behaviours are hard to change. But there does seem to be an effect in relationship to the baseline level of effectiveness, with those people already not inclined to participate being hard to move. Snyder, in a later piece, carries out a review of meta-studies, what can be called a meta-meta-analysis (Snyder, 2007). This sums up the findings of nine meta-reviews, from the US, Western Europe and less developed countries, which is about as good a summary of the effectiveness of these campaigns as it is possible to have. In the US, the effectiveness of health media campaigns is about 5%, a finding that seems to apply in Europe too. So information campaigns are a modest contribution to the effectiveness of public policies and other instruments of government, but are not a means to encourage large behaviour changes.

Using the media to effect change is only one way to communicate messages, and it may be one where the impact of the message diffuses through the large number of pieces of information the citizen gets from different sources. Better maybe to persuade the citizen directly, by a face-to-face communication on the doorstep or by telephone? Here the government tries to resemble the private sector through foot-in-the-door techniques, but with the advantage that the state or other public actor should be expected to get more respect than salesmen trying to offload their products. So the foot in the door is an effective technique in overcoming citizen barriers. State-sponsored organisations may sponsor bands of citizens or professionals to canvass the general population more directly. One example may be efforts to assist the recycling of household waste, which is important to achieve environmental objectives, such as reducing landfill and carbon dioxide emissions. Households are encouraged by recycling facilities and exhortations by government advertisement and local council leaflets; but it may take a door-to-door campaign to encourage them to carry out the activity, with the emphasis on face-to-face contact and on providing information about recycling as well as an attempt at persuasion. There have been a number of studies to test this idea. Schultz (1998) conducted a randomised controlled trial examining the impact on recycling behaviour of providing written feedback on individual and neighbourhood recycling behaviour. Cotterill et al (2009) tested for the long-term effect of an intervention to increase the level of recycling, finding that the level of recycling in the canvassed group rose by 4.3% while the control group fell by 1.1%. Schultz (1998) has shown giving feedback to recyclers increases their participation in the scheme. Feedback cards left by collection crews to highlight boxes that contain contaminated material can be effective in reducing the amount of contamination, and it also is a cheap approach (Timlett and Williams, 2008). Nomura et al (2011) show in a randomised controlled trial that giving feedback to streets about their use of food waste can raise the amount of recycling by 2.8%.

The conclusion to draw from these mobilisation exercises is that they offer potential for state-sponsored groups to engage with the citizens and to encourage them to change their behaviour, not just on the environment, but with regard to political participation and other desirable outcomes (John et al, 2011). But it is likely such attempts will not have a large impact, and affect those individuals who are more likely to carry out the preferred action anyway and have the capacity to change. Canvassing is an important aspect of communicating information and persuading, but because of the limited time to do it and the complexity of organising it, it is never going to be a major tool of government. The effects are modest and tend to be short-lived. But there is a new generation of studies that show that these effects are much stronger when delivered in a way that respects the incentive structure and biases of those for whom the message is intended.

Smart information provision: nudges

The preceding text has drawn attention to the weakness of attempts by government to persuade citizens and other actors to behave differently. Such measures to encourage citizens to act can get stronger leverage by paying attention to the techniques of persuasion. Cialdini (1993) has highlighted some of the means sponsors use to persuade consumers and other participants. The idea is that respondents often comply with requests. The secret is in the framing of the question, such as if it implies reciprocity. Getting commitment, as with pledges, might be an effective way of getting a request accepted. Cialdini's assertion of the importance of authority may be a technique that public sector actors might wish to use. For example, with an airborne disease alert, the public will listen and take notice of public information advertisements. The association of a campaign with the actions of peers will also enhance its impact.

Telling an informant his or her peers have been or will be informed about their behaviour is a powerful form of social pressure. Gerber et al (2008; 2010) carried out an experiment to find out if telling the voter that neighbours will be informed about their voter turnout would be more likely to vote, which had a strong impact. This idea can be applied to use social pressure to improve public outcomes, such as citizens contributing their resources for the good of the community. Cotterrill et al (2013) test the idea that the numbers of books citizens donate to charity will depend on the manner in which they were asked. They find the form of the request matters because people want to be recognised for their public acts. In addition to making people feel good, making them feel anxious when getting the feedback also increases compliance. Experimental work shows that if an authority becomes threatening, then removes the threat, compliance is more likely (Dolinski and Nawrat, 1998).

These examples show that policy makers can use insights from psychology to improve the leverage of existing policies. Much current thinking draws on the strides in knowledge that took place during the last 25 years or so from the work of psychologists and economists such as Slovic, Kahneman and Tverskey (Kahneman, 1973; Kahneman and Tversky, 1979; Kahneman, Slovic and Tversky, 1982; Kahneman and Tversky, 2000). The key idea is that human beings approach problems with a set of pre-set biases, which influence them toward certain kinds of behaviours. They tend not to react to changes in incentives or from the imposition of extra costs in a straightforward way. External agencies can still influence behaviour; but they need to understand the exact nature of these biases so they design highly human-centred policies that go with the grain of cognitions, which can produce strong results in the form of changed citizen behaviours. While the general provision of information might produce apathy and indifference, extra public finance might crowd out or devalue civic action, and regulation might produce resistance or passive non-compliance. Carefully tailored information signals and revisions to the exact way in which citizens interface with the institutions of the state might yield powerful results.

In recent years, the idea that information may be used in a clever or smart way to encourage citizens to behave in ways that are in their own or society's interest has been referred to by the term 'nudge', popularised by Thaler and Sunstein (2009) in their book of that name. The nudge approach uses an element of information provision to get the individual to where he or she wants to go. The state or public authority gives a signal that does not compel the person to something, but alerts them by affecting the way they carry out choices, say by altering the choice architecture, such as the default options on a website, for example.

This is what Thaler and Sunstein call liberal paternalism – not directly controlling what people do, but influencing them through reminders and cues. Important is a default option, or ensuring, if someone has to make a choice, that the default or lazy option is the more beneficial. Thaler and Sunstein give some examples of the types of changes needed. One is a red light that goes off when air conditioning filters need to be changed, so reminding consumers, or an automatic civility email reminder that sends a message to someone sending an angrily-worded email to encourage them to think again about sending it. This is not a rule in a hard sense, but the state or other public bodies arranging things for consumers so they have a chance to think about their choices.

The impact of the behavioural sciences on government

Nudge ideas have been widely discussed by local authorities and central governments across the world, such as in the UK, US and France. In 2004 the UK Cabinet Office's document, *Personal responsibility and changing behaviour: The state of its knowledge and its implications for public policy* (Halpern et al, 2004), made the case for using more knowledge about citizen behaviour, and for applying theories of interpersonal behaviour to construct better policies that engage citizens with the state. Other pioneering publications were the New Economics Foundation (NEF) report, *Behavioural economics: Seven principles for policy makers* (Dawney and Shah, 2005), and Jackson's *Motivating sustainable consumption* (Jackson, 2005). Government interest in the latest thinking was demonstrated by the work that went into MINDSPACE, produced by the Cabinet Office and the Institute for Government in March 2010 (Dolan et al, 2011). This guide gathered together key insights from behavioural economics and psychology, and listed them in its memorable acronym.

These ideas have appeared in UK government documents. For example, they appear in the *Giving* Green Paper (2010b) issued by the Cabinet Office, as well as in the Department of Health's White Paper *Healthy lives, healthy people: Our strategy for public health in England* (2010), and most recently reviewed by the House of Lords' *Behaviour change* (House of Lords, 2011). These ideas have proved popular with other governments too. The Scottish Government has carried out a review of the international evidence for behaviour change initiatives (Southerton et al, 2011). President Obama appointed Cass Sunstein, one of the authors of *Nudge*, to head up the Office of Information and Regulatory Affairs. In France, the Centre for Strategic Analysis of the Prime Minister employed a behaviour science expert, Olivier Oullier, as an advisor on behaviour change policies. The attractiveness of nudging has been due in part to its low cost, much more pertinent in an era of fiscal austerity, and also because it is a complement to conventional policy instruments, such as legislation and regulation.

The main criticism of this approach is that it appears to offer too weak a set of mechanisms to achieve sufficient behaviour change, partly from their concern not to overly burden the citizen. Changing behaviours might require a push or a 'shove' from government, rather than a mere nudge. This is the implication of the House of Lords' report. The potential problem is that given the entrenched nature of the behaviours that governments wish to alter, such as eating habits, the driving of cars and energy use, the use of defaults and information cues on their own may not be enough to shift behaviour and outcomes. Changes in behaviour usually require a combination of interventions, so it may be the case that nudges rely too much on the (important) issues of information provision and choices, rather than on the whole range of government resources. This argument has appeared in criticisms of the attempt by the Coalition government to create more participation and a collaborative approach to service provision, called the Big Society (Sullivan, 2012).

The opposing argument – the one of this chapter – is that behaviour change theory can be directed also to the traditional resources of government. For the tools of finance, organisation and law might themselves be guided by better theories and evidence on behaviour change. Thus nudge both incorporates Thaler and Sunstein's defaults and other light-touch interventions, and the techniques of behavioural economics and psychology, to redesign standard policy instruments and their informational environments. The nudge would be about the presentation of information about an economic incentive, and the way the incentive is structured, rather than the incentive itself. In fact many nudge interventions involve regulatory changes, such as changing the defaults for organ donations when citizens pay their vehicle taxes, or altering the rules on payroll giving. The problem of making strong judgements about the success of behaviour change policies is that it is difficult to maintain a hard and fast distinction between 'soft' and 'hard' tools of government (John, 2011). In addition, it is not possible to draw a clear line between authoritarian commands and informational interventions. For this reason, it is very hard to reject the claim of paternalism. The nudge agenda really assumes that the state knows best, as it involves reducing the choices – however gently – of the citizen (Sugden, 2008; 2009). In this way interventions that involve nudges are just like many other policies that reduce freedoms and choices. There is nothing necessarily light-touch about behaviour change policies.

The incorporation of the manipulation of incentives into nudge has caused controversy. The House of Lords Select Committee on behaviour change attempted its own clarification, setting out a table defining choice architecture as: the provision of information; changes to physical environments; changes to the default policy; and the use of social norms and salience (House of Lords, 2011, 10). Persuasion was seen as a distinct category to information provision, or choice architecture as a whole, and therefore is not classified as part of nudging. The Committee also placed fiscal and non-fiscal incentives outside the choice architecture. But the nudge is not the incentive, but information about the incentive, which helps it work more effectively.

The more coherent way of thinking is to see nudges and information as means to assist conventional forms of policy implementation. As the Minister of State at the Cabinet Office, Oliver Letwin, and his colleagues make clear in the report on energy use:

> These insights are not alternatives to existing policy. They complement the Government's objective to reduce carbon emissions across all sectors, and show how we can support these efforts in relatively low-cost ways. (Cabinet Office, 2011, 3)

Once government considers a new policy intervention, such as changing the default on organ donations, it involves consideration of the full range of policy tools, such as changes in the rules, as well as the softer tools. Aspects of the Green Deal, for example, are implemented by legislation some of which gives rights to tenants to demand energy efficiency in the homes they rent and changing the design of Energy Performance Certificates (EPCs).

As well as inheriting various structures and policies, the Coalition government set up the Behavioural Insights Team as its main institutional innovation in promoting behaviour change. This was created in May 2010, operating from within the Cabinet Office, and is often called 'the nudge unit'. It comprises 13 officials, takes advice from experts, such as Richard Thaler, and has set up an academic advisory panel.[2] Its work is consistent with normal practice in the centre of British government: it does not deliver policies directly, but acts as a champion and helps other departments and private sector bodies to carry out new measures. It had a two-year life, which was extended, and is being prepared for mutual status, to be partly owned by government and by another partner.

The team has pioneered a number of reforms and papers, which involves working with the private sector trying out different kinds of incentives for consumers to change behaviour (see www.cabinetoffice.gov.uk/

behavioural-insights-team). There is also a chapter on health (Cabinet Office, 2010a), which reports the work on smoking cessation, and a chapter on charitable giving, jointly written with the Office for Civil Society in the Cabinet (Cabinet Office, 2011). Particularly influential was the report *Applying behavioural insights to reduce fraud, error and debt* (Cabinet Office, 2012), which highlighted a number of trials to reduce debt from court fines and late payments on tax. Team members offer seminars across Whitehall to encourage the use of behaviour insights.

The team was influential in persuading the Driver and Vehicle Licensing Agency to require those who are renewing their driving licence to choose whether to agree that their organs may be donated in the event of their death. The Behavioural Insights Team worked with the Department for Business Innovation and Skills (BIS) on a consumer empowerment strategy, *Better choices: Better deals* (April 2011) (Department for Business and Cabinet Office, 2011). The team worked with the Department of Energy and Climate Change (DECC) on energy saving, aiding the redesign of EPCs (Cabinet Office, 2011). In keeping with the theme of this chapter, not all the insights have to be 'soft' nudges. Rather than just finding new nudges, the team is interested in identifying low-cost measures that improve public policy and demonstrably work. One example is the midata programme, set out in the Consumer Empowerment Strategy, which arises from a partnership between government and providers, energy firms, mobile providers, search engines, banks, regulators and consumer groups. This gives consumers access, in a portable electronic format, to the data businesses hold on them, which can make it easier for them to switch energy supplier. Moreover, consumers can observe their spending patterns. Here the government is helping to change access to data, which is a regulatory change even the government is working cooperatively with the industry.

One of the key activities of the unit is its use of randomised controlled trials to test interventions, which has become more a feature of its work as the team has settled in and developed its approach. The team worked with Her Majesty's Revenue and Customs (HMRC) in February 2011 to pioneer different wordings for tax return reminders. Even though the letters are a nudge, they are carried out in the context of enforcement, which involves using the legal power of government.

Most of these activities involve a redesign of the provision of information, but which is closely linked to the other kinds of regulatory powers, such as the law or tax collection or IT systems. Overall, these policies show the close connection between the application of information-based ideas, but in the context of the redesign of standard services, such as enforcement. Even though many of these interventions are not currently about information technology, it is easy to see how they may be applied to an interactive form of provision under e-government (Margetts, 2006).

The next two sections are case studies that show how conventional tools are in fact highly structured by their informational context. The first is a review of studies of tax effectiveness; the second sums up studies in restorative justice.

Example 1: taxation

One problem with using taxes as a tool of government is that is not easy to control exactly what happens as a result of the policy. Government may aim to do one thing with a new tax or a tax change, but something different often happens in the end. It is up to the individual or organisation to respond to the incentive, which is hard to tie to a preferred form of behaviour or to ensure the response is not just strategically designed to do the minimum to get the tax benefit. Also individuals may be inattentive to the incentives of the tax system. Much work in economics shows the lack of knowledge individuals have of their marginal tax rates (Lewis, 1982). If individuals do not know what their tax rates are, this effectively nullifies the effects of this instrument. In fact, people are aware of some tax rates. Research shows that tax rules tend to have an effect. For example, the timing of marriages has been found to be based on changes in marginal tax rates, as a study comparing changes in tax policy in Canada and England and Wales shows (Gelardi, 1996). But individuals often respond as much to how the message is framed as the tax itself (McCaffery and Baron, 2003; McCaffery and Slemrod, 2006). The response depends on the presentation of taxes, in particular whether they are visible or not. For example, Chetty et al (2009) carried out a field experiment in the United States on the impact of sales taxes on supermarket purchases. For a three-week period in early 2006 they put prices posted on the shelf excluding the sales tax of 7.375%. At other times consumers were shown the taxes at the checkout. The result of showing the tax in the price tag reduced consumption by 8%.

The lesson of these kinds of study is that much depends on the way in which citizens receive the signals from the tax system (Mullainathan et al, 2009). Going back to the Earned Income Tax Credit (EITC), Chetty and Saez (2009) carried out an experiment that shows better information affects the take-up of the scheme. The experiment was on 43,000 tax filers from a major company in Chicago. Half were randomly allocated to a treatment group. The treatment was a two-minute explanation about how the EITC works given by a tax professional, which was aimed at changing the understanding of the marginal incentives. The researchers found a higher take-up of the advice at the poorer end of the income distribution.

The advice led to increases of the credit by $67, and the treatment group was 2.9% more likely to report EITC amounts than the control group. Though the results were modest, the intervention was very cheap. It seems that taxes plus framing is a powerful combination.

Example 2: regulation and restorative justice

There is large body of work that argues that persuasion and dialogue are at the heart of legal effectiveness. What matters is not just the passing of a statute and the application of sanctions, but how the law is understood by those whom it is intended to affect. For example, Bardach and Kagan (1982) argue that really tough regulatory regimes do not necessarily work. Studying the environmental enforcement in the United States, they find too tough an approach to enforcement undermines the cooperative relationships needed to implement policies effectively. A more flexible approach has a better chance of working. The classic work in this tradition is by Braithwaite (1985), who studied the enforcement of safety regulations for mines in 39 disasters across the world. He discovered that most accidents could be avoided if the law was obeyed, and the best way of getting there is better communication between the owners and the unions, perhaps through deliberative arrangements. Criminal sanctions would not work. This study looked at quantitative data as well as case studies. Braithwaite also reports the selection of pits each year for training, and shows how this affected safety (though this was a non-random selection and may have involved some self-selection on the part of the pits – the ones already well disposed to the reform). Legal penalties remain important. But sanctions should build up gradually after cooperation fails. Toughness should be followed by forgiveness. With its strong results and the passion of its author, this study helped to energise a research programme on restorative justice (see the review in Braithwaite, 2002).

There is a line of work in criminology that tests the efficacy of restorative justice ideas and measures. This is about seeking to provide an alternative to conventional forms of punishment in the criminal justice system. The argument is that conventional forms of legal regulation through sentences and fines tend not to lead to individual behaviour change, and people carry on offending as before. Getting the perpetrators of crime to meet their victims may have a better effect. Note this is still a form of legal regulation, as offenders have to take these actions, but it works in a different way, which allows for more responsiveness. It can take place in different formats, such as through the offender and victim meeting each other when mediated by an expert facilitator, or it can be in a wider group involving families and other people affected – even communities. It has been adopted in a wide range of contexts, in the US, UK, Israel and South Africa (Shapland et al, 2006; Sherman et al, 2005). The core idea is that a suitable form of information provision can strengthen the effectiveness of legal regulation.

The move to examine alternatives or complements to top-down, hierarchical approaches to regulation is called responsive regulation (Ayres and Braithwaite, 1992), which involves adjusting the regulatory regime and using a balance of approaches to get to the right result. This is sometimes called smart regulation (Grabosky and Braithwaite, 1986; Gunningham, Grabosky and Sinclair, 1998), which involves a careful assessment of the strategies open to regulators rather than jumping in with too strong an intervention. These new accounts of regulation have moved the debate forward. Rather than assuming top-down control works or leaving alone is best, it examines the different ways in which legal incentives can act upon a policy problem.

Conclusion

The argument of this chapter rests on two linked propositions. The first is that there is a distinction between the provision of a tool of government, such as a law or new tax, and how the citizen or organisation receives information about it, which may vary in quality and transparency. This means that better kinds of communication affect the delivery of the policy, and this applies to all tools of government. The second is that the early generation of information studies, which showed modest effects, have been superseded by more sophisticated interventions that use the full range of psychological techniques and yield much stronger results. If both these claims are true, then governments should be able to craft information-smart tools into their interventions with the secure knowledge they can obtain better policy outcomes. And this is what governments across the world have been doing, especially in the UK since 2004. In this way, all tools are informational now because of this potential for recalibrating the instruments of the state.

One implication of the argument in this chapter is that the causal claims at the heart of the tools of government literature could be softened: it makes more sense to regard tools as closely allied in the way they communicate preferred forms of behaviour. Often there is little chance of compulsion working very well, or of incentives influencing behaviour, unless they are aligned with the preferences of the citizens or groups who are the targets of the intervention. As more and more of the activities of government are online and are being communicated through the internet, the potential for nudges should grow over time as governments start to realise their capacity to change the relationship between the citizen and the state. With digital-era governance as a likely end-point for most public agencies (Dunleavy et al, 2006), all tools really will be informational, if they were not already.

Notes

[1] This chapter was first presented as a paper to the Colloque International, Les Instruments D'action Publique Mis en Discussion Théorique, 6–8 January 2011, Sciences Po, Paris, then at the *Policy & Politics* 2012 conference: 40 Years of *Policy & Politics*: Critical Reflections and Strategies for the Future, Bristol, 18–19 September. I thank the participants at both events for their helpful questions and comments.

[2] The author is a member of the panel.

References

Ayres, I, Braithwaite, J, 1992, *Responsive regulation: Transcending the deregulation debate*, New York: Oxford University Press

Balch, GI, 1980, The stick, the carrot, and other strategies: A theoretical analysis of governmental intervention, *Law and Policy*, 2, 35–60

Bardach, E, Kagan, R, 1982, *Going by the book: The problem of regulatory unreasonableness*, Philadelphia: Temple University Press

Braithwaite, J, 1985, *To punish or persuade: Enforcement of coal mine safety*, Albany: State University of New York Press

Braithwaite, J, 2002, *Restorative justice and responsive regulation*, Oxford: Oxford University Press

Cabinet Office, 2010a, *Applying behavioural insight to health*, BehaviouralInsights Team, London: Cabinet Office

Cabinet Office, 2010b, *Giving*, Green Paper, Cm 8084, London: HM Government

Cabinet Office, Department of Energy, Climate Change and Communities and Local Government, 2011, *Behaviour change and energy use*, London: HM Government

Cabinet Office, 2012, *Applying behavioural insights to reduce fraud, error and debt*, London: Cabinet Office, www.gov.uk/government/uploads/system/uploads/attachment_data/file/60539/BIT_FraudErrorDebt_accessible.pdf

Chetty, R, Looney, A, Kroft, K, 2009, Salience and taxation: Theory and evidence *American Economic Review*, 99, 4, 1145–77

Chetty, R, Saez, E, 2009, *Teaching the tax code: Earnings responses to an experiment with EITC recipients*, NBER Working Paper No 14836, Cambridge, MA: National Bureau of Economic Research

Cialdini, R, 1993, *Influence: The psychology of persuasion,* (rev edn), New York: Morrow

Cialdini, R, 2012, *Influence: Science and practice* (1st edn), Highland Park, IL: Writers of the Round Table Press

Cotterill, S, John, P, Liu, H, Nomura, H, 2009, Mobilising citizen effort to enhance environmental outcomes: A randomised controlled trial of a door-to-door recycling campaign, *Journal of Environmental Management,* 91, 2, 403–10

Cotterill, S, John, P, Richardson, L, 2013, Pledge campaigns to encourage charitable giving: A randomised controlled trial, *Social Science Quarterly,* 94, 200–216

Dawney, E, Shah, H, 2005, *Behavioural economics: Seven principles for policy makers,* London: New Economics Foundation

Department for Business and Cabinet Office, 2011, *Better choices: Better deals,* London: BIS and Cabinet Office, www.gov.uk/government/publications/better-choices-better-deals-behavioural-insights-team-paper

Department of Health, 2010, *Healthy lives, healthy people: Our strategy for public health in England,* White Paper, London: The Stationery Office

Dolan, P, Hallsworth, M, Halpern, D, King, D, Metcalfe, R, Vlaev, I, 2011, Influencing behaviour: The mindspace way, *Journal of Economic Psychology,* 33, 1, 264–77

Dolinski, D, Nawrat, R, 1998, 'Fear-then-relief' procedure for producing compliance: Beware when the danger is over, *Journal of Experimental Social Psychology,* 34, 27–50

Dunleavy, P, Margetts, H, Bastow, S, Tinkler, J, 2006, *Digital era governance: IT corporations, the state and e–government,* Oxford: Oxford University Press

Gelardi, A, 1996, The influence of tax law changes on the timing of marriages: A two country analysis, *National Tax Journal,* 49, 17–30

Gerber, A, Green, D, Larimer, C, 2008, Social pressure and voter turnout: Evidence from a large-scale field experiment, *American Political Science Review,* 102, 1, 33–48

Gerber, A, Green, D, Larimer, C, 2010, An experiment testing the relative effectiveness of encouraging voter participation by inducing feelings of pride or shame, *Political Behavior,* 32, 409–22

Grabosky, P, Braithwaite, J, 1986, *Of manners gentle: Enforcement strategies of Australian business regulatory agencies,* Melbourne: Oxford University Press in association with Australian Institute of Criminology

Gunningham, N, Grabosky, P, Sinclair, D, 1998, *Smart regulation: Designing environmental policy,* Oxford: Clarendon Press

Halpern, D, Bates, C, Mulgan, G, Aldridge, S, with Beales, G, Heathfield, A, 2004, *Personal responsibility and changing behaviour: The state of knowledge and its implications for public policy,* London: Cabinet Office

Hood, C, 1986, *The tools of government,* London: Macmillan

Hood, C, 2007, Intellectual obsolescence and intellectual makeovers: Reflections on the tools of government after two decades, *Governance,* 20, 1, 127–44

Hood, C, Margetts, H, 2007, *The tools of government in the digital age,* Basingstoke: Palgrave Macmillan

House of Lords, 2011, *Behaviour change,* Science and Technology Sub-Committee, 2nd Report of Session 2010–12, London: The Stationery Office

Howlett, M, 2011, *Designing public policies: Principles and instruments,* Abingdon: Routledge

Howlett, M, 2005, What is a policy instrument? Policy tools, policy mixes and policy implementation styles, in Eliadis, F, Hill, M, Howlett, M (eds), *Designing government: From instruments to governance,* Montreal: McGill Queens University Press

Howlett, M, Ramesh, M, Perl, A, 2009, *Studying public policy: Policy cycles and policy subsystems* (3rd edn), Ontario: Oxford University Press

Hyman, H, Sheatsley, P, 1947, Some reasons why information campaigns fail, *Public Opinion Quarterly,* 11, 412–23

Jackson, T, 2005, *Motivating sustainable consumption,* London: Sustainable Development Research Network

John, P, 2011, *Making policy work,* London: Routledge

John, P, Cotterill, S, Richardson, L, Moseley, A, Smith, G, Stoker, G, Wales, C, 2012, *Nudge, nudge, think, think: Experimenting with ways to change civic behaviour,* London: Bloombury Academic

Kahneman, D, 1973, *Attention and effort,* Englewood Cliffs, NJ: Prentice-Hall

Kahneman, D, Slovic, P, Tversky, A, 1982, *Judgment under uncertainty: Heuristics and biases,* Cambridge: Cambridge University Press

Kahneman, D, Tversky, A, 2000, *Choices, values, and frames,* New York: Russell Sage Foundation

Kahneman, D, Tversky, A, 1979, Prospect theory: An analysis of decision under risk, *Econometrica,* 47, 2, 263–91

Kassim, H, Le Galès, P, 2010, Exploring governance in a multi-level polity: A policy instruments approach, *West European Politics,* 33, 1, 1–21

Lascoumes, P, Le Galès, P, 2004, *Gouverner par les instruments,* Paris: Presses de la Fondation nationale des sciences politiques

Lascoumes, P, Le Galès, P, 2007, Introduction: Understanding public policy through its instruments from the nature of instruments to the sociology of public policy instrumentation, *Governance,* 20, 1, 1–21

Lewis, A, 1982, *The psychology of taxation,* Oxford: Martin Robertson

McCaffery, E, Slemrod, J, 2006, *Behavioural public finance,* New York: Russell Sage Foundation

McCaffery, E, Baron, J, 2003, The Humpty Dumpty blues: Disaggregation bias in the evaluation of tax systems, *Organizational Behavior and Human Decision Processes,* 91, 2, 230–42

Margetts, H, 2006, E-government in Britain: a decade on, *Parliamentary Affairs,* 59, 2, 250–65

Mendelsohn, H, 1973, Some reasons why information campaigns can succeed, *Public Opinion Quarterly,* 37, 50–61

Mullainathan S, Congdon, W, Kling J, 2009, Behavioural economics and tax policy *National Tax Journal*, 62, 375–86

Nomura, H, John, P, Cotterill, C, 2011, The use of feedback to enhance environmental outcomes: A randomised controlled trial of a food waste scheme, *Local Environment,* 16, 637–53

Peters, B, van Nispen, F, 1998, *Public policy instruments: Evaluating the tools of public administration,* Cheltenham, UK: Edward Elgar

Salamon, L, Lund, M, 1989, *Beyond privatization: The tools of government action* Washington, DC: Urban Institute Press

Salamon, L, Elliott, O, 2002, *The tools of government: A guide to the new governance,* Oxford: Oxford University Press

Schultz, P, 1998, Changing behaviour with normative feedback interventions: A field experiment on kerbside recycling, *Basic and Applied Psychology,* 21, 25–36

Shapland, J, Atkinson, A, Atkinson, H, Colledge, E, Dignan, J, Howes, M, Johnstone, J, Robinson, G, Sorsby, A, 2006, Situating restorative justice within criminal justice, *Theoretical Criminology,* 10, 4, 505–32

Sherman, L, Strang, H, Angel, C, Woods, D, Barnes, S, Bennett, S, Inkpen, N, 2005, Effects of face-to-face restorative justice on victims of crime in four randomised, controlled trials, *Journal of Experimental Criminology,* 1, 367–95

Snyder, L, 2007, Health communication campaigns and their impact on behaviour, *Journal of Nutrition Education and Behavior,* 39, 32–40

Snyder, L, Hamilton, M, Mitchell, E, Kiwanuka, J, 2004, A meta-analysis of the effect of mediated health communication campaigns on behaviour change in the United States, *Journal of Health Communication*, 9, Suppl 1, 71–96

Southerton, D, McMeekin, A, Evans, D, 2011, *International review of behaviour change initiatives,* Edinburgh: Scottish Government

Sugden, R, 2008, Why incoherent preferences do not justify paternalism, *Constitutional Political Economy,* 19, 3, 226–48

Sugden, R, 2009, On nudging: A review of nudge: Improving decisions about health, wealth, and happiness, *International Journal of the Economics of Business*, 16, 365–73

Sullivan, H, 2012, Debate: A Big Society needs an active state, *Policy & Politics,* 40, 1, 145–8

Thaler, R, Sunstein, C, 2009, *Nudge: Improving decisions about health, wealth, and happiness* (rev and expanded edn), New York: Penguin Books

Timlett, R, Williams, I, 2008, Public participation and recycling performance in England: A comparison of tools for behaviour change, *Resources Conservation and Recycling,* 52, 622–34

CHAPTER TEN

The politics of engaged scholarship:
impact, relevance and imagination

Matthew Flinders

Just now, amongst social scientists, there is widespread uneasiness, both intellectual and moral, about the direction their chosen studies seem to be taking. This uneasiness, as well as the unfortunate tendencies that contribute to it, is, I suppose, part of a general malaise of contemporary intellectual life. Yet perhaps the malaise is more acute among social scientists, if only because of the larger promise that has guided much earlier work in their fields, the nature of the subjects with which they deal, and the urgent need for significant work today... Not everyone shares this uneasiness, but the fact that many do not is itself a cause for further uneasiness among those who are alert to the promise and honest enough to admit the pretentious mediocrity of much current effort. It is quite frankly my hope to increase this uneasiness, to define some of its sources, to help transform it into a specific urge to realize the promise of social science, to clear the ground for new beginnings... my conception stands opposed to social science as a set of bureaucratic techniques which inhibit social inquiry by 'methodological' pretensions, which congest such work by obscurantist conceptions, or which trivialize it by concern with minor problems unconnected with publicly relevant issues. These inhibitions, obscurities and trivialities have created a crisis in the social studies today without suggesting, in the least, a way out of that crisis. (Wright Mills, 1959)

The publication of the first edition of *Policy and Politics* in 1972 (the ampersand was inserted some time later) was very much in line with C Wright Mills concerns (set out above) about the direction of the social sciences and the need to retain a sense of interconnectedness, accessibility and vision. Indeed, among the contributors to the first edition were a political scientist, a social administrator, an econometrician, an economist and a historian, and their articles all contained references that drew extensively on the literatures of other disciplines. Two of the articles employed qualitative research methods, whereas three offered the results of quantitative techniques; they all, however, located the specific results of their studies within the contours of much broader debates and social concerns (and did so in a broadly engaging and accessible manner). Forty years later this commitment to: interdisciplinary research, accessibility within and beyond academe, considering politics 'as theory' *and* politics 'as practice', and a willingness to 'think big' in terms of the issues and themes it covers, remain the hallmarks of the journal. And yet at the same time it would be foolish to overlook the simple fact that *Policy & Politics* has flourished at a time when political science has become mired in an intellectual malaise about its past, present and future. Indeed, having surveyed the available evidence on the strengths and weaknesses of the discipline, John Trent (2011, 191) suggests that the basic impression 'is one of a discipline in search of its soul and out of touch with the real world of politics'.

At the heart of this disciplinary soul-searching is the growing realisation that a range of factors have conspired to ensure that political scientists generally shy away from: challenging the foundational assumptions of their discipline; undertaking theoretically-informed but also policy-relevant research that has a clear and demonstrable public benefit; focusing on specific problems with the intention of designing real-world solutions; engaging with practitioners of politics for fear of 'soiling their hands'; or writing with passion, emotion or belief that what they actually have to say matters. In this regard political science appears to have followed what might be termed a 'road to irrelevance' along with many other disciplines within the social sciences, arts and humanities. These broad intellectual historiographies have already been mapped out and lamented in a range of influential texts – not least Bent Flyvbjerg's *Making Social Science Matter* (2001), Stephen Toulmin's *A Return to Reason* (2001) and Ian Shapiro's *Flight From Reality* (2005) – which in their own ways harp back to long-standing concerns about the evolution of the social sciences – concerns that were laid bare in C Wright Mills' *The Sociological Imagination* and are clear from the extract at the head of this chapter. What *is* novel about the current state of political science (and the social sciences more broadly) is not so much the existence of internal disciplinary schisms and frictions but the markedly different 'post-crisis' external context.

The global financial crisis has acted as something of a 'game-changer' in the sense that academics and universities are now under far more public pressure to account for the money they receive from the public (in either fees or grants). The specific form of this pressure has varied from country to country. In the United States concerns about the irrelevance of the discipline has taken the form of a congressional decision to remove political science from National Science Foundation funding eligibility; in Canada research funding has explicitly targeted 'community engagement'; in the United Kingdom it has taken the form of the introduction of 'Impact Case Studies' as part of the external research funding allocation system; on the other side of the world the Australian government is experimenting with a new model of 'Star Metrics' in order to try and gauge both the social and economic returns of research funding. More radically calls have been made to democratise the distribution of government research funding – in, for example, Dan Hind's *The Return of the Public* (2010) – through the introduction of public commissioning which would allow citizens to decide upon the allocation of resources. The direction of travel is therefore relatively clear and consistent in the sense that publicly funded scholars are increasingly expected to demonstrate the social value and relevance of their work. For many scholars such external demands represent 'the tyranny of relevance' (that is, an illegitimate threat to academic freedom or little more than the next step in the pathology of systematic commercialisation) or of increasing the risk of 'shooting (or ignoring) the messenger' as politicians pick and choose the research that best supports their positions (see Rogowski, 2013). It is at exactly this point that the ritual invocation of John Henry Newman's *The Idea of a University* (1854) is generally offered as the paradigm of intellectual form, structure and purpose. And yet, as Stefan Collini (2012) has outlined, Newman's vision was and always will be something of a false construct and a poor defence against the pressure of change and social adaptation. Others have argued that the 'relevance debate' provides an opportunity for political science rather than a threat; possibly even the chance to redefine not only the *limits* of the discipline but also the *nature* of the discipline (see Flinders, 2013a).

Such emotive posturing tends to create more heat than light, and one of the most basic problems with what might be termed 'the politics of engaged scholarship' at the present moment is that it lacks any firm conceptual or theoretical underpinning through which to understand the origins, opportunities, risks or challenges of the demand to exhibit greater intellectual *and* social relevance within political science. The central aim of this chapter is therefore to tease apart the nature of contemporary scholarship in order to reveal its component parts, historical shifts in emphasis, the topography of contemporary debates and – most importantly – how the emphasis on relevance should not automatically be viewed as the imposition of a market-based and instrumental logic, but might more productively be viewed as an opportunity to showcase exactly why the study of politics matters, to forge a deeper and more reflective model of scholarship, and to increase the leverage position of the discipline vis-à-vis external research funders.

More specifically, this chapter engages in a form of *conceptual travelling* (hopefully not *conceptual stretching*) by drawing out the insights of the recent 'public sociology wars' and transferring the notion of the 'four sociologies' into the sphere of political science. This provides a novel, fresh and arguably more balanced lens through which to understand and reconceptualise a multilevelled set of debates that include (at the micro-political level) the skills agenda within political science, the incentives that promote certain forms of scholarly activity above all others, and the design and capture of research grants. At the meso- or mid-range level this grasp of *different forms* of scholarship flows into a more sophisticated understanding of *different forms* of relevance, *different forms* of engagement and *different forms* of 'impact'; a discussion about the role of departmental chairs and journal editors as professional and intellectual gatekeepers; and a discussion about the strange depoliticisation of political science. At the macro-political level the disaggregation of different forms of scholarship (each with their own logic, values and styles) exposes the link between the debate concerning the relevance of the political and social sciences and a set of far broader questions concerning (*inter alia*): the need to cultivate public, practitioner, media or any other form of non-academic interest; in the changing role and influence of public intellectuals; and what universities are actually for in the 21st century. The aim of this chapter is not therefore to contribute to the contemporary flaying of political science but to contribute a cure for the ailments that appear to be afflicting the discipline. The cure rests with a plea for a rediscovery of the political imagination, both individually and collectively, and a curious call for scholars to become 'more wobbly'.

This chapter is divided into three interrelated sections that are designed to provoke and stimulate in equal measure. The first section offers a very brief history of political science and attempts to understand what David Ricci (1984) termed 'the tragedy of political science' and how this contributed to the current debate concerning relevance, impact and engagement. The 'tragedy' – for those who want to skip the opening section and go straight to the substantive section on forms of impact and engagement – is that the dominant mode of inquiry within political science was almost (and frequently explicitly) designed to minimise public or practitioner engagement. And, even in sub-fields or countries where rational choice-theoretic and quantitative methods were not dominant, a broader process of 'professionalisation' fuelled a drift towards what Matthew Flinders (2013b) has labelled 'methodological masturbation, theoretical fetishism, sub-disciplinary balkanisation and the development of esoteric discourses' that did little to demonstrate the relevance of the study of politics. As Edward Fullbrook's (2003; 2007) writing on the 'post-autistic economics movement' and the 'crisis' in economics illustrates, political science was by no means alone in evolving in this manner. The second section, however, shifts not to economics but to sociology in order to drill down still further into the relationship between scholarship and relevance. 'Knowledge for what and knowledge for who?' therefore provide basic but central questions that reveal, drawing upon Michael Burawoy's work (see, for example, Burawoy 2005, 2008, 2009), at least four types of scholarship that each cast a quite distinct shadow (or should that be *light?*) upon the notions of relevance, engagement and impact. The third and final section then looks at the implications of this broader approach to scholarship for political science. This chapter concludes that the 21st century will generally reward those scholars and disciplines with the capacity to 'trespass across borders' and who nurture intellectual imagination.

The tragedy of political science

There is something completely wrong (and yet at the same time strangely enjoyable) about attempting to sum up the history of a discipline in just a few short paragraphs. Moreover, the eclectic and fragmented nature of political science makes this a particularly difficult challenge and any interpretation is but one of several possible historiographies. And yet there are also relatively clear and well-recognised schisms within the field that provide important reference points that allow us to explore very much *intus, et in cute* (that is, 'underneath, and in the flesh'). The central cut, however, can only be the demarcation between *political science* and *political studies* that occurred from around the middle of the 20th century. The critical (yet under-acknowledged) aspect of the birth of the behavioural revolution was, however, itself designed to respond to an anxiety that political science had become increasingly irrelevant and detached. David Easton's arguments in *The Political System* (1953) concerning 'the decline of modern political theory' and the 'malaise' of political science', David Truman's sweeping critique in his *The impact on political science of the revolution in the behavioral sciences* (1955), on the alleged failure of the discipline to keep pace with the other social sciences, and Robert Dahl's *Epitaph for a Monument to a Successful Protest* (1961), were each in their own ways crafted with an emphasis on the need for political science to demonstrate a more ambitious and explicit social relevance.

From the 1950s the study of politics became 'a divided discipline' at which a set of scholars who remained committed to a more humanist and socially engaged approach to the study of politics sat at one table, and those 'young Turks' who advocated a more fundamental shift towards the 'scientific' (or even 'economic') study of politics sat at another (see Almond, 1988). This latter approach became synonymous with a notion of 'professionalism' and 'professionalisation' that argued in favour of (*inter alia*): the injection of a clearer separation between academics and policy makers; the rapid development of an esoteric language of politics; a focus on quantitative analysis and data collection; and an attempt to inject a sharp divide between 'facts' and 'values'. There is, as always, a need to inject a degree of caution into claims of such magnitude, and it is undoubtedly true that the behavioural revolution was far less influential beyond North America (and even within the United States it was far less hegemonic than is commonly thought).[1] Nevertheless it is impossible to deny the fact that during the second half of the 20th century political science shifted significantly in terms of its dominant theories, methods, values and aspirations. Whether this complex and multifaceted shift was the result of 'physics envy' (in the 1950s and 1960s) or 'economics envy' (1970s and 1980s) the outcome was that deductive, game theoretic formal modelling and quantitative analysis enjoyed a privileged position in terms of appointments, publication opportunities and funding. Even those political scientists who were not swept along in the behavioural revolution, and retained a commitment to a pluralistic methodology and a humanistic set of values, reacted to an environment that incentivised the production of increasingly esoteric vocabularies and the production of scholarly publications over teaching or public service. The 'tragedy of political science' as David Ricci (1984) argued three decades ago is therefore that as the study of politics became more 'professional' and 'scientific', the weaker it became in terms of both its social relevance and accessibility and as a social force supportive of democracy and democratic values.

To abridge the history of political science in such terms is to work within the parameters of a wide set of accounts of the discipline from Stefan Collini, Donald Winch and John Burrow's *That Noble Science of Politics* (1983), Raymond Seidelman's *Disenchanted Realists* (1985), James Farr and Raymond Seidelman's *Discipline and History* (1993), James Farr, John Dryzek and Stephen Leonard's *Political Science in History* (1995), Jack Hayward, Brian Barry and Archie Brown's *The British Study of Politics* (1999), Sanford Schram and Brian Caterino's *Making Political Science Matter* (2006), Wyn Grant's *The Development of a Discipline* (2010) or Guy Peters, Jon Pierre and Gerry Stoker's *The Relevance of Political Science* (2014) – to name just a few leading texts – and it is hard to review the history of the discipline and not come away with a rather discomforting view of a profession that appears to lurch from crisis to crisis and that has generally evolved in a muddled manner and upon the assumption that, as Heinz Eualau suggested (1959, 94; see also 1977), 'if you don't know where you are going, any road will take you there'. Political science has never been, as Gabriel Almond (1990) succinctly noted, 'a happy discipline' but it would appear to be one that dovetails – to a greater or lesser extent – with Shapiro's (2005) arguments concerning 'the flight *from* reality'. The aim of this section, however, is to look beyond and beneath this relatively well-known narrative and tease out three specific threads of thought that each in their own ways relate to the subtitle of Ricci's (1984) book (that is, scholarship, democracy and politics).

The theme of scholarship brings the 'Perestroika movement' centre stage by revealing the implicit (and sometimes) explicit evolution of a clear 'methodological pyramid' within political science that is based on a narrow 'scientific' idiom, and which places practitioners of rational choice and formal modellers using statistical tests and mathematical proofs at the apex, and single-case studies at the bottom (and all other theories, methods and approaches in between) (see Smith, 2006). This methodological pyramid – first publicly explicated and defended by Arendt Lijphart (1971) in the year before *Policy & Politics* was first launched – remains central to the discipline today, and explains the long-standing criticism of many of the discipline's leading and most prestigious journals by scholars who either do not work within this idiom or simply prefer a more pluralistic approach to theory and methods (for a discussion see Pion-Berlin and Cleary, 2005). The methodological pyramid therefore prizes and (as a result) incentivises a form of scholarship and writing that – irrespective of its contested intellectual value – is highly inaccessible, to the level of parody. The monopoly claim of the scientific trope in the social sciences may not be specific to political sciences – as revealed by the 'post-autistic economics movement'[2] – but its implications are far-reaching in the sense that graduate students and new entrants to the profession are well aware that decisions over prizes, hiring, tenure and promotion depend primarily upon publications and that journals that emphasise formal, mathematical or quantitative approaches tend to be more highly regarded. Viewed from this intradisciplinary perspective, the Perestroika movement was not (and is not) about 'relevance' or 'engagement' or similar social concerns, but remains primarily an *epistemological dispute* that calls for the methodological pyramid to be tipped on its side so that a broader range of theories and approaches (notably 'thick' descriptive methods) can be recognised as valuable and legitimate techniques in their own right. Put slightly differently, the Perestroikans have been less concerned with the *social role* of scholarship beyond academe, and in this sense are a very different intellectual movement to the Caucus for a New Political Science that was formed in 1967 as a response to the perceived 'depoliticisation' of the discipline.

As Clive Barrow (2008) has emphasised, the Caucus for a New Political Science was established to re-emphasise the link between scholarship and democracy, 'to help make the study of politics relevant to the struggle for a better world'. 'Relevance' in this context contained both internal and external dimensions that not only take us *back* to the 'methodological pyramid' (above) but also take us *forward* to a more detailed analysis of different forms of relevance, impact or engagement (as well as fundamental questions about the role of a professor of politics in the 21st century, discussed below). The idea of a 'New' Political Science was forged on the notion of academic-community linkage and the role of political science in promoting public debate, cultivating engaged citizenship and having some form of impact *beyond* academe. The normative implication of this external role was, however, heretical to the apolitical behaviouralists, who by the late 1960s were dominant within the American Political Science Association (APSA). Moreover the organisation's constitution stated that APSA 'will not commit its members on questions of public policy nor take positions not immediately concerned with its direct purpose', which was 'to encourage the study of political science'. The tragedy of political science was, to return to Ricci's (1984) terminology, that at a time when the American public was beset with a range of social challenges (race politics, gay rights, Vietnam, Watergate, etc.) political science appeared institutionally trapped within a myth of value-free science.

The deeper *internal* ambition of the Caucus for a New Political Science was therefore to reveal this myth and, as Christian Bay (1965, 39) argued, 'how much of the current work on political behaviour generally fails to articulate its very real value biases, and that the political impact of this supposedly neutral literature is generally conservative and in a special sense anti-political'. This line of argument was subsequently developed to great effect in Charles McCoy and John Playford's influential *Apolitical Politics* (1967), but can also be taken back to C Wright Mills' critique in *People, Power and Politics* (1963) and Bernard Crick's *The American Science of Politics* (1959). The real aim of highlighting the role and arguments of the Caucus is, however, to emphasise: firstly, that, in terms of its core aims and ambitions, it failed (the methodological pyramid was not toppled), and this is reflected in the rise of the Perestroika movement in 2000. Secondly, the Caucus was as much *a sociological critique* of the relationship between political science and society as it was a methodological critique of behaviouralism; and (finally) taking this sociological perspective still further leads Colin Hay to suggest that political science may, to some extent, have fuelled the growth in 'disaffected democrats' and declining levels of public trust in political processes, political institutions and politicians. Put slightly differently, the discipline's implicit acceptance of a set of baseline assumptions about the generally self-interested nature of human behaviour could only ever really cultivate a degree of cynicism, distrust and negativity. In this sense rational choice theory became less of a predictive science of politics or deductive method and more of a self-fulfilling prophecy which is why Hay (2009, 587) concludes 'political scientists have contributed significantly to the demonisation of politics.... [T]hey trained us, in effect, to be cynical. And in that respect at least, we have been excellent students'.

This focus on the relationship between democracy and scholarship (specifically the role of the latter in supporting the former) leads us neatly to the issue of power, and the simple fact that any call for reform within any institution or profession is in itself a demand for a redistribution of power. This, in turn, forces us to reflect on different forms of power within higher education and the actors who control those resources. What is interesting about the Perestroika movement is the manner in which it has explicitly focused attention on the power of the 'East Coast Brahmin', based at a small number of research-intensive universities, and a behaviouralist hegemony that effectively controls the distribution of jobs, prizes, journal editorships and research monies. The perceived power and reach of this small *über*-elite is so great that many Perestroikans have maintained a veil of anonymity for fear of professional retribution. More broadly, however, it is clear that dominant power structures exert a latent effect on the behaviour of any profession, and in the case of political science (in the United States and beyond) the path of least resistance and maximum reward involves a primary focus on scholarly publications (preferably with a strong quantitative emphasis), and evidence of success in securing competitive research grants (teaching, administrating or contributing to a broad array of 'public goods' beyond the academy are generally secondary concerns). The incentives and sanctions system within political science has therefore traditionally placed little emphasis on the professional responsibilities of scholars *to the public*; the strategy for those who want to progress swiftly through the academic ranks remains one of cultivating a niche (that is, hyper-specialisation), writing specialist books and papers that very few people will ever read, and perfecting the art of learned helplessness and general incompetence so that they are rarely disturbed when teaching and administrative duties have to be allocated.[3] The problem appears to be that the rest of the world has noticed.

In making such strident accusations I am by no means a lone scholar. Theda Skocpol, for example, has underlined the need for ambition, energy and fresh thinking within the discipline, and has defined the current state of the art as being defined by 'navel gazing and talking to ourselves' (*Inside Higher Education*, 7 September 2010). Robert Putnam has similarly highlighted the need for the discipline to reconnect and to 'focus on things that the rest of the citizens of our country are concerned about' (*Inside Higher Education*, 7 September 2010). Jeffrey Isaac, editor of *Perspectives on*

Politics, adopts a similar position when he states 'we're kidding ourselves if we think this research typically has the obvious public benefit we claim for it... We political scientists can and should do a better job of making the public relevance of our work clearer and of doing more relevant work' (*New York Times*, 19 October 2009). The problem is, however, that the dominant scholarly tradition of political science generally rejects such an emphasis and as a result, as Joseph Nye has argued, 'the danger is that political science is moving in the direction of saying more and more about less and less' (*New York Times*, 19 October 2009). And the fact that Isaac and Nye made these comments not in an academic journal or professional magazine but in the *New York Times* illustrates the manner in which the issue of relevance has mutated from a disciplinary sideshow to a very public debate. 'To read many political science journals is to enter an enclosed and often narcissistic world of academics writing for each other', Peter Riddell, the former political commentator for *The Times* and currently director of the Institute for Government, wrote (2010, 552), 'It is self-referential as well as self-reverential, and often unreadable to anyone but a specialist. Real politicians seldom feature in these articles. Indeed the authors seem to feel they would be corrupted by contact with politicians. But politics is not, or should not be, about mathematics or neo-Marxist jargon. Some political scientists do try to bridge the gap with the world of politics. But they are a minority.' The current emphasis on relevance and impact is therefore a response to what C Wright Mills once described (with his typical flourish) as 'the entrance into fruitlessness' (1959, 2000, 22) or what Shapiro (2005) has more recently labeled 'the flight from reality'.

The question is not so much then 'Should political science be more relevant?' for the simple reason that these questions ultimately lead us away from the real issues that will shape the future of the discipline in the 21st century. To even question whether political science should be more relevant, in the sense of being more visible to and engaged with the public, belies a failure to grasp the seriousness of the challenges that face the discipline. The more urgent and pressing questions concern 'knowledge for who and knowledge for what?'; they concern the identification of different forms of engagement and different levels of impact; they concern an awareness that a 'return to reason' will only be achieved by reconsidering the essence of scholarship in the 21st century; and by cultivating a more sophisticated and ambitious political imagination amongst the next generation of scholars. It is for exactly these reasons that the next section embarks upon a little interdisciplinary learning and explores the outputs and outcomes of 'the public sociology wars'.

Public sociology

The starting point for this section can only really be Ernest Boyer's seminal analysis of the historical shift in the role and values of higher education throughout the 20th century. *Scholarship Reconsidered: Priorities of the Professoriate* (1990) represents a damning and far-reaching critique of the gradual withdrawal of academics from the public sphere. A focus on research and publication had, Boyer (1996, 19) argued, undermined the capacity of universities and academics to:

> challenge the established order... act appropriately both as conscience and social critic in the service of the nation. The academy must become a more vigorous partner in the search for answers to our most pressing social, civic, economic and moral problems, and must affirm its historic commitment to what I call the scholarship of engagement.

In a sense, then, by calling for the essence and values of scholarship to be reconsidered, Boyer was re-emphasising the sociological dimension of political science and the civic duty of academics – not to any specific political party, candidate, decision or debate – but to society more generally in terms of viewing knowledge as a civilising and progressive force that could be used to engage and stimulate and, through this – as C Wright Mills (1959, 5) had argued – the 'indifference of publics' might be 'transformed into involvement with public issues'. For Boyer a new paradigm of scholarship had to recognise (and incentivise) four general areas of endeavour (Table 10.1).

The simple fact was, according to Boyer, that universities had evolved to an almost pure focus on 'the scholarship of discovery' to the detriment of their capacity for integrating, sharing or explaining the relevance of that research. The important element of this taxonomy, however, is not that it

Table 10.1: Ernest Boyer's taxonomy of scholarly endeavours

1. The scholarship of discovery	Pushing back the frontiers of human knowledge through research
2. The scholarship of integration	Placing discoveries into their larger scientific and social context
3. The scholarship of sharing knowledge	Disseminating the findings of research and its implications within and beyond the lecture theatre and seminar room
4. The application of knowledge	Rejection of any false wall between 'pure' and 'applied' knowledge and the capacity to demonstrate some notion of social relevance

identifies four forms or types of scholarship, but that they are mutually self-reinforcing or interdependent (even to some degree parasitical). Put slightly differently, the overall standard of *any* scholarship could only be refined, strengthened and improved by stress-testing it against the demands and pressures of the second, third and fourth elements. Research that was tested in the crucible of academic *and* practitioner *and* public arenas was therefore likely to be more sophisticated and robust; it would also be more visible and relevant in terms of informing public debates, promoting engaged citizenship, or assisting in the design of public policy. This interrelationship between different forms of scholarship, with different potential audiences and forms of impact, leads us from the general to the specific and to Michael Burawoy's (see, for example, Burawoy 2005, 2008, 2009) work on the notion of 'public sociology' as a way of further disaggregating and understanding the challenges and opportunities of engaged scholarship.

In 2004 Burawoy used his Presidential Address to the American Sociological Association to offer a powerful critique of the discipline, and to offer a *cri de coeur* in favour of a model of engaged scholarship that dovetailed with Boyer's call for a reconsideration of the meaning of scholarship.[4] 'Responding to the gap between the sociological world and the world we study', Burawoy suggested, 'the challenge for sociology is to engage in multiple publics in multiple ways'. In this regard his thesis was simple and clearly resonates with a set of parallel debates within political science. In its beginning, sociology had aspired to play a positive and progressive role in social change, but by the middle of the 20th century the search for academic prestige and respect had led it to cultivate its own specialised vocabularies and an emphasis on statistical creativity and systemic theory (exactly the 'grand theory' and 'abstracted empiricism... parasites living off the classic social science tradition' that C Wright Mills would rally against in *The Sociological Imagination*). By the early 1960s Seymour Martin Lipset and Neil Smelser triumphantly declared the end of sociology's prehistory, and that the path to a real science was fully open.[5] *Professional sociology* therefore became dominated by a specific 'scientific' paradigm of scholarship that was generally insular, statistical, distant, had pretensions towards objectivity, and was directed exclusively to a scholarly audience. Although it would be wrong to portray Burawoy as a one-man Perestroika movement, it would be fair to suggest that his research and writing stands at the forefront of debates concerning the relevance, impact and future of the social sciences, and in this regard it is necessary to examine his analysis of the interdependency between four types of knowledge or what he labels 'the four sociologies' (Table 10.2).

The link with Boyer's 'taxonomy of scholarly endeavours' (Table 10.1, earlier) and Burawoy's 'four sociologies' are clear, with both attempts to

Table 10.2: Michael Burawoy's four sociologies

	Academic audience	*Extra-academic audience*
Instrumental knowledge	**PROFESSIONAL SOCIOLOGY** Seeks to emulate the natural sciences in the pursuit of knowledge	**POLICY SOCIOLOGY** Seeks to provide knowledge that can be used to solve, help or understand a specific problem, issue or challenge in society
Reflexive knowledge	**CRITICAL SOCIOLOGY** Seeks to expose the values and hidden assumptions that professional sociology seeks to bring to bear on social issues and social relationships. The idea of value-free 'objective' social science is exposed as a dangerous chimera	**PUBLIC SOCIOLOGY** Emphasises accountability to the public and engagement with the public. This may take the form of 'traditional' public sociology in a top-down 'public intellectual' model, or a deeper form of engagement based upon a dialogue and the co-production of knowledge

disaggregate scholarship being tied to a normative attempt to encourage scholars, in general, and academic sociologists, in particular, to engage beyond academe and to risk participating (directly or indirectly) in social and political debates, in order to demonstrate not simply why the social and political sciences matter but also to improve the standard and reflective qualities of that scholarship. The existence of a major and often bruising (and unfortunately often personalised) international debate concerning the 'public sociology *wars*', however, underlines the simple fact that (irrespective of the discipline) the demand for a shift in the nature of scholarship from one dominant tradition or scholarly idiom to another will inevitably lead to the digging of trenches, the loading of weapons and a full-blooded debate about the underlying nature and ambitions of the discipline, as has occurred in relation to the Perestroika debate in political science and the 'post-autistic economics' debate (see Turner, 2005; Piven, 2007; Burawoy, 2009). What really matters for the argument of this chapter, however, is not so much the output or outcome of the public sociology wars but their implications for political science, in terms of understanding the politics of engaged scholarship at a deeper level than has currently been achieved. British political studies, in particular, is in danger of becoming locked into a polarised and potentially pathological intellectual cul-de-sac between those who highlight a 'relevance problem', and those who claim the discipline has never been more relevant and engaged.[6] Such black and white dualisms shed little light on those more interesting and subtle shades of grey that reveal new options and roads to relevance. What then are the implications or lessons for political science that can be gleaned from the public sociology wars, in general, and Burawoy's typology in particular? An answer might focus, very briefly, on at least six issues.

1. Burawoy's 'four sociologies' *maps across* onto political science in several ways.
2. Producing engaged scholarship is about *working smarter not harder.*
3. Engaging with non-academic audiences does *not involve 'dumbing-down'* but *up-skilling.*
4. Engaged scholarship is *reflective and complements* traditional academic scholarship and is needed for the discipline to flourish.
5. Many scholars will feel threatened by an approach to scholarship that *separates the wheat from the chaff.*
6. The social sciences are currently dealing with *a clash of cultures* that are to some extent antagonistic and pathological.

Taking each of these points in turn, it is clear that Table 10.2 is to a great extent transferable across a number of social sciences, and particularly to political science. As a number of histories of the discipline make clear, the study of politics evolved out of an engaged and civic-minded view of the potential of the discipline to educate and shape society for the public good. This emphasis was to some extent lost during the middle of the 20th century and, as a result, the Caucus for a New Political Science emerged in the 1960s to promote a focus on what we might (employing Table 10.2) call *policy* or *public political science.* By the turn of the century the state of the discipline had evolved (or arguably narrowed) to the extent that the reform movement (in this case the Perestroika movement) focused on an academic debate concerning the value of *critical* political science, in the sense of those methods or theories that departed from or criticised the dominant paradigm (discussed above). The current emphasis on demonstrating relevance, cultivating user-engagement and achieving some form of social impact (broadly defined), is therefore an attempt to shift the balance of professional priorities *back* beyond a solely academic audience. This in itself (secondly) highlights the manner in which engagement, relevance and impact take many forms that, in turn, demand the cultivation of new skills and modes of communication. Just as there is no such thing as 'the public', but a range of different groups and communities with differing interests and demands, so are there also a vast number of 'pathways to impact'. Taking this forward, if we draw upon Giovanni Sartori's (1970) famous dictum that 'three slices are sufficient for the purposes of logical analysis' and collapse Burawoy's two academic audiences into one, we can begin to identify the manner in which engaged scholarship requires that academics diversify in a manner that involves working *smarter* but not necessarily *harder* (Table 10.3).

Table 10.3: Pathways to impact and triple writing

Audience	Writing form	Examples
Academic	Phase 1: Research results, findings and implications are written up into traditional academic outputs (i.e. *single writing*)	Books, articles, conference papers, etc.
Practitioner	Phase 2: The same research then forms the basis of a short research-note that is intended to be both accessible and of value to a range of user-groups (i.e. *double writing*)	Professional magazines, pamphlets, practitioner notes, evidence to parliamentary or official inquiries, etc.
Public	Phase 3: In the final stage the research forms the focus of a number of succinct, pithy and even controversial articles for newspapers, magazines or popular websites (i.e. *triple writing*)	Books, social media, blogs, twitters, newspaper articles, etc.

This three-stage 'cascade approach' take us to a third and particularly controversial point: the view amongst many academics that writing for a non-academic audience is synonymous with 'dumbing-down' or 'painting by numbers'. In reality, writing for a broad audience of non-specialists is a challenging endeavour that forces the author to reflect on the meaning and structure of every word, sentence and paragraph, in a manner that is rarely experienced in academic life. Bereft of the intellectual safety blankets of copious references, footnotes and jargon, academics are required to approach their topic in a completely new manner. Engaged scholarship therefore requires a crisp, clear and precise writing style that resonates with George Orwell's counsel in 'Politics and the English Language' (1946), but which subsequently became highly unfashionable within academe. Pushing this point still further, it is more than possible that a talented scholar might produce works that are at-one-and-the-same-time both of interest to and accessible to the professor, the politician, the practitioner and the public. Double and triple conversations across and between various parts of society can be sparked by very special books – WEB Du Bois' *The Souls of Black Folk* (1903), David Riesman's *The Lonely Crowd* (1950), Hannah Arendt's *The Human Condition* (1958), C Wright Mills' *The Sociological Imagination* (1959), Bernard Crick's *In Defence of Politics* (1962), Robert Bellah's *Habits of the Heart* (1985), Gunnar Myrdal's *An American Dilemma* (1944), James C Scott's *Seeing Like a State* (1999), Robert Putnam's *Bowling Alone* (2000)

– that are written by academics and draw upon scholarly research in a manner that reveals a deftness of touch and mind that forges a connection with readers far beyond academe. In a sense they carry academic research into the public realm.

This flows into the fourth reason that 'the public sociology wars' are relevant to the current debate within political science: engaged scholarship is *reflective and complements* traditional academic scholarship. This is a critical point. Burawoy's 'four types' of sociology are not independent or self-contained but are, in fact, interdependent and mutually reinforcing. The same is true for political science, and yet many scholars continue to see *policy* or *public* political science as little more than a cosmetic 'add-on', as a second-class endeavour undertaken solely to secure funding to do 'real' research (that is, traditional academic scholarship). In reality the *academic-practitioner-public* spectrum (Table 10.3, above) is more akin to a set of concentric circles or an intellectual ecosystem, in which a failure to nourish one element draws the whole system into a precarious state. My own experience has taught me that engaged scholarship tends to become dynamic and self-sustaining in often quite unexpected ways: a newspaper column or memorandum to a parliamentary committee might lead to an invitation to sit on a review panel that, in turn, opens up new research opportunities (and funding); a pamphlet written for a think tank is picked up by a foreign government and suddenly reveals virgin intellectual terrain; or – most recently – an appearance at a major international book festival forces me to reflect on my own assumptions about public attitudes to politics.[7] The politics of engaged scholarship is about opening up new horizons, not about closing them down. And yet it can also be brutal and unforgiving in many different ways.

The politics of engaged scholarship tends to be more immediate and personal than is generally experienced within a narrow and traditional approach to scholarship, for the simple fact that it forces scholars to place their heads above the parapet in one way or another. This is neither 'good' nor 'bad' but is more a symptom of the fact that the modern academic cannot survive without a thick skin. There are broadly three dimensions to this fifth point (one political, one technical, one scholarly). The first is a point that Burawoy (see, for example, Burawoy 2005, 2008, 2009) arguably underplays: to become 'relevant' is to a great extent tied to adopting a public position on a topic; it is therefore, to some extent, to become a public figure, even a political player in a game you may not really understand or want to play. The insatiable appetite of the modern media's need to generate a constant flow of 24/7 news, the technical revolution and real-time immediacy of new forms of social media, combined with a general shift towards an increasingly aggressive model of 'attack politics', produce a situation in which unprepared and isolated academics can suddenly find themselves at the centre of a media feeding frenzy. Just as public sociology is to some extent politicised sociology, then so too are the risks that academics will become drawn into unexpected debates, misrepresented, used and abused, but the appropriate response to this risk has to be a review of our professional skills and support, notably in relation to public engagement and media management, rather than a hasty retreat to our ivory towers.[8]

The *politics of* engaged scholarship may also, however, emerge in quite different and unexpected ways. The requirement to communicate beyond academe is a great extinguisher of verbose jargon that, in turn, facilitates an arguably more measured assessment of the intellectual value of any research. The political dimension of this point is that I have long wondered, of much modern political science, whether there is actually any fire beneath the smoke? Is much of our scholarship simply confused verbiage or is there, after all, something there? The answer, I think, is: something is there, but it is buried so deep – 'with all the author's chaff on everything' as Crick (1962) put it 'before ever the grain is reached' – and it demands so much in terms of translation, that *what* that germ of relevance actually *is* or *why* it matters is rarely uncovered. Phrased in this manner, *public* or *policy* scholarship is completely compatible with the very highest standards of academic research, because it is simply concerned with teasing out and making clear exactly why the research is in some way relevant to modern concerns, what exactly it has found out, and why those findings matter against any number of benchmarks. The politics of engaged scholarship therefore revolves around the art of translation, and this *may* leave some disciplinary emperors with very few clothes.

And yet, at the broadest level, what the public sociology wars really reveal is the existence of a cultural gap, gulf – possibly even a chasm – between the *internal culture* of academic life and the external pressures that are being placed upon it. Phrased in this manner, a rhetoric–reality gap has emerged between the pressure to shift from an exclusive focus on *the scholarship of discovery* (Table 10.1, above) or academic forms of engagement (Table 10.2, above) towards a more balanced approach that, while still focusing on the pursuit of knowledge as the core function of a university, is equally concerned with promoting and disseminating the discovery, relevance and value of that knowledge to a range of audiences. The tension occurs from the simple fact that the pathway to professional success, promotion and esteem within higher education remains tightly wedded to a focus on the production of peer-reviewed publications in international journals, and research monographs with university presses. The incentives for pursuing any other mode of scholarship are slim, and might arguably have been almost designed to squeeze the creative life and energy – that spark of playful or daring imagination – out of all but the most confident scholar. On top of this there appears to be an odd tendency, within those British academic circles concerned with the arts, humanities and social sciences, to stigmatise and demonise any academic whose work becomes popularised or useful to non-academics. From AJP Taylor to Niall Ferguson – and many others in between – the label of the 'media don' who has 'sold out' has done little to encourage scholars to reach out to wider audiences. And yet the paradox of this cruel and spiteful barb is that the truly 'hard' sciences enjoy a rich tradition in exactly those forms of writing and dissemination that the social sciences appear loath to embrace. From Ernst Mayr to Carl Sagan, and from Roger Penrose to Francis Crick – not to mention Lewis Wolpert, Erwin Schrödinger, Stephen Hawking, Stephen Jay Gould and Richard Dawkins – modern science appears to have been well-nourished by an emphasis on the scholarship of integration, the scholarship of sharing knowledge and the application of knowledge.[9] *Public science* is therefore an integral and highly respected element of professional science.

There is, of course, a second paradox to any comparison between the 'hard' sciences and the social sciences that has very specific implications for political science, and which allows this chapter to move towards its conclusion and a single focus. In *Making Political Science Matter* (2006), Sanford Schram and Brian Caterino outline the impact of 'physics envy' on the discipline and how this led to an attempt to produce objective, empirically testable, generalisable knowledge about political phenomena. 'By the end of the twentieth century', they note (2006, 3), 'interest had clearly increased in a political science that produced scientific knowledge *regardless of its relevance* for doing something about the problems political actors confronted [emphasis added]'. The paradox being that just as political science turned towards physics for intellectual direction and sustenance physics was itself entering a period of intense self-doubt.[10] As Lee Smolin notes in *The Problem with Physics* (2007, viii),

> The story I will tell could be read as a tragedy. To put it bluntly – and to give away the punch line – we have failed. We inherited a science, physics, that had been progressing so fast for so long that it was often taken as the model for how other kinds of science should be done. For more than two centuries, until the present period, our understanding of the laws of nature expanded rapidly. But today, despite our best efforts, what we know for certain about these laws is no more than we knew back in the 1970s.

It would appear that physics is itself experiencing an intense period of post-Cartesian anxiety as theoretical physics and the new science of cosmology

– neutron stars, geons, quantum foam, quasars, dark energy, etc. – seem to have exhausted experimental science's capacity to test and validate certain propositions within the standard model or paradigm.[11] And yet Smolin's arguments concerning the future of physics lay not with a plea for new institutions or increased funding but in a more subtle plea for a different form of capital; that is, an intellectual capital born out of an appreciation of the need to 'embrace creative rebels'. The implication appears to be twofold: firstly, that physics has stumbled into a *revolutionary* period but is attempting to understand and navigate this period through the tools of an outdated model of *normal* science (*qua* Kuhn 1962) that is inadequate to the task at hand; and secondly, that the capacity for physicists to respond has been eviscerated by the dominance of a professionalised and fairly narrow single model of 'good science' during the second half of the 20th century. Foundational thinkers who were willing to challenge certain self-evident truths or work beyond the mainstream were not tolerated, independence was not encouraged, and as a result the discipline created an academy of highly trained technicians and jettisoned those 'seers' with daring ideas and muscular minds. 'Without being aware of it' Smolin argues (2007, 328) '[the vast majority of physicists have] remained prisoners in those invisible and despotic circles which delimit the universe of a certain milieu in a given era'. The 'trouble with physics' appears to be quite simple: it has lost its intellectual mojo, its creative *joie de vivre* and – most of all – *its imagination*.

And yet there is arguably a strange symmetry between the challenges confronting physics and those confronting the social and political sciences. Indeed, it is hard to read Smolin's analysis of the 'sociology of knowledge' within physics and the 'hegemonic dominance of string theorists' without being reminded of the Perestroika movement's complaints about quantitative methods and formal modelling. It is also difficult to comprehend Smolin's analysis of the manner in which many scientists have become 'prisoners in those invisible and despotic circles which delimit the universe of a certain milieu in a given era' (2007, 329) without recalling possibly the most powerful defence of engaged scholarship within the social sciences – C Wright Mills' *The Sociological Imagination* (1959). Pressing this point still further, Burawoy (2008, 369) has argued that, 'In addition to a sociological imagination we also need a *political imagination*' [italics in the original]. It is for exactly this reason that the next and concluding section briefly locates the rediscovery of the political imagination at the heart of the politics of engaged scholarship.

The political imagination

In many ways the 40th anniversary of *Policy & Politics* represents far more than an opportunity to mark the achievements of a journal, but an opportunity to review the broader intellectual landscape within which that journal exists and, through this, identify those qualities of thought and mind which have cultivated such undoubted success. With this in mind this chapter has focused on what has been termed *the politics of engaged scholarship*, and has sought to set this pressure against 'the tragedy of political science' (first section, above) and its drift to a dominant mode of scholarship that is almost designed to cultivate *a politics of disengagement*. In this regard political science is by no means unique within the social sciences, and for this reason the second section of this chapter drew upon recent debates and controversies within sociology in order to tease apart a number of different forms of scholarship. Each of these highlighted the existence of different forms of relevance, different audiences with which to engage, and different 'pathways to impact'. More broadly, what Boyer's focus on shifting the priorities of the professoriate, and Burawoy's analysis of the 'four sociologies' reveal is not a zero-sum relationship between engagement and accessibility, on the one hand, and world-class intellectual endeavour, on the other, but a positive-sum relationship that builds its own momentum and to some extent become self-sustaining through engagement as a form of leverage. Seen from this perspective, engaged scholarship is not a recipe for creating 'tame academics' or for blunting intellectual ambition or horizons, but a recipe to return to a model of scholarship with a broader social purpose and visibility, one that can play a positive role in 'cultivating our humanity', to paraphrase Martha Nussbaum (1997). Put simply, a form of scholarship that actually matters.

To make such an argument is not to make a plea for a new form of punk political science – some Hunter S Thompson inspired model of scholarship – but it is to make a plea for a new phase of political science that is more obviously and explicitly infused with *the political imagination*. To make such an argument is clearly to work within the contours of C Wright Mills' *The Sociological Imagination* but, as Mills noted, 'political scientists who have read my manuscript suggest "the political imagination"; anthropologists, "the anthropological imagination" – and so on. The term matters less than the idea.'[12] The aim of this final section, then, is to locate Mills' 'idea' within this chapter's focus on the politics of engaged scholarship, and in this regard it might simply be noted that the political imagination is concerned with *bridging*, *accessibility* and *morality*.

1. The task and the promise of the political imagination is to form and sustain, through intellectual endeavour, social and political relationships (that is, *bridging*).
2. The political imagination therefore demands a degree of clarity in style and diversity in terms of outputs (that is, *accessibility*).
3. The political imagination is morally significant, optimistic and relevant (that is, *morality*).

The notion of *bridging* takes us back to *the scholarship of discovery* and its second, third and fourth-order relationships with *the scholarship of integration, the scholarship of sharing knowledge* and *the application of knowledge* (Table 10.1, above). The bridging role is not concerned with – and indeed must vigorously reject - naïve assumptions about the generation of simple solutions to complex sociopolitical problems, but is concerned with helping individuals, communities and groups make sense of their position in the world and the nature of the challenges that confront them, in a way that forges some form of reconnection. Scholarly knowledge, from this perspective, has academic value in its own right, but it also has (or should have) a social value in the sense of a meaningful relevance, demonstrable impact or simply some visibility beyond academe. The political imagination isn't for *the market of commerce* – as many academics fear - but concerns *the market of ideas*. Those who possess the political imagination are therefore able to see the bigger picture in terms of structural transformations in society (political, economic, technological, psychological, etc.), but are then able to use this not only as a contribution to academic knowledge but as a contribution *to* society. In this sense the political imagination cannot promise to give individuals greater control over their lives, but it does offer a form of linkage and a way of cultivating social understanding and political literacy.

This emphasis on *integrating, sharing* and *applying,* as sub-components of a focus on bridging, provides insights with which to further understand the political imagination. Those leading academics who might be defined as demonstrating such an imagination in their work are almost without fail 'hyphenated scholars' in the sense that they have mastered Hirschman's emphasis on 'the art of trespassing' across disciplinary borders.[13] Elinor Ostrom, Andrew Gamble, Amartya Sen (political economy); Zygmunt Bauman, Ulrick Beck, Richard Sennet, and Anthony Giddens (political sociology); Onora O'Neill, Thomas Pogge, Martha Nussbaum (political philosophy); Mary Warnock (philosophy and education); Cass Sunstein, Richard Thaler (behavioural psychology, economics and law); the disciplines matter less than the breadth of perspective and daring of thought. The notion of *sharing* seems to dovetail with this approach, as a capacity to talk to (or write for) a variety of audiences is an element that each of these scholars appears to have mastered (as revealed in the number who have been invited to give the Reith Lectures). It would also appear that hyphenated scholars are also adept at *applying* the insights of their research to a range of social problems. Take, for example, Anthony Giddens' intellectual relationship with the 'third way', Amartya Sen's research on the problems of society's poorest members, Mary Warnock's contribution to the regulation of human fertilisation and embryology, Cass Sunstein and Richard Thaler's research on public policy and 'nudging', and Elinor Ostrom's focus on the 'tragedy of the commons'. What this reveals is not so much the value of a problem-focused approach akin to that promoted by advocates of Bent Flyvbjerg's (2001) phronetic social science, but a richer, more subtle and essentially more imaginative approach to demonstrating why the social sciences matter.

A focus on *bridging* obviously therefore demands some comment on the issue of *accessibility*, and in this regard much has already been said about the arguably divorced and mystifying nature of modern political science. In a sense what I am throwing out is a question about the relationship between language, clarity and deceit. 'Any fool can make the simple complex' Albert Einstein famously suggested 'but it takes a real genius to discuss complex issues in simple terms'. The problem is that the current cultural emphasis within academe encourages students and faculty to 'tech-up' their research and writing at every turn, to the extent that *what* that germ of relevance actually *is* or *why* it matters is rarely uncovered. (In this regard Mills' translation of segments of Talcott Parson's *The Social System* (1951) into plain English provided a devastating insight into the art of abstraction.) The simple fact is that writing for multiple audiences demands creativity and the capacity to take risks, and even a certain playfulness of mind; it requires skills and attributes – ways of looking at the world – that most established political scientists have either arguably lost (or never had), and that new entrants to the profession are rarely encouraged to develop. It also demands that scholars understand Mills' emphasis on *intellectual craftsmanship* and the need to approach their political writing in terms of it being an art *as well* as a science.[14] An art, that is, that connects, inspires and which possesses *entheos* in the true sense of the term, and it is for exactly this reason that the final strand of the political imagination focuses on political morality and values *vis-à-vis* political science.

'Politics is the master science, both as an activity and as a study' Bernard Crick (1962, 164) argued exactly fifty years ago '[but] neither the activity nor the study can exist apart from each other'. In making this point Crick sought to highlight a link between *the health of democratic politics* and *the health of the study of politics*. A quarter of a century later Samuel Huntington

(1988, 7) would seek to re-emphasise this link in his argument that, 'Where democracy is strong, political science is strong… where democracy is weak, political science is weak'. In making this point, Crick and Huntington were attempting to expose the deeper social purpose of political science, in the sense of cultivating public understanding and promoting engaged citizenship by daring to emphasise the inescapable moral dimension of politics in both theory and practice. In doing so Huntington quoted Albert Hirshman's (1981, 305) adage that 'Morality belongs [at] the centre of our work; and it can get there only if social scientists are morally alive and make themselves vulnerable to moral concerns – then they will produce morally significant works, consciously or otherwise.' To be morally alive, and to be willing to say what you think matters, is to possess the political imagination; it is therefore forged upon the existence of some notion or belief in a *political purpose* or 'a desire to push the world in a certain direction, to alter other people's ideas of the kind of society that they should strive after' (Hirschman, 1981). This, in itself, brings us back full circle and to a focus on what has made *Policy & Politics* such a success over the last four decades.

Viewed from the perspective of this chapter, *Policy & Politics* has cultivated the political imagination in terms of both the approach of successive editors, and in the general perspective of its contributors. It has therefore been willing to take risks, look across disciplinary boundaries and identify future trends, in a manner that has prevented the gap between politics 'in theory' and politics 'in practice' that has emerged across the social and political sciences. In doing so it has retained a sense of drive, ambition and creativity that many other journals have lost as they slipped towards an increasingly dry, lifeless and irrelevant mode of scholarship. Phrased in the language of Shapiro's critique, *Policy & Politics* has not engaged in a 'flight *from* reality' and is therefore well positioned within the current 'relevance debate' (for a review of this debate see Trent, 2011). Indeed, the real questions concern not the past or the present but the future, and in this regard *any* journal would do well to reflect upon Mills' emphasis on 'being wobbly'. 'I am a Wobbly, personally, down deep, and for good… I am outside the whale' (cited in Mills and Mills, 2000, 252). By this Mills meant he was unwilling to be bound by academic or professional dogma, by those 'invisible and despotic circles' that Smolin (2007, 329) argued had acted to define and delimit the boundaries of modern science. To possess the political imagination is therefore, to some extent, to assume the position of an outsider (or as Mills referred to himself, 'an outlander') and a noteworthy feature of the careers of all the 'hyphenated scholars' listed above is that they have each in their own ways dared to exist 'outside the whale'. The political economy of academic journals will, like political science itself, reward those journals that are both optimistic and open minded, and who see opportunities where others see threats. The *next 40 years* will reward those journals who lead from the front and are willing to take risks; those journals that bridge boundaries, challenge common assumptions, and think anew; those journals that are willing to cultivate curiosity and shape debates; those journals that are themselves content to exist to some extent 'outside the whale'; but most of all it will reward those journals that possess *the political imagination*.

Notes

[1] For a discussion see Hayward et al, 2003; Dunleavy et al, 2001

[2] 'An autistic science with no relation to real life' – see www.paecon.net

[3] It is for exactly this reason that Russell Jacoby observes that the visibility and influence of public intellectuals has declined precisely because academic life has become structured by a set of demands that are almost designed for suffocating growth of academic careerism. See Jacoby, 2000

[4] Boyer, 1996; Wright Mills, 1959, 5; see Burawoy, 2005

[5] Boyer, 1996. Wright Mills, 1959, 5; see Burawoy, 2005; Lipset and Smelser, 1961

[6] For a range of opinions and perspectives see the special issue of *Political Science Review* (2013) 'The Politics of Impact', 11, 2

[7] See http://blog.oup.com/2012/08/matthew-flinders-defending-politics-menzies-campbell/

[8] For an interesting case study of these risks see Stacey, 2004

[9] Any modern political scientist would benefit from reading the various pieces of accessible scholarship contained within Dawkins, 2008

[10] A phenomenon examined in more detail by Keating and della Porta, 2008

[11] On this see Stefan Collini's introduction to Cambridge University Press's 1998 re-print of CP Snow's *The Two Cultures*.

[12] Wright Mills, 1959, 19 fn 2

[13] Hirschman, 1981, 305

[14] An oblique but relevant text on this topic is Sennett, 2009

References

Almond, G, 1990, *A discipline divided*, London: Sage

Almond, G, 1988, Separate tables: Schools and sects in political science, *PS: Political Science & Politics*, 21, 4, 828–42

Arendt, H, 1958, *The human condition*, Chicago, IL: University of Chicago Press, 1998

Barrow, C, 2008, The intellectual origins of new political science, *New Political Science*, 30, 2, 215–44

Bay, C, 1965, Politics and pseudopolitics, *American Political Science Review*, 54, 1, 39–51

Bellah, R, 1985, *Habits of the heart*, University of California Press

Boyer, E, 1990, *Scholarship reconsidered: Priorities of the professoriate,* Carnegie Foundation for the Advancement of Teaching, New York: John Wiley and Sons

Boyer, E, 1996, The scholarship of engagement, *Journal of Public Service and Outreach*, 1, 1, 11–20

Burawoy, M, 2005, For public sociology, *American Sociological Review*, 70, 4–28

Burawoy, M, 2008, Open letter to C Wright Mills, *Antipode*, 40, 3, 365–76

Burawoy, M, 2009, The public sociology wars, in Jeffries, V (ed), *Handbook of Public Sociology*, New York: Rowman and Littlefield

Collini, S, 2012, *What are universities for?,* London: Penguin

Collini, S, Winch, D, Burrow, J, 1983, *That noble science of politics*, Cambridge: Cambridge University Press

Crick, B, 1959, *The American science of politics*, Berkeley, CA: University of California Press

Crick, B, 1962, *In defence of politics,* London: Penguin, 2000

Dahl, R, 1961, The behavioral approach in political science: Epitaph for a monument to a successful protest, *American Political Science Review*, 55

Dawkins, R (ed), 2008, *The Oxford Book of Modern Science Writing,* Oxford: Oxford University Press

Du Bois, WEB, 1903, *The souls of black folk*, Chicago, IL: AC. McClurg and Co; Cambridge, MA: University Press, John Wilson and Son

Dunleavy, P, Kelly, P, Moran, M, 2001, *British political science: Fifty years of political studies,* London: Wiley-Blackwell

Easton, D, 1953, *The political system: An inquiry into the state of political science*, New York: Alfred A. Knopf

Eulau, H, 1959, Political science, in Hoelitz, B (ed), *A reader's guide to the social sciences*, Glencoe, IL: Glencoe Free Press

Eulau, H, 1977, Drift of a discipline, *American Behavioral Scientist*, 21, 1, 5–10

Farr, J, Seidelman, R (eds), 1993, *Discipline and history: Political science in the United States,* Ann Arbor, MI: University of Michigan Press

Farr, J, Dryzek, J, Leonard, S (eds), 1995, *Political science in history: Research programs and political traditions,* Cambridge: Cambridge University Press

Flinders, M, 2013a, The tyranny of relevance and the art of translation, *Political Studies Review*, 11, 2, 149–67

Flinders, M, 2013b, The political imagination, in Peters, G, Pierre, J, Stoker, G (eds), *The relevance of political science*, Basingstoke: Macmillan

Flyvbjerg, B, 2001, *Making social science matter,* Cambridge: Cambridge University Press

Fullbrook, E, 2003, *The crisis in economics,* London: Routledge

Fullbrook, E, 2007, *Real world economics,* London: Anthem

Grant, W, 2010, *The development of a discipline: The history of the Political Studies Association,* Hoboken, NJ: Wiley-Blackwell

Hay, C, 2009, Academic political science: Understanding politics differently, *Political Quarterly,* 80, 4, 587–91

Hayward, J, Barry, B, Brown, A (eds), 2003, *The British study of politics in the twentieth century,* Oxford: Oxford University Press

Hind, D, 2010, *The return of the public,* London: Verso

Hirschman, A, 1981, *Essays in trespassing: Economics to politics and beyond,* Cambridge: Cambridge University Press

Huntington, S, 1988, One soul at a time: Political science and political reform, *American Political Science Review,* 82, 1, 3–10

Isaac, J, 2009, *New York Times,* 19 October

Jacoby, R, 2000, *The last intellectuals,* London: Basic Books

Keating, M, della Porta, D, 2008, *Methods and approaches in the social sciences,* Cambridge: Cambridge University Press

Kuhn, T, 1962, *The structure of scientific revolutions,* Chicago: University of Chicago Press

Lijphart, A, 1971, Comparative politics and comparative method, *American Political Science Review,* 65, 3, 682–93

Lipset, SM, Smelser, J, 1961, *Sociology: The progress of a decade,* Englewood Cliffs, NJ: Prentice Hall

McCoy, C, Playford, J (eds), 1967, *Apolitical politics: A critique of behavioralism,* New York: Cromwell

Mills, K, Mills, P (eds), 2000, *C Wright Mills: Letters and autobiographical writings,* Berkeley, CA: University of California Press

Myrdal, G, 1944, *An American dilemma: The negro problem and modern democracy,* New York and London: Harper and Brothers

Nussbaum, M, 1997, *Cultivating humanity,* Harvard, MA: Harvard University Press

Nye, J, 2009, *New York Times,* 19 October

Peters, G, Pierre, J, Stoker, G (eds), 2014, *The relevance of political science,* Basingstoke: Palgrave

Pion-Berlin, D, Cleary, D, 2005, Methodological bias in the American political science review, in Renwick Monroe, K (ed), *Perestroika!* New Haven, CT: Yale University Press

Piven, F, 2007, *Public sociology,* Irvine, CA: University of California Press

Putnam, R, 2000, *Bowling alone: The collapse and revival of American community,* New York: Simon and Schuster

Putnam, R, 2010, *Inside Higher Education,* 7 September

Ricci, D, 1984, *The tragedy of political science*, New Haven, CT: Yale University Press

Riddell, P, 2010, In defence of politicians, *Parliamentary Affairs*, 63, 3, 545–57

Riesman, D, 1950, *The lonely crowd*, New Haven, CT: Yale University Press

Rogowski, R, 2013, Shooting, or ignoring, the messenger, *Political Studies Review*, 11, 2, 216–21

Sartori, G, 1970, Concept misformation in comparative politics, *American Political Science Review*, 64, 4, 1033–53

Schram, S, Caterino, B, 2006, *Making political science matter: Debating knowledge, research and method*, New York and London: New York University Press

Scott, JC, 1999, *Seeing like a state: How certain schemes to improve the human condition have failed*, New Haven, CT: Yale University Press

Seidelman, R, 1985, *Disenchanted realists*, Albany, NY: State University of New York Press

Sennett, R, 2009, *The craftsman*, London: Penguin

Shapiro, I, *The flight from reality*, 2005, Princeton, NJ: Princeton University Press

Skocpol, T, 2010, *Inside higher education*, 7 September

Smith, RM, 2005, Of means and meaning, in Renwick Monroe, K (ed), *Perestroika!* New Haven, CT: Yale University Press

Smolin, L, 2007, *The problem with physics: The rise of string theory, the fall of a science, and what comes next*, Boston, MA: Houghton Mifflin Harcourt

Stacey, J, 2004, Spin-sters: The unwittingly conservative effects of public sociology, *Social Problems*, 51, 1, 131–45

Talcott, P, 1951, *The social system*, Glencoe, ILL: The Free Press

Toulmin, S, 2001, *A return to reason*, Harvard, MA: Harvard University Press

Trent, J, 2011, Should political science be more relevant?, *European Political Science*, 10, 191–209

Truman, DB, 1955, The impact on political science of the revolution in the behavioral sciences, in Bailey, SK, et al (eds), *Research frontiers in politics and government*, Washington, DC: Brookings Institute

Turner, J, 2005, Is public sociology a good deal?, *The American Sociologist*, 36, 3–4, 27–45

Wright Mills, C, 1959, *The sociological imagination*, London: Penguin, 2000

Wright Mills, C, 1963, Power, politics, and people, New York: Oxford University Press

CHAPTER ELEVEN

Reflections on contemporary debates in policy studies

Sarah Ayres and Alex Marsh

Introduction

The journal *Policy & Politics* occupies unique intellectual terrain. From the outset it has sought to foster a dialogue between the discipline of political science and the field of public administration. It has recognised the ambiguity in the nature of public administration: it is both a field of academic endeavour and a set of professional practices. The journal has a foundational commitment to ensuring that the products of the academy are informed by the insights of practice, while making sure those products are accessible to reflexive practitioners. The journal has worked with the grain of policy studies in emphasising the importance of all the components of policy making: it views politics as relevant throughout the policy process, rather than being contained within the complex choreography of the institutions of representative democracy. There has consequently been limited support for models relying on a simplistic division between politics and administration; the journal has been associated with significant contributions to debates over policy implementation and policy in action (notably Barrett and Hill, 1984). The journal has been open-minded on questions of methodology: it has accommodated a broad range of quantitative, qualitative and mixed methods. It has responded sympathetically to significant shifts in the intellectual terrain such as increasing emphasis upon inter-professional and joint working, the arrival of the discourses and practices of public management, and more recent preoccupations with questions of governance beyond the state.

The 40th anniversary of the journal is an opportunity to reflect upon both its achievements and the current state of the debates. Interest in appraising the current state of the field of policy studies is evident elsewhere (Nowlin, 2011). There have recently been calls for greater consideration of how researchers go about their work and what it is they are seeking to achieve (Raadschelders, 2011; Cairney, 2013a). The lack of reflection on the philosophical foundations of alternative analytical perspectives is highlighted as problematic. Detailed work exploring important philosophical currents in thinking continues (Whetsell and Shields, 2013) but this type of reflection is yet to be routinely integrated into research activity. Embracing deeper reflection can, however, be uncomfortable. It can surface significant problems. Calls for new thinking which challenges dominant approaches can generate considerable hostility, as is evident in the initial responses to Luton's (2007) relatively modest call for greater awareness of the role social construction plays in shaping our knowledge base (Meier and O'Toole, 2007; Andrews et al, 2008). Yet, the discomfort induced by close questioning can open up opportunities for significant theoretical and empirical development.

This chapter aims to locate the contributions to this book in relation to key debates. It starts by mapping the key contours of the terrain covered by *Policy & Politics* over the last 40 years. It does so under four broad headings: (1) theorising policy, (2) evidence and the policy process, (3) transforming structures and processes, (4) implementation and practice. The third section uses these headings and draws out some key themes from the chapters comprising this book. The fourth section concludes with five key arguments. First, we advocate greater tolerance of diversity in theoretical and empirical enquiry. Second, we encourage an open mind in relation to the production and utilisation of research evidence in the policy process. Third, we feel the academy has a public duty to work with practice to generate the 'big ideas' and more expansive thinking currently lacking in austerity politics. Finally, we suggest that further theoretical and empirical examination of the role of individuals, leadership and 'agency' would be valuable. Finally, we note *Policy & Politics* aims to rise to the challenge of remaining reflexive and open minded in responding to future trends and setting research agendas.

Key themes in policy studies

This section briefly reviews four interrelated themes that we consider have been central to policy studies over the life of *Policy & Politics*. We start by considering the broad topic of theorising policy. We then focus on the more specific issue of the role of evidence in the policy process. Our third topic is the reconfiguration of structures and processes of governance and delivery. This issue has taken on a new urgency in the context of austerity politics. Finally, we consider implementation and practice. Cross-cutting these four themes are some recurrent, more fundamental, analytical issues such as the analysis of structure and agency.

Theorising policy

John (2012) proposes that we can bring order to the profusion of competing accounts of policy and policy change by identifying five broad explanatory approaches. His framework has resonance across several debates within policy studies. John argues that theory will tend to draw concepts, variables and causal explanations from one of the following approaches: institutions; groups and networks; exogenous factors; rational actors; and ideas. John is also an advocate for evolutionary explanations for policy (2003; 2012, 165–71). Each of these families of theory in turn covers a number of more subtly differentiated approaches. This is perhaps clearest in institutionalism where historical, sociological and rational choice variants are identified (following Hall and Taylor, 1996). These have now been joined by discursive institutionalism (Schmidt, 2008; 2012).

Giving theoretical primacy to one of John's five approaches can deliver 'pure' explanations for policy. More common in policy studies are synthetic explanations. The three explanatory frameworks that dominated the theorisation of the policy process during the 1990s (Sabatier and Jenkins-Smith, 1993; Baumgartner and Jones, 1993; Kingdon, 1995) were all, to varying degrees, synthetic approaches. Attempts to provide synthetic explanations have subsequently become more elaborate: they seek to encompass an ever greater array of variables drawn from more of John's five approaches (John, 2003; Real-Dato, 2009).

Cairney (2013a) has recently asked some probing questions about the way in which theories in policy studies are brought into dialogue. Producing synthetic explanations is only one possibility. Theories can be used to complement each other: providing different perspectives on the same issue. Or we may recognise that theories potentially contradict each other: they offer conflicting explanations and the analytical task is to compare theories in order to select the most effective. The key point we draw from Cairney's article is that authors are not always sufficiently clear in distinguishing situations of theoretical contradiction from situations of theoretical synthesis. Synthesis may be attempted where theories make incompatible assumptions about the nature of social or policy processes or are using nominally similar concepts to signify different things. This can lead not to successful synthesis but the risk of theoretical incoherence. Cairney's point is well made. Theory inevitably entails ontological and epistemological commitments, but these are explicitly examined less frequently than would be desirable. Recent calls for closer examination of the philosophical foundations of policy studies resonate with earlier arguments in political science (Hay, 2006; Schram and Caterino, 2006), and similar debates are being played out in parallel in different strands of the literature.

At the core of this discussion is methodological monism: can and should policy studies pursue knowledge of the type assumed to be accessible to the natural sciences? Different answers to this question rest on different ontologies. They deliver different epistemologies and hence different views on, for example, the scope and nature of intellectual progress and knowledge accumulation within policy studies. In practice, positivist thinking had a strong grip on policy studies for many years, as it did on political science and public administration. This resulted in a premium being placed upon hypothesis testing, quantitative methods and the statistical estimation of models. However, counter-currents of postpositivism have not only developed but arguably continue to strengthen (Fischer, 2003; Fischer and Gottweis, 2012; Bevir and Rhodes, 2003). Poststructuralist arguments around the potential contribution of governmentality to policy studies have assumed particular prominence (Bevir, 2011). A strand of the current policy literature explicitly takes the argument a step further. It embraces Law and Urry's (2004) argument that social science is performative: it does not simply describe the social world but also has the power to transform it (Newman, 2012).

One intriguing current development is the occurrence of an apparent theoretical bifurcation. On the one hand, authors are looking more explicitly for inspiration from the natural sciences. On the other hand, research is developing in strongly qualitative and interpretivist directions. The former move is most clearly evident in the rise of concepts such as 'complexity' and 'evolution'. Both concepts have origins in natural science, and are used in myriad different ways in policy theory (Cairney, 2013b; Geyer and Rihani, 2010). Much of the use is allusive or metaphorical: there is limited direct importation of theoretical models and mechanisms from natural science. There have, however, been direct attempts to use concepts from complexity science and synthesise them with established concepts such as path dependency (Room, 2011; 2012). The debate over what has been, and what can be, achieved by these borrowings from natural sciences has increased in sophistication (Prindle, 2012; Little, 2012).

Approaches that look to the natural sciences can be contrasted with moves towards policy anthropology (Shore et al, 2011) and policy ethnography (Rhodes, 2011). Such approaches take a very different stance on ontological questions such as the nature of social structures or the explanation of continuity and change. They favour detailed qualitative research which seeks to unlock meaning. Micro-level analysis of subjectivity, ambiguity, and interpretation provides insights into how policy actors construct and reconstruct their world and act within it and upon it. The potential and achievements of this approach to policy studies continue to be appraised (Hay, 2011). Here again we encounter arguments in favour of theoretical synthesis. For example, McKee (2009) has argued for the synthesis of governmentality theory with ethnographic approaches, as a means of unravelling the activity of governing and the intricacies of the struggles inherent in much contemporary policy.

The terrain of policy studies is, if anything, becoming ever more varied. It remains an open question whether the field is characterised by vibrant pluralism and dialogue or by a series of parallel conversations with limited interaction. There would be considerable value in developing this discussion further. However, our objective here is simply to provide a brief overview highlighting some of the issues at stake and some of the directions in which the debates are developing.

Evidence and the policy process

Since the turn of the millennium a key strand of the debate has examined the idea of evidence-based policy, both in theory and practice (Parsons, 2002; Sanderson, 2002; Bochel and Duncan, 2007). Evidence-based policy lies squarely within the tradition of rational, technocratic policy making. It implies that certain types of generalisable, non-context specific knowledge are not only achievable but have been achieved. While the literature addresses both the demand for and supply of evidence (Duncan and Harrop, 2006; Nutley et al, 2007), greater focus has been on producing evidence in forms that are sufficiently digestible and timely to influence policy. The primary audience for such advice is academic researchers. Yet, academic researchers speaking directly to policy makers is only one mechanism by which ideas are imported into policy. Think tanks have significant success in making timely and digestible inputs – grounded in evidence of wildly varying quality – into policy. Similarly, key actors in the policy process – such as special advisors – can play a vital translation role (Gains and Stoker, 2011).

The scope for practising evidence-based policy has been widely questioned, as has its desirability on normative grounds. The question of the context-specificity of policy knowledge comes most sharply into focus in the related literature on policy transfer (Ettelt et al, 2012). The debate has moved on to ideas of evidence-informed policy and policy-based evidence. This move signifies a recognition that evidence sits alongside many other influences upon policy (Mulgan, 2005) and, indeed, a greater sensitivity to the role of power and politics in constructing 'evidence' (Sullivan, 2011). These developments echo broader debates about the fragility of social scientific knowledge, and the strategic role of ignorance in social processes

(McGoey, 2012). The acknowledgement that evidence can sit in a range of different relationships with the policy process represents something of a rediscovery of themes well-established in the research utilisation literature (following Weiss, 1979), although new dimensions have been added to the debate (Sanderson, 2009; Downe et al, 2012).

Transforming structures and processes

An ever-present theme over the last 40 years has been the transformation of the organisational structures through which policy is developed and delivered. One strand of this discussion relates to changing political structures and processes: reconfiguration of the institutions of representational democracy and the rise of participative and direct democracy. The other strand of the discussion examines changing modes of policy and service delivery. The connection between these two strands is of increasing significance (Copus et al, 2013), but here we focus upon changing modes of delivery.

The ideas corralled under the heading of New Public Management (NPM) (Hood, 1991) challenged Weberian bureaucracy, the dominant models of organisation within the public sector. They led central governments across the globe to separate policy from delivery in processes of agencification (Pollitt and Talbot, 2004) and a recurrent debate over the so-called Quango State (Skelcher, 1998; Flinders, 2008). NPM also inspired the unbundling, market testing and contracting out of public services. Following Osborne and Gaebler (1993), the mantra 'steering not rowing' was frequently invoked to encapsulate the appropriate role for government; novel organisational forms such as the quasi-market evolved.

Analytically the discussion of organisational design was initially structured around the relative merits of markets, hierarchies and networks. One core question is the conditions under which moving services to the market is likely to deliver enhanced performance (Greener, 2008). A second strand of the discussion framed the issues more broadly and debated whether we have moved from the era of government, dominated by public bodies directly under political control, to an era of governance, in which a more fragmented landscape of independent organisations is responsible for both policy and delivery (Kooiman, 2003). The dominant logic of organisation was characterised as shifting from hierarchy to network.

However, empirically it became apparent that markets, hierarchies and networks are ideal types. They are rarely observed in pure form in practice (Exworthy et al, 1999). Organisational fragmentation gives rise to new types of coordination problem that must be overcome. Framing analysis around ideal types risks misreading organisational change and continuity.

While the NPM project has proved highly problematic in practice (Hood and Peters, 2004) and possible successors have been identified (Dunleavy et al, 2006; Bennington and Moore, 2010), it has also been argued that the rejection of traditional bureaucratic models fails to recognise both their resilience (Olsen, 2008) and value(s) (du Gay, 2000; 2005; Clegg et al, 2011). Recent developments such as the putative emergence of a 'new public governance' (Osborne, 2010) have led to a perceived need to reformulate well-established frameworks (Klijn and Koppenjan, 2012) or to explore the scope for new dialogues (Bevir, 2011).

Current debates over structures and delivery encompass both extensions of familiar themes and the emergence of new currents of thinking. The arrival of individual budgets and personalisation has moved quasi-market mechanisms closer to genuine market mechanisms. Initial use in adult social care delivered somewhat mixed results, but there are strong advocates for extensions to other areas of public services (Glasby et al, 2009). At the same time, alternative forms of delivery such as coproduction have increased in prominence (Bovaird, 2007; Thomas, 2012), as has discussion of alternatives to state-centric means of organising. This is a process that accelerated with the onset of recession and austerity politics: as the state sought to scale back involvement in service delivery by professional public servants, the focus has increasingly shifted to other means of meeting need (Lowndes and Pratchett, 2011; Farnsworth, 2011; Hancock et al, 2012).

Implementation and practice

The concept of implementation rose to prominence at around the same time as *Policy & Politics* was founded. The 1970s and 1980s witnessed a proliferation of models of implementation (Hill and Hupe, 2009). However, interest in the topic then waned somewhat. In the late 1990s the discussion was rekindled in more nuanced form (Hill, 1997), seeking to integrate implementation with broader policy process theories and sensitivity to institutional structures (Exworthy and Powell, 2004). Similarly, Lipsky's (1980) concept of street-level bureaucracy provided a revealing perspective on frontline service delivery (Maynard-Moody and Musheno, 2003) which can be embedded into broader frameworks to shed light on, for example, the implications of frontline discretion for accountability (Hupe and Hill, 2007).

Academic debates over implementation and, more recently, over the conditions for policy success (McConnell, 2010), are complemented by the literature exploring the practice of policy, although much remains to be done to link the analysis of implementation with an understanding of how policy is negotiated at the micro-level. There has been a longstanding interest in the reflexive practitioner (Schon, 1983) and how practitioners can reframe problems in ways that allow progress to be made on the ground (Schon and Rein, 1994). It offers a route to understanding not only what and how policy delivers, but also the scope for creativity within policy processes. This literature demonstrated a postpositivist sensibility before postpositivism rose to popularity.

More recently there has been considerable interest in the sorts of knowledge policy makers and practitioners draw on in order to form their own basis for action. Freeman (2007) deploys the concept of 'epistemological bricolage' to capture the way in which diverse knowledges are integrated as a basis for practice. This resonates with the way in which policy can be constructed at a notionally more strategic level (Dwyer and Ellison, 2009). A much broader ranging discussion of the nature of quotidian policy work is also under way (Colebatch et al, 2010), including examining practice at the highest levels of government (Rhodes, 2011). An outstanding task is to meld a concern with public management, frontline policy work and broader thinking on the policy process (Howlett, 2011).

Finally, alongside debates over the intricacies of structure and process, the tools of government literature seeks to assess the substance of policy: the effectiveness of the different classes of policy instrument (Hood, 1986; Hood and Magretts, 2007; Salamon, 2002; John, 2011). The aim is to provide a critical overview of the options available to policy makers seeking to shape the social world. Authors use classifications of differing levels of granularity. Hood (1986) offers a very broad categorisation of the tools available, while others embed their assessment in considerably more institutional detail which results in a rather more disaggregated picture (Salamon, 2002). This literature has been re-energised in part as a result of technological change, in part by evolving thinking about effective regulatory design, and in part by the rise of 'nudge' economics and behaviour change, which raise significant questions about both effectiveness and normative desirability (Jones et al, 2013; Leggett, 2013).

Advancing the debates

This section takes the four themes introduced above and provides a perspective on the contribution of the chapters in this book. We also identify areas in which we consider there are analytical issues ripe for further development.

Theorising policy

The contributions to this book give a flavour of the theoretical diversity within contemporary policy studies, as well as communicating some of the foundational issues currently being contested. Both Rhodes (2013) and Flinders (2013) make the case for tolerance of greater diversity in theoretical and empirical enquiry. Flinders (page 625) notes that:

> during the second half of the 20th century political science shifted significantly in terms of its dominant theories, methods, values and aspirations… the outcome was that deductive, game theoretic formal modelling and quantitative analysis enjoyed a privileged position in terms of appointments, publication opportunities and funding.

He calls for considered resistance to this dominant set of beliefs and values. He draws on the Perestroika movement in political science which mounted an epistemological challenge that called 'for the methodological pyramid to be tipped on its side so that a broader range of theories and approaches (notably "thick" descriptive methods) can be recognised as valuable and legitimate techniques' (page 626).

Here it is useful to distinguish the profile of the research that is being carried out in policy studies from the hierarchy of value that is ascribed to that work. It may well be the case that a certain type of hypothetico-deductive, quantitative research is ascribed particular value, even while the majority of the research being conducted is not rooted in that approach. This tells us something important about the sociology of a discipline. Flinders gives us a flavour of this distinction. If access to the most prestigious journals and conferences is controlled by those with particular methodological preferences and perspectives, and publication and participation in such outlets has significant career benefits, then those favoured models and modes of thought come to be valorised and replicated. But that does not necessarily tell us much about the theoretical and methodological preferences held by the majority of the community's members. Positivist methodologies may be championed as the gold standard in one part of the field, while in practice the majority of researchers work with more idiographic, qualitative methods. This may not be comfortable, but it is not contradictory.

In fact, if we look across the contributions to the book it is notable that the sort of positivist, quantitative research that authors such as Rhodes and Flinders are questioning does not feature prominently. That could be no more than a selection effect. But it also reflects the profile of presentations at the 40th anniversary *Policy & Politics* conference. *Policy & Politics* welcomes a broad range of approaches, believing that there is strength in diversity and pluralism, but the bulk of the papers at the conference were qualitative. The examples included in this issue are a powerful reminder of the value of theoretically informed case study approaches that enable in-depth explorations of 'the local'. Intensive research methodologies that seek to capture the richness of the 'real world' often produce unexpected results and subtleties that would elude more extensive methods.

John (2013) perhaps has the greatest sympathy with positivist epistemologies, in the sense that nudge techniques draw on psychological results that are taken to have general applicability. John's example shows that the social sciences still have much to learn from the natural sciences in particular contexts. Van der Steen et al's (2013) chapter makes explicit reference to a range of concepts drawn from natural sciences, particularly complex adaptive systems (Mitchell, 2011). However, these concepts from natural science are invoked primarily for the qualitative insights they can provide. When set alongside Rhodes' (2013) chapter deploying ethnographic methods we have an illustration of the bifurcation in perspectives referred to earlier. In addition, Newman (2013) provides a valuable illustration of the application of the concept of performativity to pressing policy issues.

The only chapter in the book that adopts the approach of drawing explicitly on complementary perspectives, as suggested by Cairney (2013a), is Peters' (2013) examination of coordination. The chapter represents an illuminating attempt to take a phenomenon of key theoretical and practical significance and explore the insights offered by very different analytical perspectives. This approach – placing theories into dialogue with each other – has considerable unexplored potential both in its own right and as a stepping stone to more thoughtful and coherent theoretical synthesis.

Across the book we can identify most of the approaches to theorising policy identified by John (2012). Pollitt (2013) explicitly frames his work as institutionalist, whereas Peters (2013), while recognising the significance of institutions, draws on both rational actor models and the role of ideas. The chapters based around local responses to austerity have a strong group and network sensibility, while also reflecting on the importance of ideas. Davies (2013) reminds us of the significance of broader structural and exogenous factors.

Even though the authors have different theoretical starting points, a theme underpinning most of the chapters is the relative significance of structure and agency in determining policy and its outcomes. Peters (2013), for example, refers to the structural features of political reputation, professional traditions and communities, and the 'rigidity' of policy frames or belief systems in influencing policy coordination. At the same time, he identifies agency as vital: the role of policy entrepreneurs, leaders, boundary spanners and instigators shapes outcomes. The complex interplay between structure and agency is noted. A number of the other chapters examine the structure/agency issue in a variety of contexts. One message to emerge strongly is the importance of social agency in shaping implementation and determining policy outcomes. We return to this issue below.

Evidence and the policy process

Evidence-based policy typifies a rational, technocratic approach to policy making. However, despite developments in the production and use of evidence, several chapters in this book identify potential barriers to policy-relevant research and the limitations of the social sciences in informing our understanding of contemporary policy and politics. These include the inadequacy of available research methods (Pollitt, 2013), the political motivations of policy makers (Rhodes, 2013), the inaccessibility of research findings (Flinders, 2013), preconceived ideas about the nature of the policy process (Van der Steen et al, 2013), different epistemological foundations preventing knowledge transfer between the academy and practice (Peters, 2013), and a lack of reflexive and critical analysis to inform crisis management in times of austerity (Lowndes and McCaughie, 2013).

Four chapters provide more focused engagements with the issue of evidence and policy. First, Pollitt's central argument is that there is a glaring lack of evidence about the impact or success of reforms in the UK over the past 40 years. Pollitt contextualises his observation by noting that there are 'considerable technical and methodological problems in evaluating such reforms... . Two interconnected problems are that the design of reforms does not stand still, and neither does the context in which they are being implemented' (2013, 471). This means that orthodox evaluation models based on *ex ante* objectives and quantifiable performance indicators often cannot be applied. In addition, Pollitt highlights the role of a general lack of sustained political interest in reform: without the demand for rigorous assessment of the consequences of reform the supply of robust evidence on outcomes is not forthcoming. Pollitt recognises that *ideas* from the social sciences are often adopted (or more likely adapted) by policy makers. But that falls far short of evidence-based policy. Pollitt draws on the work of Chris Skelcher (2008, 41) who contends that 'at the level of generalisable, empirically supported causal statements, social science research has been able to contribute little to the normative project of designing governance institutions'.

Second, Rhodes (2013) considers the limitations of the dominant tradition of modernist-empiricism in political science. He refers to 'genre mixing' as some social scientists, recognising the limitations of a positivist epistemology in policy studies, have turned away from law-like generalisations to a more interpretivist approach. Here he sees his use of ethnographic method to examine the practices of Whitehall departments as bringing something new and valuable to the analysis. He contends that the:

> rational, managerial approach has predominated since 1968, producing little beyond the civil service reform syndrome. We do not need more of the same. We need a different approach to reform. The storytelling approach is a contender. A bottom-up approach to reform rooted in the everyday knowledge of departments is a lone voice in this wilderness, but it can hardly do worse. (2013, 493-4)

These two contributions operate from rather different epistemological starting points. Pollitt's argument invites us to reflect upon whether the barriers to evidence-based policy identified are intrinsic to the UK policy process, and hence insurmountable, or whether a different structural alignment and different incentives could bring evidence in closer dialogue with policy in reality. Even if that were possible, the initiative would have to originate within the policy system, because whether 'social scientists can intervene to insist on a more evidence-based approach to public management reform must be doubted – there has been no sign of that so far' (Pollitt, 2013, 477). Rhodes' analysis raises questions for both the academy and practice about what constitutes useful evidence and how its merits might be weighed and set against real world problems requiring solutions.

The concept of evidence-based policy and practice presupposes the existence of relevant evidence, either from past local experience or imported from elsewhere via policy transfer. In their analysis of local government responses to recent austerity measures, Lowndes and McCaughie (2013) identify a surprising lack of evidence or big ideas about how to manage the crisis. They observed creative behaviours and coping strategies at a local and individual level in a bid to offset the negative effects of austerity:

> [W]hile cost-cutting and efficiency measures dominate, creative approaches to service redesign are also emerging, based upon pragmatic politics and processes of 'institutional bricolage'. While the absence of radical new ideas and overt political conflict is

surprising, local government reveals a remarkable capacity to reinvent its institutional forms to weather the storm. (2013, 534).

Their study showed that some public officials actually discovered a greater capacity for creative thinking within the constraints of the current economic crisis. Interestingly, it indicates that creative and resilient policy responses can be found in the absence of evidence or external guidance. Their study provides clear illustrations of practice-based policy – whereby the act of 'doing' shapes policy bottom-up. The concept of 'institutional bricolage' captures the recombination and reshuffling of preexisting components to serve new purposes (Lanzara, 1998). This serves as an important reminder: the academy has much to learn from practice and must continue to nurture a two-way dialogue in the production of knowledge and evidence.

Finally, Flinders returns to a core theme: how the academy should engage with policy and practice. He argues for reconnecting with practice at several levels and issues a challenge to the academic community. Flinders calls for 'engaged scholarship' that is 'more visible and relevant in terms of informing public debates, promoting engaged citizenship, or assisting in the design of public policy' (2013, 629). The challenge will be to overcome the barriers to engagement. Some barriers are about disciplinary priorities: engagement may be advocated but it is not necessarily valued. Some barriers are about approaches to research: academics need to utilise the full range of tools available in order to produce meaningful and relevant knowledge to help 'individuals, communities and groups make sense of their position in the world and the nature of the challenges that confront them' (2013, 637). Some barriers are about communication: Flinders advocates 'triple writing' for academic, practitioner and public audiences to extend the influence of social science beyond the academy.

Flinders argues forcefully that engaged scholarship cannot be considered an optional extra. Rather he conveys a sense of urgency: extending and strengthening the links between social science research and practice is of fundamental importance to the survival of the academy. In order to fully grasp the engagement agenda Flinders calls for scholars to realise their 'political imagination' by embarking on a different type scholarship: not only more accessible but also more expansive. One does not have to accept Flinders' claim that engagement is essential to disciplinary survival to agree that it is important. One aspect of this discussion we lack is extended examples of what this model of engaged scholarship looks like in practice. There are those within the academic community who are willing, and no doubt able, but do not have a clear idea of what to do or how to get started. Flinders sketches some illuminating, albeit fleetingly brief, examples from his own experience. There is a strong case for developing fuller statements of what this model of scholarship looks like in the digital age.

Transforming structures and processes

The majority of the chapters in this book explore some aspect of transforming structures. Several authors offer new insights relating to well-established debates about the balance between modes of governance – markets, hierarchy and network – in pure and hybrid forms (Peters, 2013; Martin and Guarneros-Meza, 2013; and Pollitt, 2013). Others explore structural transformation in a new policy environment, characterised by austerity and crisis (Newman, 2013; Davies, 2013; and Lowndes and McCaughie, 2013).

A strong theme is hierarchy and hybridity. Pollitt (2013) observes that the strongly centralised top-down style of UK politics makes possible the repeated introduction of large scale public management reform. Guy Peters (2013, 571) reflects on the challenges of achieving coordination in multi-agency partnerships and observes that often 'hierarchical coordination is the default option'. In other words, networking or collective action might not happen in the absence of hierarchy where 'central actors have the capacity to produce the behaviours that they demand from other actors' (2013, 571). While this may preserve the dominance of the State, hierarchical methods for producing coordination are also resource intensive. This provides a clear incentive for governments to promote self-steering when possible. Martin and Guarneros-Meza (2013, 585-603) also argue central government can play a key role in catalysing local collaboration, but here the emphasis is upon 'soft steering' in the form of advice, expertise, legitimacy and resources. Strategically deployed, these can have a powerful and positive effect on the success of local partnerships and networks. These two examples demonstrate, in different ways, the resilience and continuing value of hierarchy in the so-called transition to networked governance.

These contributions provide further evidence of the complex interplay between different governance modes. Pollitt (2013, 468) notes that transition from hierarchy, market to network as a ' "parade of the paradigms", though not entirely fictitious, and certainly handy for textbooks and classrooms ... is flawed'. This parade of 'label changes' and 'counter-trends' can undoubtedly result in tensions and contradictions both in practice between modes of governance, as one overlaps another, and at the level of mapping analysis on to practice. However, contributors to this issue also point to the complementarity of governance modes: one mode supporting or enabling another in the right environment or context. What is clear is that questions of coherence, contradiction and complementarity across governance modes are evolving, and much remains to be done to arrive at a broad-based, robust conclusion.

From a different perspective, there is no doubt that the global financial crisis and austerity politics have prompted critical reflections on modes of governance and dominant ideologies. At first glance, the recent economic downturn and austerity measures have done little to quell the apparent appeal of market-based solutions to contemporary governance problems. Davies (2013, 497) argues that 'despite a profound and enduring economic crisis, neoliberalism continues to dominate'. He endorses Colin Crouch's (2011) contention that we are likely to remain trapped in neoliberalism for many years. Indeed, it is arguably the case that neoliberalism has not simply survived the crash. Rather we have witnessed an intensification and extension of neoliberal practices and market-based solutions. In the UK, as elsewhere in Europe, at all governance levels there is a drive to implement austerity measures and do more for less (Lowndes and McCaughie, 2013; Martin and Guarneros-Meza, 2013; Newman, 2013).

The absence of an alternative to the neoliberal narrative at a macro-political level has been noted for at least a decade (Watson and Hay, 2003). In the absence of a credible challenge to neoliberalism, attention has increasingly turned to the potential for change at the local level. This contemporary turn is well represented in this book. Newman (2013, 518), in particular, explores the spaces and possibilities for radical or progressive interventions that can 'help generate new performances within the constraints of the present, and how those with a commitment to progressive politics might engage with the policy process in hard times'. Rather than portray a system that is beaten and broken by neoliberal ideology, Newman searches for new possibilities that evoke collective action, entrepreneurship and citizenship as an antidote to marketisation and the politics of austerity.

Likewise, Lowndes and McCaughie (2013) refer to the creative responses of local government in managing austerity. Interestingly, Lowndes and McCaughie agree with Newman (2013) and Davies (2013) in observing a surprising lack of overt political crisis so far in the UK. Given the impact austerity measures are having on formal governance structures, public actors and vulnerable citizens, one might have anticipated greater resistance or open contestation. Instead, local initiative and strong leadership appear to be producing resilient responses to wicked issues and austerity politics (Martin and Guarneros-Meza, 2013). These chapters demonstrate that the lack of a well-articulated political vision or unifying ideology does not necessarily preclude positive, creative and effective action.

Davies (2013) develops an argument of a different order. He notes the turn to the concept of 'everyday making'. Everyday makers see 'doing things differently' as a means of contesting the existing social order and charting a path beyond capitalism (Holloway, 2010). Rather than trying to contest neoliberalism at a systemic level, everyday maker-activists instead enact political action and resistance by changing small behaviours which might in turn have some cumulative impact. However, Davies rejects the idea that we need to choose between everyday and systemic orientations, arguing that they are complementary. Retaining a perspective on capitalism as an unstable and crisis-prone social system has value. Davies argues that 'the challenge for policy and politics is not to jettison "everyday" or "system" but rather to grasp the enduring relationship in different contexts' (2013, 498). For Davies, one of the future challenges is 'grasping the dynamics of scale: the systemic implications of everyday struggles and vice versa' (497).

Davies' chapter represents an important counterpoint to chapters focusing on the local and everyday. There is a real danger that the busyness associated with responding to the acute problems generated by budget cuts means that service providers and communities have no time to reflect upon the broader context. The agenda is reactive. This places greater responsibility upon scholars to render the broader context legible and provide additional intellectual resources to facilitate proactivity. Davies' contribution raises the issue of the aspirations for progressive politics. Has the ground upon which systemic analysis and critique can occur been vacated too readily? Or, in highlighting the link between the everyday and systemic transformation, has Davies pinpointed the most likely route through which to effect transformation? If so, then does it represent an area urgently requiring more rigorous theoretical and empirical interrogation?

Implementation and practice

The chapters in this book touch on several of the dimensions of the implementation debate. Both the role of central government in shaping policy top-down and the role of local resistance in shaping policy bottom-up feature prominently.

Regarding the influence of central government, Pollitt (2013, 465) refers to the 'almost ceaseless procession of reforms' in the UK over the past 40 years. One of his key findings is the apparent ease with which reform can take place is a result of the institutional characteristics of the political system: light touch legal procedures, one-party governments, powerful prime ministers and submissive parliaments mean that 'the window of opportunity for large-scale management reform is almost always at least half-open' (2013, 475). Likewise, Rhodes (2013) affirms the enduring nature of the Westminster model in shaping policy and politics in Whitehall. At the top of government departments, Rhodes (2013, 485) describes 'a class of political-administrators. ... Their priority and their skills are about surviving in a world of rude surprises. The goal is willed ordinariness.' He suggests that 'civil service reform is not, therefore, a matter of solving specific problems but of managing unfolding dilemmas and their inevitable unintended consequences. ... Strategic planning is a clumsy add-on to this world' (2013, 485).

A strong theme of the chapters in this book is the significance of individual action and the local in shaping policy and its outcomes. Davies (2013), Lowndes and McCaughie (2013) and Newman (2013) all argue that within old narratives and ideologies, new 'local' spaces for creativity, repositioning and survival open up. Lowndes and McCaughie (2013) refer to the work of Coleman et al (2010, 290) who suggest that processes of 'local sense making' are 'required to reconcile old assumptions and identities with new realities'. Their study of local government offers an intriguing insight into how 'practice' and 'doing' can drive change at local level and lead to creative responses to implementation problems and resource shortfalls. Newman also 'highlights the significance of local authorities as creative and innovative actors' (2013, 520), while Davies (2013, 497) suggests that 'everyday making seeks to accomplish small-scale, gradual changes by constructing new ways of living and doing politics from the bottom up.'

Van der Steen et al (2013) similarly focus on the local and contingent. Their analysis of 'weak schools' in the Netherlands poses two central questions: What causes the differences in outcomes of similar policies in similar contexts? Can patterns and causation be found in what seem to be unpredictable, unstable, and chaotic systems? Their study shows that contextual factors and local circumstances can have a substantial, and sometimes unintended, impact on policy implementation and outcomes. In their view, only local actors are in a position to identify, predict and ultimately manage these causal influences and outcomes. This 'moves the attention of policy makers from analysis *ex ante* towards the local knowledge of the process as it emerges' (Van der Steen et al, 2013, 565). This position raises fundamental questions about policy implementation and analysis. It suggests a move from the rational, rigid, managerial approach to the use of a more interpretivist sensibility that can account for complexity, emergent knowledge and context-specificity. This position resonates with Rhodes' (2013) justification for the use of ethnography to study Whitehall.

The central role of individuals, leadership and 'agency' in shaping policy emerges clearly from the chapters. In this respect they echo recent developments in the theorisation of policy change (Mahoney and Thelen, 2010). Lowndes and McCaughie (2013) recognise the importance of specific people (or agency) in developing creative responses to austerity.

However, they also recognise the conceptual limitations in examining the role of individuals and understanding the characteristics, traits and behaviours that make their actions so important in context. They observe (2013, 545) that:

> Our case study revealed the importance of 'special people' in undertaking the work of institutional bricolage, but we have very few conceptual tools to deal with this finding. Despite our academic obsession with the structure/agency relationship, we are actually not very good at analysing agency, particularly in its embodied form. There is a tendency for academics and practitioners alike to feel embarrassed when confronted with the truism that personality and passion and individual qualities matter.

While several chapters in this book signal the role of public entrepreneurs, boundary spanners and leaders, there is perhaps less detail on what those characteristics look like in practice. This observation leads to a bigger set of questions, including: Can these characteristics be satisfactorily identified and categorised? Can skills be taught and replicated? Can they be incentivised by organisational structures and procedures? What shapes the scope of agency and in what circumstances can agency transform structure? If one accepts the important role of the 'individual' in policy studies then these questions require further exploration. While agency – including 'leadership' – is repeatedly noted as important, Lowndes and McCaughie (2013) rightly highlight the challenges we face in coming to terms with this theoretically. This is, perhaps, in part the shadow of the prolonged theoretical dominance of historical institutionalism and a preoccupation with structure. However, this is an area of active theoretical development (Sullivan et al, 2012). The contributions to this issue strongly point to this as a fruitful area not only for further theoretical refinement but also for detailed empirical inquiry.

Finally, Peter John's (2013) work on the 'tools of government' captures the technological, methodological and scientific developments that have taken place in this field over the past 40 years. John notes that it is typically argued that the range of tools available to policy makers has been supplemented by the use of ideas such as 'nudging'.

> The attractiveness of nudging has been due in part to its low cost, much more pertinent in an era of fiscal austerity, and also because it is a complement to conventional policy instruments, such as legislation and regulation. (John, 2013, 612)

In essence nudge is the idea that 'information may be used in a clever or smart way to encourage citizens to behave in ways that are in their own or society's interest' (John, 2013, 611). Nudge is about shaping the choice architecture and providing decision makers with cues that take advantage of known decision-making biases. But basic to the nudge argument is the point that any choice will be affected by the way information is provided, whether designed or not. John's key argument is that this distinction between nudge and traditional tools of government becomes hard to sustain once this central role for information is recognised.

Conclusion

The 40th anniversary of *Policy & Politics* provides an opportunity to reflect on critical debates in policy studies. The past 40 years have witnessed significant changes in the social sciences, policy and practice. This chapter has sought to reflect on theoretical and practical developments pertinent to *Policy & Politics* during this period and to suggest some steps to advance the debate. We conclude with five key arguments.

First, we urge the academy to be continuously reflexive in relation to foundational assumptions. We do not advocate a particular approach. We stand with Rhodes (2013) and Flinders (2013) in supporting the call for tolerance of greater diversity in theoretical and empirical enquiry and advocate the appropriate use of the full range of available research methods. While positivist, hypothesis-driven research might be ascribed preeminence in some quarters, chapters in this book demonstrate once again the valuable insights to be gleaned from qualitative and interpretivist approaches (Newman, 2013; Lowndes and McCaughie, 2013; Martin and Guarneros-Meza, 2013; Rhodes, 2013). Yet other contributions have worked productively with non-linear approaches to policy analysis (Van der Steen et al, 2013) and have drawn inspiration from the natural sciences (John, 2013). These very different approaches have served to produce knowledge appropriate to task. The chapters serve as a useful reminder that one's choice of research method should be dictated by a judicious mix of a rigorous ontology and the nature of the research problem. It should not be driven simply by disciplinary presumptions.

Second, several chapters in this book have identified potential barriers to evidence-based policy and the limitations of the social sciences in informing contemporary policy and politics. This prompts reflection on what appropriate evidence should look like and whether current approaches are fit for purpose. It raises significant epistemological questions: can orthodox evaluation models based on *ex ante* objectives can be relied upon in politically charged (Pollitt, 2013; Rhodes, 2013) and complex (Van der Steen et al, 2013) environments? The importance of practice-informed knowledge emerges clearly; it demonstrates that the academy has much to learn from colleagues working in the field. Indeed, in the absence of evidence and big ideas, practitioners' capacity for creative behaviours and coping strategies can deliver valuable learning by doing (Lowndes and McCaughie, 2013; Newman, 2013; Davies, 2013). The challenge for the academy is to strengthen the link between research and practice to look for innovative solutions to complex problems.

Third, we reaffirm the enduring importance of the analysis of governance structures and processes in policy analysis. Indeed, such analysis forms the basis of the majority of chapters in this book. One aspect of this discussion warrants further consideration. A number of authors have referred to an absence of an alternative to the neoliberal narrative at a macro- political level and the importance of the 'local' as an environment for progressive politics, resistance and change (Newman, 2013; Lowndes and McCaughie, 2013; Davies, 2013). Davies (2013, 497), in particular, argues that a future challenge for the academy is to think about 'grasping the dynamics of scale' – how micro-level activity can have a cumulative impact on macro-ideology and practice and vice versa. Indeed, we feel the academy has a public duty (Flinders, 2013) to offer insights that harness local knowledge and set it within its broader context. Thinking about 'scalability' could serve to generate the 'big ideas' and vision deemed lacking in the current period of austerity politics.

Fourth, the central role of individuals, leadership and 'agency' in shaping policy implementation emerges strongly from this issue. In particular, Lowndes and McCaughie's (2013) observation that there are few conceptual tools to examine the role of agency in context suggests a potentially rewarding avenue for future investigation. If agency represents such a significant driver for change, resistance and entrepreneurship, then we need to develop our theoretical and conceptual understanding of this phenomenon. In doing so, it could also address Davies' (2013) calls for a closer consideration of scalability by examining the link between 'structure' and 'agency'.

Finally, as Flinders (2013, 636) notes, 'the 40th anniversary of *Policy & Politics* represents far more than an opportunity to mark the achievements of a journal but an opportunity to review the broader intellectual landscape within which that journal exists'. *Policy & Politics* has made significant contributions to the debate over the past four decades, and this chapter has identified a number of areas for advancing the debate in the coming years. The challenge for the future will be to remain reflexive, open minded, responsive to trends while proactive in setting research agendas – a challenge the journal warmly welcomes.

Acknowledgement

We would like to thank two referees for helpful comments on a previous draft as an article in *Policy & Politics*. Any remaining errors are the responsibility of the authors.

References

Andrews, R, Boyne, G, Walker, R, 2008, Reconstructing empirical public administration: Lutonism or scientific realism, *Administration and Society*, 40, 3, 324–30

Barrett, S, Hill, M, 1984, Policy, bargaining and structure in implementation theory: Towards an integrated perspective, *Policy & Politics*, 12, 3, 219–40

Baumgartner, F, Jones, B, 1993, *Agendas and instability in American politics*, Chicago: University of Chicago Press

Bennington, J, Moore, M (eds), 2010, *Public value: Theory and practice*, Basingstoke: Palgrave MacMillan

Bevir, M, 2011, Governance and governmentality after neoliberalism, *Policy & Politics*, 39, 4, 457–71

Bevir, M, Rhodes, R, 2003, *Interpreting British governance*, London: Routledge

Bochel, H, Duncan, S (eds), 2007, Making policy in theory and practice, Bristol: Policy Press

Bovaird, T, 2007, Beyond engagement and participation: User and community coproduction of public services, *Public Administration Review*, 67, 5, 846–60

Cairney, P, 2013a, Standing on the shoulders of giants: How do we combine the insights of multiple theories in public policy studies, *Policy Studies Journal*, 41, 1, 1–21

Cairney, P, 2013b, What is evolutionary theory and how does it inform policy studies?, *Policy & Politics*, 41, 2, 279–98

Clegg, S, Harris, M, Höpfl, H (eds), 2011, *Managing modernity: Beyond bureaucracy?*, Oxford: Oxford University Press

Colebatch, H, Hoppe, R, Noordegraaf, M (eds), 2010, *Working for policy*, Amsterdam: Amsterdam University Press

Coleman, A, Checkland, K, Harrison, S, Hiroeh, U, 2010, Local histories and local sensemaking: A case of policy implementation in the English National Health Service, *Policy & Politics*, 38, 2, 289–306

Copus, C, Sweeting, D, Wingfield, M, 2013, Repoliticising and redemocratising local democracy and the public realm: Why we need councillors and councils, *Policy & Politics*, 41, 3, 389–408

Crouch, C, 2011, *The strange non-death of neoliberalism*, Cambridge: Polity Press

Davies, J, 2013, Just do it differently? Everyday making, Marxism and the struggle against neoliberalism, *Policy & Politics*, 41, 4, 497–513

Downe, J, Martin, S, Bovaird, T, 2012, Learning from complex policy evaluations, *Policy & Politics*, 40, 4, 505–23

Du Gay, P, 2000, *In praise of bureaucracy*, London: Sage

Du Gay, P (ed), 2005, *The values of bureaucracy*, Oxford: Oxford University Press

Duncan, S, Harrop, A, 2006, A user perspective on research quality, *International Journal for Social Research*, 9, 2, 159–74

Dunleavy, P, Margetts, H, Bastow, S, Tinkler, J, 2006, New Public Management is dead: Long live digital-era governance, *Journal of Public Administration Research and Theory*, 16, 3, 467–94

Dwyer, P, Ellison, N, 2009, 'We nicked stuff from all over the place': Policy transfer or muddling through?, *Policy & Politics*, 37, 3, 389–407

Ettelt, S, Mays, N, Nolte, E, 2012, Policy learning from abroad: Why it's more difficult than it seems, *Policy & Politics*, 40, 4, 491–504

Exworthy, M, Powell, M, 2004, Big windows and little windows: Implementation in the congested state, *Public Administration*, 82, 2, 263–81

Exworthy, M, Powell, M, Mohan, J, 1999, The NHS: Quasi-market, quasi-hierarchy and quasi-network?, *Public Money and Management*, 19, 4, 15–22

Farnsworth, K, 2011, From economic cuts to a new age of austerity, in Farnsworth, K, and Irving, Z (eds), *Social policy in challenging times*, Bristol: Policy Press

Fischer, F, 2003, *Reframing public policy: Discursive politics and deliberative practices*, Oxford: Oxford University Press

Fischer, F, Gottweis, H (eds), 2012, *The argumentative turn revisited: Public policy as communicative practice*, Durham, NC: Duke University Press

Flinders, M, 2008, *Delegated governance and the British state: Walking without order*, Oxford: Oxford University Press

Flinders, M, 2013, The politics of engaged scholarship: Impact, relevance and imagination, *Policy & Politics*, 41, 4, 621–42

Freeman, R, 2007, Epistemological bricolage: How practitioners make sense of learning, *Administration and Society*, 39, 4, 476–96

Gains, F, Stoker, G, 2011, Special advisors and the transmission of ideas from the policy primeval soup, *Policy & Politics*, 39, 4, 485–98

Geyer, R, Rihani, S, 2010, *Complexity and public policy: A new approach to 21st Century politics, policy and society*, London: Routledge

Glasby, J, Le Grand, J, Duffy, S, 2009, A healthy choice? Direct payments and healthcare in the English NHS, *Policy & Politics*, 37, 4, 481–97

Greener, I, 2008, Markets in the public sector: When do they work, and what do we do when they don't?, *Policy & Politics*, 36, 1, 93–108

Hall, PA, Taylor, R, 1996, Political science and the three new institutionalisms, *Political Studies*, 44, 5, 936–57

Hancock, L, Mooney, G, Neal, S, 2012, Crisis social policy and the resilience of communities, *Critical Social Policy*, 32, 3, 343–64

Hay, C, 2006, Political ontology, in Goodin, R, Tilly, C (eds), *The Oxford Handbook of Contextual Political Analysis*, Oxford: Oxford University Press

Hay, C, 2011, Interpreting interpretivism interpreting interpretations: The new hermeneutics of public administration, *Public Administration*, 89, 1, 167–82

Hill, M, 1997, Implementation theory: Yesterday's issue?, *Policy & Politics*, 25, 4: 375–85

Hill, M, Hupe, P, 2009 (2nd edn), *Implementing public policy*, London: Sage

Holloway, J, 2010, *Crack capitalism*, London: Pluto Press

Hood, C, 1986, *The tools of government*, London: Sage

Hood, C, 1991, A public management for all seasons?, *Public Administration*, 69, 1, 3–19

Hood, C, Magretts, H, 2007, *The tools of government in the digital age*, Basingstoke: MacMillan

Hood, C, Peters, G, 2004, The middle aging of New Public Management: Into the age of paradox?, *Journal of Public Administration Research and Theory*, 14, 3, 267–82

Howlett, M, 2011, Public managers as the missing variable in policy studies: An empirical investigation using Canadian data, *Review of Policy Research*, 28, 3, 247–63

Hupe, P, Hill, M, 2007, Street-level bureaucracy and public accountability, *Public Administration*, 85, 2, 279–99

John, P, 2003, Is there life after policy streams, advocacy coalitions, and punctuations: Using evolutionary theory to explain policy change?, *Policy Studies Journal*, 31, 4, 481–98

John, P, 2011, *Making policy work*, London: Routledge

John, P, 2012, *Analysing public policy*, London: Routledge

John, P, 2013, All tools are informational now: How information and persuasion define the tools of government, *Policy & Politics,* 41, 4, 605–20

Jones, R, Pykett, J, Whitehead, M, 2013, *Changing behaviours: On the rise of the psychological state*, Cheltenham: Edward Elgar

Kingdon, JW, 1995, *Agendas, alternatives and public policies*, Boston, MA: Little Brown

Klijn, E-H, Koppenjan, J, 2012, Governance network theory: Past, present, and future, *Policy & Politics*, 40, 4, 587–606

Kooiman, J, 2003, *Governing as governance*, London: Sage

Lanzara, G, 1998, Self-destructive processes in institutional building and some modest countervailing mechanisms, *European Journal of Political Research,* 33, 1–39

Law, J, Urry, J, 2004, Enacting the social, *Economy and Society,* 33, 3, 390–410

Leggett, W, 2013, The politics of behaviour change: Nudge, neoliberalism, and the state, *Policy & Politics,* forthcoming, DOI: http://dx.doi.org/10.1332/030557312X655576

Lipsky, M, 1980, *Street-level bureaucracy: dilemmas of the individual in public services,* New York: Russell Sage Foundation

Little, A, 2012, Political action, error and failure: The epistemological limits of complexity, *Political Studies,* 60, 1, 3–19

Lowndes, V, McCaughie, K, 2013, Weathering the perfect storm? Austerity and institutional resilience in local government, *Policy & Politics,* 41, 4, 533–49

Lowndes, V, Pratchett, L, 2011, Local governance under the coalition government: Austerity, localism and the Big Society, *Local Government Studies,* 38, 1, 21–40

Luton, L, 2007, Deconstructing public administration empiricism, *Administration and Society,* 39, 527–44

Mahoney, J, Thelen, K (eds), 2010, *Explaining institutional change: Ambiguity, agency and power,* Cambridge: Cambridge University Press

Martin, S, Guarneros-Meza, V, 2013, Governing local partnerships: Does external steering help local agencies address wicked problems?, *Policy & Politics,* 41, 4, 585–603

Maynard-Moody, S, Musheno, M, 2003, *Cops, teachers, counselors: Stories from the frontline of public services,* Ann Arbor, MI: University of Michigan Press

McConnell, A, 2010, Policy success, policy failure and grey areas in-between, *Journal of Public Policy,* 30, 3, 345–62 delete?

McGoey, L, 2012, Strategic unknowns: Towards a sociology of ignorance, *Economy and Society,* 41, 1, 1–16

McKee, K, 2009, Post-Foucauldian governmentality: What does it offer critical social policy?, *Critical Social Policy,* 29, 3, 465–86

Meier, K, O'Toole, L, 2007, Deconstructing Larry Luton: Or what time is the next train to reality junction?, *Administration and Society,* 39, 6, 786–96

Mitchell, M, 2011, *Complexity: A guided tour,* Oxford: Oxford University Press

Mulgan, G, 2005, Government, knowledge and the business of policy making: The potential and limits of evidence-based policy, *Evidence & Policy,* 1, 2, 215–26

Newman, J, 2012, *Working the spaces of power: Activism, neoliberalism and gendered labour,* London: Bloomsbury

Newman, J, 2013, Performing new worlds? Policy, politics and creative labour in hard times, *Policy & Politics,* 41, 4, 515–32

Nowlin, MC, 2011, Theories of the policy process: State of the research and emerging trends, *Policy Studies Journal,* 39, 1, 41–60

Nutley, S, Walter, I, Davies, HTO, 2007, *Using evidence: How research can inform public services,* Bristol: Policy Press

Olsen, J, 2008, The ups and downs of bureaucratic organisation, *Annual Review of Political Science,* 11 13–37

Osborne, SP, 2010, Introduction: The (new) public governance: A suitable case for treatment? in Osborne, SP (ed), *The new public governance?* London: Routledge

Osborne, D, Gaebler, T, 1993, *Reinventing government: How the entrepreneurial spirit is transforming the public sector,* New York: Plume

Parsons, W, 2002, From muddling through to muddling up: Evidence-based policy making and the modernisation of British government, *Public Policy and Administration,* 17, 3, 43–60

Peters, BG, 2013, Towards policy coordination: Alternatives to hierarchy, *Policy & Politics,* 41, 4, 569–84

Pollitt, C, 2013, 40 Years of public management reform in UK central government: promises, promises…, *Policy & Politics,* 41, 4, 465–80

Pollitt, C, Talbot, C (eds), 2004, *Unbundling government: A critical analysis of the global trend to agencies, quangos and contractualisation,* London: Routledge

Prindle, D, 2012, Importing concepts from biology into political science: The case of punctuated equilibrium, *Political Studies Journal,* 40, 1, 21–44

Raadschelders, J, 2011, The future study of public administration: Embedding research object and methodology in epistemology and ontology, *Public Administration Review,* 71, 6, 916–24

Real-Dato, J, 2009, Mechanisms of policy change: A proposal for a synthetic framework, *Journal of Comparative Policy Analysis: Research and Practice,* 11, 1, 117–43

Rhodes, RAW, 2011, *Everyday life in British government,* Oxford: Oxford University Press

Rhodes, RAW, 2013, Political anthropology and public policy: Prospects and limits, *Policy & Politics,* 41, 4, 481–96

Room, G, 2011, *Complexity, institutions and public policy,* Cheltenham: Edward Elgar

Room, G, 2012, Evolution and the arts of civilisation, *Policy & Politics,* 40, 4, 453–72

Sabatier, P, Jenkins-Smith, H, 1993, *Policy change and learning: An advocacy coalition framework,* Boulder, CO: Westview

Salamon, LM (ed), 2002, *The tools of government: A guide to the new governance,* New York: Oxford University Press

Sanderson, I, 2002, Evaluation, policy learning and evidence-based policy making, *Public Administration*, 80, 1, 1–22

Sanderson, I, 2009, Intelligent policy making for a complex world: Pragmatism, evidence and learning, *Political Studies*, 57, 699–719

Schmidt, V, 2008, Discursive institutionalism: The explanatory power of ideas and discourse, *Annual Review of Political Science*, 11, 303–26

Schmidt, V, 2012, Discursive institutionalism: Scope, dynamics and philosophical underpinnings, in Fischer, F, Gottweis, H (eds), 2012, *The argumentative turn revisited: Public policy as communicative practice*, Durham, NC: Duke University Press

Schon, D, 1983, *The reflexive practitioner: How professionals think in action*, New York: Basic Books

Schon, D, Rein, M, 1994, *Frame reflection: Towards the resolution of intractable policy controversies*, New York: Basic Books

Shore, C, Wright, S, Pero, D (eds), 2011, *Policy worlds: Anthropology and the analysis of contemporary power*, Oxford: Berghahn

Schram, SF, Caterino, B (eds), 2006, *Making political science matter: Debating knowledge, research and method*, New York: New York University Press

Skelcher, C, 1998, *The appointed state: Quasi-governmental organisations and democracy*, Buckingham: Open University Press

Skelcher, C, 2008, Does governance perform? Concepts, evidence, causalities and research strategies, in Hartley, J, Donaldson, C, Skelcher, C, Wallace, M (eds), *Managing to improve public services*, Cambridge: Cambridge University Press, 27–45

Sullivan, H, 2011, Truth junkies: The use of evaluation in UK public policy, *Policy & Politics*, 39, 4, 499–512

Sullivan, H, Williams, P, Jeffares, S, 2012, Leadership for collaboration: Situated agency in practice, *Public Management Review*, 14, 1, 41–66

Thomas, JC, 2012, *Citizen, customer, partner: Engaging the public in public management*, Armonk, NY: ME Sharpe

Van der Steen, M, van Twist, M, Fenger, M, Le Cointre, S, 2013, Complex causality in improving underperforming schools: A complex adaptive systems approach, *Policy & Politics*, 41, 4, 551–67

Watson, M, Hay, C, 2003, The discourse of globalisation and the logic of no alternative: Rendering the contingent necessary in the political economy of New Labour, *Policy & Politics*, 31, 3, 289–305

Weiss, CH, 1979, The many meanings of research utilisation, *Public Administration Review*, 39, 5, 426–31

Whetsell, T, Shields, P, 2013, The dynamics of positivism in the study of public administration: A brief intellectual history and reappraisal, *Administration and Society*, forthcoming, DOI: 10.1177/0095399713490157

Index